Military Intelligence

A History

Military Intelligence

A History

PETER GUDGIN

SUTTON PUBLISHING

First published in 1999 by
Sutton Publishing Limited · Phoenix Mill
Thrupp · Stroud · Gloucestershire · GL5 2BU

British Library Cataloguing in Publication Data
A catalogue record for this book is available from the British Library.

ISBN 0-7509-1870-5

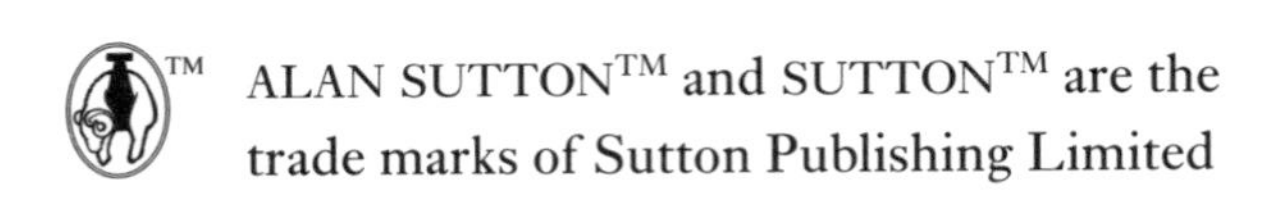

Typeset in 11/15pt Ehrhardt.
Typesetting and origination by
Sutton Publishing Limited.
Printed in Great Britain by
Biddles, Guildford, Surrey.

Contents

List of Plates

(between pages 140 and 141)

List of Charts

Acknowledgements

Source notes have been deliberately omitted from this book, in order to make the text more continuous and easier for a layperson to read. Instead, reliance has been placed upon the Bibliography to provide the reader who wishes to go into greater detail regarding specific aspects of British military Intelligence with details of sources for such information.

For detail concerning the history of British military Intelligence up to 1914, I am greatly indebted to Brigadier B.A.H. Parritt's excellent privately published book *The Intelligencers*, and to Lieutenant-Colonel Thomas G. Fergusson's equally valuable work on the development of a modern Intelligence organisation, *British Military Intelligence, 1870–1914*, published by Arms and Armour Press.

For information concerning British Intelligence in the period from the beginning of the First World War to the end of the Second World War, I am particularly grateful to the excellent series of books on the British covert Intelligence agencies by Nigel West (former MP Rupert Allason), whose published work in this field is unique and whose sources are impeccable. Much useful background is also contained in Dr Christopher Andrew's well-researched book on the same organisations, *Secret Service*. These books were of great value in the writing of Chapter 5, dealing with covert military Intelligence and counter-Intelligence. Good sources of more detailed information on the covert agencies of both the UK and the USA and their operational techniques were 'Kim' Philby's *My Silent War*, John Ranelagh's *The Rise and Decline of the CIA* and *Inside the Company: CIA Diary* by Philip Agee. For general background as well as for detailed information regarding British Intelligence as a whole during the Second World War, the official history produced in five volumes by Professor Sir Harry Hinsley's team is unique; it does, however, contain relatively little concerning the Second World War contribution of either SIS or the Security Service and tends to over-emphasise that of GC & CS at their expense. Michael Howard's contribution to this series, *Strategic Deception in the Second World War*, was particularly valuable as the basis for the information contained in Chapter 6. For background technical information, Mario de Arcangelis's book *Electronic Warfare* and Max Whitby's *Space Technology* were very helpful.

All the books listed in the Bibliography have been useful in one respect or another, and will be valuable to the reader seeking more detail on particular aspects of military Intelligence.

The assistance of the Public Record Office at Kew and the Ministry of Defence Central Library in providing documents covering the organisation of the War Office's Military Intelligence Directorate and its overseas outposts is gratefully acknowledged. For permission to publish their photographs I am grateful to:

Barry Jones of Stoneleigh Visual Aids
The Director of the National Army Museum, Chelsea, London
British Aerospace
Marconi Avionics
Pilkington PE Ltd
Dunlop Ltd Archive Project
EMI Electronics Ltd
The Director of the Royal Signals Museum, Blandford, Dorset
US Air Force
Associated Press

Abbreviations and Acronyms

AAG	Assistant Adjutant-General
ABDA	Australia-Britain-Dutch-American command
ACA	Allied Commission for Austria
ACofS	Assistant Chief of Staff
ADI(Sc)	Assistant Director of Intelligence (Science)
AFV	Armoured Fighting Vehicle
AG	Adjutant-General
AMAN	Israeli Military Intelligence Organisation
APS	Axis Planning Section
AQMG	Assistant Quartermaster-General
ASIO	Australian Security & Intelligence Organisation
AVO	államvédelmi Osztály – Hungarian Intelligence and Security Organisation (later AVH – államvédelmi Hatósag)
BAOR	British Army of the Rhine
BCRA(M)	Bureau Centrale de Renseignements et d'Action Militaire
BEF	British Expeditionary Force
BfV	Bundesamt für Verfassungsschutz – West German Office for the Protection of the Constitution
BND	Bundesnachrichtendienst – West German Intelligence service
BOSS	Bureau of State Security (South Africa)
BRIXMIS	British Commander-in-Chief's Mission
BRUSA	Britain–USA Pact
'C'	Head of British Secret Intelligence Service
CBME	Combined Bureau, Middle East
CCG	Control Commission for Germany
CCG(BE)	Control Commission for Germany (British Element)
CDS	Chief of the Defence Staff
CELD	Central External Liaison Department (China)

CESID	Centro Superior para la Informacion de la Defensa – Spanish Intelligence Service
CF	Cameron (Folkestone) – British First World War tactical Intelligence network
CIA	Central Intelligence Agency (USA)
CIG	Central Intelligence Group (USA)
CIGS	Chief of the Imperial General Staff
C-in-C	Commander-in-Chief
COI	Coordinator of Information; Central Office of Information
COMINT	Communications Intelligence
COS	Chief(s) of Staff
COSSAC	Chief of Staff, Supreme Allied Commander
CPGB	Communist Party of Great Britain
CRMP	Corps of Royal Military Police
CRPO	Combined Research & Planning Office; Command Regimental Pay Office
CSDIC	Combined Services Detailed Interrogation Centre
CSIS	Canadian Secret Intelligence Service
CSS	Chief of the Secret Intelligence Service
DAAG	Deputy Assistant Adjutant-General
DAA & QMG	Deputy Assistant Adjutant- & Quartermaster-General
DDA	Deputy Director Administration
DDI	Deputy Director of Intelligence
DDMI	Deputy Director of Military Intelligence
DDO	Deputy Director Operations
DDR	German Democratic Republic
DDS&T	Deputy Director, Science & Technology
DF	Direction-Finding
DGER	Direction Général des Études et Recherches
DGSE	Direction Général de Securité Extérieure
DGSS	Direction Général des Services Spéciaux
DIA	Defense Intelligence Agency (USA)
DIS	Defence Intelligence Staff
DMI	Director of Military Intelligence
DMO	Director of Military Operations
DMO & I	Director of Military Operations & Intelligence
DMP	Dublin Metropolitan Police
DORA	Defence of the Realm Act

DQMG	Deputy Quartermaster-General
DS	Darjavna Sugurnost – Bulgarian State Security Service
DSI	Defence Security Intelligence
DSO	Distinguished Service Order
DST	Direction de la Surveillance du Territoire
ECCMs	Electronic Counter-Counter-Measures
ECMs	Electronic Counter-Measures
EEF	Egypt Expeditionary Force
ELINT	Electronic Intelligence
EMP	Electro-Magnetic Pulse
EOKA	National Organisation of Cypriot Fighters
EW	Early Warning; Electronic Warfare
EWI	Economic Warfare Intelligence
FAPSI	Federal'noe Agentstvo Pravitel'stvennoi Sviazi i Informatsii – Russian SIGINT organisation
FBI	Federal Bureau of Investigation (USA)
FH(O)	Fremde Heer (Ost) – Foreign Armies (East) – Eastern Intelligence branch of the OKH
FH(W)	Fremde Heer (West) – Foreign Armies (West) – Western Intelligence branch of the OKH
FOES	Future Operations Enemy Section
FRG	Federal Republic of Germany
FSB	Federal'naya Sluzhba Bezopasnosti – Russian Federal Security Service
FSK	Federal'naya Sluzhba Kontrazvedki – Russian Federal Counter-Intelligence Service
FUSAG	First US Army Group
GC & CS	Government Code & Cipher School
GCHQ	Government Communications Headquarters
Gestapo	Geheime Staatspolizei – German Secret State Police
GHQ	General Headquarters
G(Int)	General Staff (Intelligence)
GPU	Gosudarstvennoe Politicheskoye Upravlenie – Soviet State Political Administration
GRU	Glavnoe Razvedyvatelnoe Upravlenie – Chief Intelligence Directorate of the Soviet General Staff
GSFG	Group of Soviet Forces Germany
GS(I)	General Staff (Intelligence)

HQ	Headquarters
HUMINT	Human Intelligence
IMINT	Imaging Intelligence
IRA	Irish Republican Army
ISIC	Inter-Service Intelligence Committee
ISLD	Inter-Service Liaison Department
IS(O)	Intelligence Section (Operations)
ISSB	Inter-Service Security Board
ISTD	Inter-Service Topographical Department
JIB	Joint Intelligence Bureau
JIC	Joint Intelligence Sub-Committee
JSC	Joint Security Control
JSSIC	Joint Service Specialised Interrogation Centre
KGB	Komitet Gosudarstvennoe Bezopasnosti – Soviet Committee for State Security
Kripo	Kriminalpolizei – German Criminal Police
LASP	Low-Altitude Surveillance Platform
LCS	London Controlling Section
MAD	Magnetic Anomaly Detection; Militärische Abschirmdienst – German Field Security Organisation
MB	Soviet Ministry of Security
MEF	Mediterranean Expeditionary Force (1914–18); Middle East Forces (1939–45)
MEW	Ministry of Economic Warfare
MGB	Ministerstvo Gosudarstvennoe Bezopasnosti – Soviet Ministry of State Security
MGO	Master-General of the Ordnance
MI	Military Intelligence
MIR	Military Intelligence (Russia)
MIRS	Military Intelligence Research Section
MO	Military Operations
MoD	Ministry of Defence
Mossad	Israeli Secret Intelligence Service
MPI	Mean Point of Impact
MVD	Ministerstvo Vnutrennikh Del – Soviet Ministry of Internal Affairs
NASA	National Aeronautics and Space Administration (USA)
NATO	North Atlantic Treaty Organisation

NBC	Nuclear, Biological and Chemical
NCO	Non-Commissioned Officer
ND	Nachrichtendienst des Heeres – German military Intelligence organisation
NIA	National Intelligence Authority (USA)
NID	Naval Intelligence Department
NIS	National Intelligence Service (South Africa)
NKVD	Narodnyi Komissariat Vnutrennikh Del – Soviet People's Commissariat for Internal Affairs
NSA	National Security Agency (USA)
NV	Normal Vetting
OB	Order of Battle
OGPU	Obedinennoe Politicheskoe Upravlenie – Soviet Unified State Political Administration
OKH	Oberkommando des Heeres – German Army HQ
OKW	Oberkommando der Wehrmacht – German Armed Forces HQ
ONI	Office of Naval Intelligence (USA)
OP	Observation Post
ORBAT	Order of Battle
ORPO	Ordnungspolizei – German police branch
OSS	Office of Strategic Services (USA)
POW	Prisoner of War
PR	Photographic Reconnaissance
PV	Positive Vetting
PW	Prisoner of War
PWE	Political Warfare Executive
QMG	Quartermaster-General
RAF	Royal Air Force
RCMP	Royal Canadian Mounted Police
RFC	Royal Flying Corps
RIC	Royal Irish Constabulary
RN	Royal Navy
RPV	Remotely Piloted Vehicle
RSHA	Reichssicherheitshauptamt – German security service
RSS	Radio Security Service
RTR	Royal Tank Regiment
RUC	Royal Ulster Constabulary
SAMOS	Satellite And Missile Observation System

SAS	Special Air Service
SAVAK	Iranian Intelligence & Security Service
SBS	Special Boat Squadron
SD	Sicherheitsdienst – German Security Service
SDECE	Service de Documentation Extérieure et de Contre-Espionage
SEAC	South-East Asia Command
SHAEF	Supreme Headquarters Allied Expeditionary Force
SHAPE	Supreme Headquarters Allied Powers in Europe
SIB	Special Investigation Branch
SIFAR	Italian Counter-Intelligence Service
SIGC	Spanish Guardia Intelligence Servce
SIGINT	Signals Intelligence
SIME	Security Intelligence Middle East
SIPAN	Spanish Security Police
SIS	Secret Intelligence Service (MI 6)
SISME	Italian Secret Intelligence Service
SLU	Special Liaison Unit
SO	Staff Officer
SOE	Special Operations Executive
SOXMIS	Soviet Commander-in-Chief's Mission
STB	Statni Tajna Bezpecnost – Czechoslovak Secret Intelligence Service
SVR	Sluzhba Vneshnei Razvedaki – Russian Foreign Intelligence Service
T	Agent Network
TA	Traffic Analysis
TAVR	Territorial Army and Volunteer Reserve
T & S	Topographical and Statistical; Technical and Scientific Department
UB	Urzad Bezpieczenstva – Polish Secret Intelligence Service
UKUSA	United Kingdom-United States of America Pact
UN	United Nations
USSR	Union of Soviet Socialist Republics
V(-Weapon)	Vergeltungswaffe ('reprisal weapon')
VCIGS	Vice-Chief of the Imperial General Staff
VIP	Very Important Person
WL	Wallinger (London) – British First World War Intelligence Network

XX	Twenty Committee/Double-Cross
Y	Tactical Signals Intelligence Organisation
Z Org	Duplicate MI 6 Agent Network (Z Organisation)

Introduction

The profusion of stories of Intelligence and counter-Intelligence coups, confessions of former spies, accusations and counter-accusations against the various Intelligence services of NATO and the former Warsaw Pact countries has produced confusion among the general public; this has been exacerbated since the break-up of the USSR and the end of the Cold War by the many new organisations which have arisen as a result. These events have led many to question the purpose of Intelligence and the need for it in the relaxed atmosphere now supposed to be prevailing; in the UK particularly there have been calls for the abolition of secrecy in matters relating to the Intelligence services and for the drastic reduction, if not the total abolition, of the Intelligence-gathering organisations in the alleged absence of need for their continued existence.

This book is an attempt to clarify for the lay reader the reasons behind the need for Intelligence and the organisations responsible for its collection, collation and dissemination. What is Intelligence? What are the types of Intelligence and the methods used in their collection? Who collects it, collates it and makes use of the finished product? How are the various services involved organised? How have these organisations evolved, and why? What is the meaning of the many abbreviations and acronyms which appear with monotonous regularity in the press?

To many people, the phrase 'military Intelligence' conveys a sense of mystery and intrigue coupled with a glamorous James Bond lifestyle, while to many others it is a contradiction in terms. The first group has formed a greatly over-glamorised picture of Intelligence work by reading too much spy fiction, while the second, which tends in any case to be anti-military in its thinking, refuses to credit the military with much intelligence, either as individuals or in the mass. There has also, until recently, always been a large body of opinion within the armies of many civilised countries which has regarded Intelligence and those who collect it as being beneath the dignity of an officer and gentleman; needless to say, this body of opinion has tended to be found among the less intelligent, but often the more senior and therefore the more influential officers.

The reader will have realised that these three groups of people are using the word 'intelligence' in two different senses: those spelling it with a capital 'I' usually mean 'information communicated', 'news' or 'a department of a State or armed service for securing information, openly or secretly, and collating it'. With a lower-case 'i' it is taken to mean 'the faculty of understanding; mental brightness', in the words of *Chambers' Etymological Dictionary*. This convention has been followed in this book.

The word 'military' can be taken to mean either all armed services or, in its original sense, the Army alone; in this book the word is used in the latter sense, other services and providers of Intelligence being mentioned only in passing as they impinge upon the military scene.

Frequent mention will be made throughout the text of tactical and strategic Intelligence, and some definition of these two terms is necessary. *Strategic Intelligence* is that Intelligence required at the national level by strategic planners, government policy-makers and high-level military commanders; it will normally include all categories of Intelligence bearing on national strategy, such as military, political, economic, technical, scientific, geographic and sociological. In the British Army, for example, strategic Intelligence has normally been collated in and disseminated from London. *Tactical Intelligence*, which may also be known as field or combat Intelligence, is collected, collated and disseminated within the theatre of operations; it consists of that Intelligence required by a commander in the field to fight a battle successfully, and is concerned with enemy strengths, dispositions, commanders, state of training, equipment, morale and intentions, as well as with the terrain and communications in the theatre of operations. With the rapid improvements in the range of weapons and communications, mobility, means of reconnaissance and the advent of global war in the twentieth century, the distinction between strategic and tactical Intelligence has become somewhat blurred, and the modern field commander in a theatre of operations requires much Intelligence that would formerly have been considered as strategic; nevertheless, these definitions still apply in principle.

This book is about military Intelligence world-wide; but as this is a vast field to cover in detail and one which is beyond the capacity of a book of this size to contain, only the workings of British military Intelligence and counter-Intelligence organisations will be considered in detail, those of other countries being compared in outline only. While some armies may have had better Intelligence organisations than those of the British, and others have organised their military Intelligence agencies on British lines, it is the British organisation that has been the subject of so many leaks, prosecutions and sensation-seeking books in recent years. These have been cryptic, outdated or just plain inaccurate, so that a need has emerged for a simple guide to the confusing list of organisations, acronyms and abbreviations involved.

The Intelligence machine collects, collates and evaluates Intelligence from a wide variety of sources, and interprets it to provide both facts and forecasts for its customers; contrary to the impression held by a large proportion of the public, its sources are mostly overt, and their information is already in the public domain, if one knows where to find it. Some sources, however, are covert and must therefore be carefully protected. The popular idea of Intelligence as being supplied almost entirely by intrepid secret agents could not be further from the truth, particularly where military Intelligence is concerned. While a great deal of espionage is undoubtedly carried on in the modern world, secret agents rank low in the hierarchy of useful sources, providing perhaps five per cent or less of the mass of information which floods into a modern Intelligence agency. As Admiral Wemyss, the British First Sea Lord at the end of the First World War, is reported to have said, the product of secret Intelligence is 'uncertain information from questionable people'.

A military Intelligence organisation is a user of most types of Intelligence, but must rely upon others to provide much of it. Advances in warfare and the means of gathering Intelligence have been increasing ever more rapidly since the mid-eighteenth century, until today the sheer enormity of the processing task, even with the assistance of modern data-processing equipment, requires the maintenance of a very large Intelligence organisation in peacetime. The fact that a large peacetime Intelligence organisation, or even *any* peacetime Intelligence organisation, has not always been available in the UK will become obvious from a study of the historical chapters which follow; in fact the history of British Intelligence is one of peaks of organisational plenty alternating with troughs of extreme government stringency. It is virtually only since the Boer War that the British Government has seen the necessity for the maintenance of an adequate Intelligence organisation in time of peace.

This book serves as a guide to the many facets and functions of military Intelligence, both past and present. It contains no sensational revelations and uncovers no secrets, but aims to provide useful background to the multitude of books on specific aspects of Intelligence which are currently available.

CHAPTER 1

British Military Intelligence to 1919

The use of Intelligence by armed forces throughout the world is as old as warfare itself, and military Intelligence was probably the earliest form of this arcane art. No military commanders would willingly commit their forces against an enemy in terrain of which they knew little or nothing. In any military operation in war it is essential for a commander of an armed force to be able to appreciate all relevant information concerning the enemy and terrain, as well as a summary of the courses of action open to the enemy commander and which of these the commander is most likely to take. This applies only in time of war, however; in times of peace the need for military Intelligence has been much less obvious to governments and soldiers, particularly in the UK.

The British Army, like most armies, tends to be somewhat conservative in outlook, and has never really liked the idea of covert Intelligence; indeed it is only in comparatively recent times that it has overcome its aversion to something so ungentlemanly and unsporting as spying on one's enemies. Intelligence, in the sense of information about a potential or actual enemy, has always been associated with spies, informers and traitors, and the British Army's attitude to such people was aptly summed up by Colonel G.A. Furse who, in his book *Information in War*, published in London in 1895, wrote:

> The very term 'spy' conveys to our mind something dishonourable and disloyal . . . his underhand dealings inspire us with such horror that we would blush at the very idea of having to avail ourselves of any information obtained through such an agency.

Not all Intelligence is provided by covert means, however. The more overt methods of gathering information by means of scouts, reconnaissance patrols and observation have always been accepted as a military responsibility by the British Army, and the techniques for gathering such information have always been included in the military training curriculum. The British Army's recorded use of Intelligence certainly antedates the formation of the New Model Army, which many historians regard as the birth of the British Army, in the mid-seventeenth century; its unrecorded use undoubtedly goes back very much further.

The appointment of Scoutmaster, the third most senior appointment in the British Army, was initiated by Henry VIII. It was the Scoutmaster's responsibility, as Chief Reconnoitier of the Army, to provide tactical military Intelligence for his commander, and his brief, as laid down by the King in 1518, stated:

> It is the Office of the Scoutmaster when he cometh to the field to set and appoint the scourage, he must appoint some to the high hills to view and see if they can discover anything. Also the said Scoutmaster must appoint one other company of scouragers to search, and view every valley thereabouts, that there be no enemies laid privily for the annoyance of the said camp, and if they do discover any, they are to advertise the Scoutmaster; and he must either bring or send word to the high marshal of the advertisement with speed.

Such a simple brief emphasises the simplicity of warfare in those days; the range of the weapons used was short, the speed of movement was limited to those of the horse and the marching soldier, visual reconnaissance was limited to the range of the human eye (assisted in some cases by a primitive telescope) and the size of an army was limited by the ability of a commander to control it with the primitive means of communication available. The rate of progress in the improvement of weapons, mobility and means of communication was so slow that a hundred years later, the duties of the Scoutmaster remained unchanged.

With the outbreak of the Civil War, however, the Scoutmaster's duties became more complicated and extensive. Both sides appointed their own Scoutmasters, that of the Earl of Essex, Sir Samuel Luke, being particularly successful. Luke ran a network of scouts and agents who provided such detailed and accurate information concerning the Royalist forces that he was described as: 'this noble commander who watches the enemy so industriously that they eat, sleep, drink not, whisper not but he can give us an account of their darkest proceedings'. For all his successes, however, he suffered the occasional failure, and he was bitterly criticised for his lack of Intelligence before the Battle of Edgehill. The opposing armies had marched in the same direction for ten days, never more than twenty miles apart, without either side being aware of the other's proximity. Such an episode emphasises the limitations of the means available in the seventeenth century for gathering tactical Intelligence.

In 1643, Luke had been promoted to Scoutmaster-General to the Parliamentary forces and given the responsibility for co-ordinating the activities of three Deputy Scoutmasters, one with the Earl of Manchester's Army in eastern England, one with Sir William Waller in the south, and the third with the City of London forces. Although the Royalists also had scoutmasters, they had no Scoutmaster-General, and therefore no centralised control of their Intelligence organisation.

In 1649, after the Battle of Worcester and the consequently declining need for tactical Intelligence, one of the periodic reductions in defence expenditure so beloved of British governments down the centuries reduced the Scoutmaster's allowance to only 20*s* a day, compared to the £8 he had received daily during the war. Six months later, in April 1650, when the young Charles Stuart crossed the Scottish border marching south at the head of an avenging Scottish Army, they raised it again to £4 per day, only to reduce it again three years later after the Prince's defeats at Dunbar and Worcester. Thus was the precedent set for the many alternations of government generosity and parsimony which have recurred at frequent intervals since then, whereby in time of war an efficient military Intelligence organisation has been built up, only to be knocked down again, frequently to nothing, in the peace which followed.

In December 1652, Cromwell appointed John Thurloe, a 36-year-old lawyer, as Secretary of State with additional responsibility for Intelligence. In the seven years during which he held the appointment, Thurloe spent some £70,000 annually on building up and maintaining a network of spies and informers in all the European capitals as well as Britain, and supplying both military and political Intelligence, in an organisation which has never been equalled. The British people were suspicious of one another as a result of a civil war fought primarily about politics and religion, and information of real and imaginary plots and conspiracies was plentiful. It was not only the plentiful supply of information which made Thurloe's organisation so successful, however; two other factors were also of contributory importance, namely Cromwell's confidence in his Secretary of State and the availability of virtually unlimited finance. Dictatorships are dependent for their survival on good Intelligence, and are therefore more generous to Intelligence, organisations than are democracies. In comparative terms, no British government since the period of Cromwell's rule has made so much money available for Intelligence. It was an outstanding example, amply fulfilled, of the generosity which, as mentioned earlier, can follow a period of parsimony.

On Cromwell's death, Thurloe's Intelligence organisation lapsed, largely because when Thomas Scott, a previous incumbent, was appointed in 1659 to succeed him, Thurloe refused to pass on to Scott the list of his agents, on the grounds that it would be treachery to reveal them without their consent. Thurloe's place in the history of British military Intelligence is unique: despite his appointment having been political, he was able to make such a success of the post by virtue of the environment characteristic of totalitarian rule, whereby one man could control the whole range of military Intelligence from the overt to the covert, from the tactical to the strategic. Nevertheless, it is from this period that the British public's natural antipathy to military rule and the British Army's inherent mistrust of professional Intelligence officers can be dated.

In 1660, King Charles II appointed Sir Theophilus Jones as Scoutmaster-General for the Irish campaign at a salary of 6*s* 8*d* a day and £100 a year besides, with duties, like Luke's, quite different from the tactical reconnaissance duties of the forward cavalry and infantry units. His role was well summarised by Sir James Turner in 1671:

> The English have a General Officer whom they qualify with the title of Scoutmaster-General . . . I hear in some places of Italy they have something very like him and that is Il Capitoni di Spioni, i.e., the Captain of Spies. I cannot believe that this Scoutmaster has anything to do with that intelligence which I call publick and is obtained by parties whether of horse or foot, for the commanding of these . . . belongs properly to the Major Generals and the several Majors of Regiments both of the Cavalry and Infantry, none of which I conceive will suffer the Scoutmaster to usurp their office. They must then only have the regulation of private intelligence, wherein no doubt they may ease the General of the Army very much.

On 6 July 1685, the last battle between Englishmen on English soil was fought on Sedgemoor in Somerset. King James's victory over the Duke of Monmouth was attributable mainly to poor terrain Intelligence on the part of the Duke's Army, and illustrates well the unwisdom of relying for military Intelligence upon a single untrained, uncorroborated civilian source. In this case the source was a farm labourer, one Richard Godfrey, who, having alerted Monmouth to the presence of the Royalist Army only three miles away, was asked by Monmouth to return to the Royalist lines and discover the exact enemy positions. This Godfrey did creditably, giving an extremely detailed and accurate picture, but he omitted to tell Monmouth that the Royalists' north and west flanks were protected by a wide canal, known locally as the Bussex Rhine, which had been widened and deepened by exceptional rainfall. Godfrey's further information that the Royalists had been drinking and carousing decided Monmouth to stage an immediate night attack – a risky procedure at the best of times, but much more so when carried out by inexperienced troops across boggy and unfamiliar ground. His cavalry were pulled up short by the canal, and the Royalist troops, alerted by the noise, regrouped and pursued and slaughtered Monmouth's followers. Colonel John Churchill, later to be Duke of Marlborough, was caught asleep, his own spy in Bridgwater having failed to warn him of Monmouth's plans to attack that night. It was a lesson he never forgot, and in all his subsequent great battles and marches from 1702 to 1711, he was never again surprised by the enemy.

In 1686, the post of Scoutmaster-General was abolished, and the duties formerly carried out by the Scoutmaster-General, the Harbinger (the officer responsible for the provisioning of the Army) and by the Provost-Marshal were combined in the post of Quartermaster-General. When John Churchill, by now the Earl of Marlborough, was appointed Captain-General of the allied armies in the Low Countries by King William III on his deathbed in 1702, he paid close attention to the organisation of his Intelligence; he was not again to be caught napping as had happened at Sedgemoor. He divided his Intelligence organisation into two distinct parts, one covering close tactical Intelligence and the other responsible for strategic Intelligence, both military and political. Already the increased range and accuracy of weapons and the increased mobility insisted upon by Marlborough were revealing a need for longer-range military Intelligence than the purely tactical, short-term Intelligence requirements of his predecessors.

The man responsible for Marlborough's tactical Intelligence was William Cadogan, who had fought as a boy cornet in the Irish campaign, both under King William at the Battle of the Boyne and later with Marlborough at the sieges of Cork and Kinsale. James II had collected a small French army and landed in Ireland, where the army, whose officers were predominantly Catholic, was thought likely to support him. A few weeks later he had laid siege to the Protestants in Londonderry. Although the Royal Navy raised the siege in July 1689, William's army was able to do little more than hold on to the Protestant enclave in Ulster. It was poorly trained, badly equipped and badly supplied, and was no match for the French troops. In the following year, therefore, William was forced to dispatch a much larger army, including Dutch and Danish as well as English troops, which defeated James at the Battle of the Boyne in July 1690 and drove his army south. After a series of sieges, all resistance was finally crushed in 1691; James returned to France, leaving William free to concentrate on wider issues.

On these occasions Cadogan had so impressed Marlborough that the latter took Cadogan with him to The Hague in 1701 as his Quartermaster-General, despite Cadogan being twenty-five years Marlborough's junior and only a Major in rank. Cadogan soon revealed an aptitude both for logistics and the provision of reliable Intelligence. As a result, he was promoted to Colonel in 1703, to

Brigadier-General in 1704, to Major-General in 1706 and to Lieutenant-General in 1709, a rate of promotion seldom equalled before or since.

Responsibility for the coordination of strategic military and political Intelligence reports in the field was given by Marlborough to his private secretary, Adam de Cardonnel. In making use of his private secretary in this way, Marlborough was setting a precedent which was followed until the early years of the twentieth century. De Cardonnel was fortunate in having at his disposal the network of spies and agents throughout Europe built up gradually over the years by Marlborough. Thus he was able, for example, to learn the complete order of battle and the battle plans of the French Army from a letter received during the march to the Danube. The secret of the success of Marlborough's Intelligence service was, again, the availability of adequate funds, although in this instance the funds had not been provided for that purpose by the British Government. Marlborough had felt compelled to resort to a practice adopted many times, both before and since: he misappropriated to his Intelligence organisation funds allotted for other purposes. At a subsequent enquiry, he was shown not only to have failed to account for some £280,000 allocated for the payment of foreign soldiers in British service, but also to have accepted more than £60,000 from suppliers of bread and bread wagons to the Army.

In his defence, Marlborough said that the money had been constantly applied to one of the most important parts of the service there: 'I mean the procuring of Intelligence and other secret service.' He also showed the expenditure to have been an economy – 'I may venture to affirm that I have, in the article for secret services, saved the Government near four times the sum this deduction amounts to – which I must reckon so much money saved to the public' – and further stated: 'no war can be conducted successfully without early and good Intelligence, and . . . such services cannot be had but at a very great expense'. True though these statements were, Marlborough was nevertheless condemned by Parliament, and left for exile in Europe. His fate is a salutary reminder to Intelligence officers that it is not enough to obtain good Intelligence; the methods by which it is obtained must be capable of justification in court, and the money used to obtain it capable of being shown to have been allocated for the purpose.

Marlborough's practice of making his Quartermaster-General responsible for the gathering of military Intelligence was continued in the British Army throughout the eighteenth century, and the story of British military Intelligence during this period is interwoven with the stories of successive Quartermasters-General. During the Seven Years War, Marlborough's sensible separation of tactical from strategic and political Intelligence was repeated by Prince Ferdinand; his Quartermaster-General, Friedrich von Bauer, and his Private

Secretary, Christian von Westfalen, carried out the functions performed for Marlborough by Cadogan and de Cardonnel, respectively. Neither was nominated as Head of Intelligence; this function was carried out by the commander himself.

This principle, whereby the field commander himself acted as Head of Intelligence, was also observed by General Wolfe in the battle for Quebec in September 1759. Wolfe carried it further, however, by undertaking all reconnaissances and interrogations of deserters himself, to the exclusion of his Quartermaster-General and his Intelligence staff. Admittedly this was partly because he had fallen out with his three most senior officers, but by thus reducing the number of officers who knew details of his plans in advance, Wolfe effectively increased the security of the operation and thereby achieved both complete surprise and a famous victory.

James Wolfe was an exceptionally good commander of men, which explains why, at the age of only thirty-two, the age at which officers in the present British Army are promoted from Captain to Major, he had reached the rank of Major-General. He was also a good tactician and a natural Intelligence officer; he realised that to capture Quebec, he had to force General Montcalm, the French commander, to leave the safety of the city's fortifications and do battle on the Plain of Abraham. To do this, however, Wolfe had first to cross the St Lawrence River and scale the cliffs on the opposite bank, and every attempt he had made to do so had been frustrated by the French moving troops up the opposite side of the river to his proposed crossing-point. From four unrelated snippets of information he learned: first, that there was a path leading up the cliff at his preferred crossing-point; second, that the French officer in charge of the defence of this path had been court-martialled for neglect of his duties; third, that of the militiamen guarding the path, one half had been sent home to help with the harvest, and finally, that the French regiment previously in the area had been posted to Montreal. He therefore reconnoitred the site personally, wrapped in his cloak as a disguise, from a rowing-boat on the river, to confirm the reports and the suitability of the site for a surprise crossing.

Having confirmed that his chosen crossing-point was suitable, Wolfe returned to the site the following day with ten of his staff officers, suitably disguised with soldiers' greatcoats to hide their gold braid, and over the next two days, personally supervised preparation of the thirty-five flat-bottomed boats in which the 1,700-strong attacking force would drift some thirteen miles down-stream to the landing site on the opposite shore. Although they had all personally seen the landing area and cliff path, Wolfe's three brigade commanders wrote a joint letter to him on the afternoon preceding the attack, complaining that they were insufficiently informed as to both the place and the plan of attack on the morrow. In Wolfe's reply, he pointed out that it was not customary either to point out in public orders the direct spot of an attack or for an inferior officer not charged with a particular duty to ask instructions on that point. That his tight security was fully justified was demonstrated when a sergeant of the 60th Royal American Regiment (later to become the 60th King's Royal Rifle Corps) deserted on the same day as Wolfe's crushing reply to his brigadiers; although under interrogation he revealed that the British were preparing to re-embark for an attack, he was unable to say where the attack would begin. As a result, Montcalm in his diary dismissed the information as mere verbiage, shedding no light on British intentions. As a diversion to divide the defending French force, with the probable bonus of providing prisoners for interrogation and captured documents for translation, Wolfe despatched his Quartermaster-General, Colonel Guy Carleton, in command of a detachment, to another site upstream of the proposed landing site.

Wolfe's brilliant night attack was outstandingly successful, although sadly he fell fatally wounded in his hour of victory. He had demonstrated that as long as available information can be assimilated and interpreted by one person and the resulting Intelligence incorporated into the plan, there need be neither a Head of Intelligence nor an Intelligence staff. However, it should be borne in mind that in the wars in both Canada and North America, the British Army was operating among a population which spoke mainly English. The gathering and interpretation of Intelligence was thus very much easier than when the inhabitants speak a different language or are of a different race or colour.

After America gained independence from Britain in 1781, by 1793 the large British Army had been reduced to some 17,000 men and the militia had also fallen into decline. However, when a militant, strong and revolutionary France arose to shatter the British Government's dream of perpetual peace by declaring war in 1793, the belated but familiar change of heart, almost traditional among British politicians, occurred. The pendulum of government again swung away from parsimony towards generosity to the Army. Emergency measures were rushed through Parliament in an effort to repair the damage caused by past neglect, but these came too late: when an expeditionary force commanded by the King's second son, Frederick, Duke of York, was sent to Flanders as part of an Allied Army to contain French expansionism, it found itself outmanoeuvred and outclassed. As ever in peacetime, the collection and collation of military Intelligence had been neglected, as had training in the traditional arts of reconnaissance and outpost duty, by which means much tactical Intelligence was normally gathered.

Humiliated, alone, outnumbered both at sea and on land, virtually defenceless thanks to the past neglect of the armed forces by Parliament, and by now desperate in the face of the very real threat of invasion, Britain struggled to rearm itself. The nation was called to arms in a dramatic speech to Parliament by Pitt, the young Prime Minister, in March 1794, and, throughout the country gentlemen formed themselves into military regiments of volunteers who bought their own uniforms, supplied their own horses, paid their soldiers from their own pockets and drilled twice weekly, to remarkable effect and with a minimum of government help. The names of famous regiments raised in this manner live on today in the Territorial Army and Volunteer Reserve (TAVR), particularly the Yeomanry, and since then they have formed a major part of the British Army in time of war.

The war drifted on without the feared invasion of Britain materialising. The nearest thing to an invasion occurred when the French landed a small force in Pembrokeshire which was captured by the Pembroke Yeomanry, who were awarded the battle honour 'Fishguard' as a result. This is still the only battle honour ever awarded to a British Army unit for service in the United Kingdom.

Eventually, the war was brought to an end by the signing of the Treaty of Amiens in March 1802; literally within days the government had again lost interest in home defence and set about disbanding the Yeomanry, Fencible and Guides units. Napoleon had not lost his interest in invasion, however, and between 1803 and 1805 he built up a concentration of 100,000 men in camps along the Channel coast, together with a fleet of flat-bottomed boats. In Britain, spy scares were rife, and Dover fishermen brought back alarming stories of French troops practising embarkation and disembarkation drills. This activity alarmed the British Government, which was forced, yet again, to set about making anti-invasion preparations.

There was a special need for both tactical and strategic Intelligence, because there was a grave lack in London of information concerning Napoleon's strength, capabilities and intentions; as always in peacetime, the collection of information about friendly foreign countries is not only the first service to be cut back on financial grounds, but is also often strenuously and successfully opposed on political grounds. In March 1803, therefore, the then Quartermaster-General, General Sir Robert Brownrigg, proposed the formation of a repository or 'Depot of Military Knowledge' within his own department, based upon the French Depôt de la Guerre. He suggested that this repository should comprise four branches: one for Plans, another for Movements, a Military Library, and a Topographical Branch for the preparation of maps; topography had been one of the Quartermaster-General's responsibilities throughout the eighteenth century. This idea was enthusiastically supported by both the Duke of York and the Secretary of State for War, and the Depot of Military Knowledge (see Chart 1) was established with all speed, to be the first of a long line of organisations in the British Army formed to gather military Intelligence in peacetime. The Library

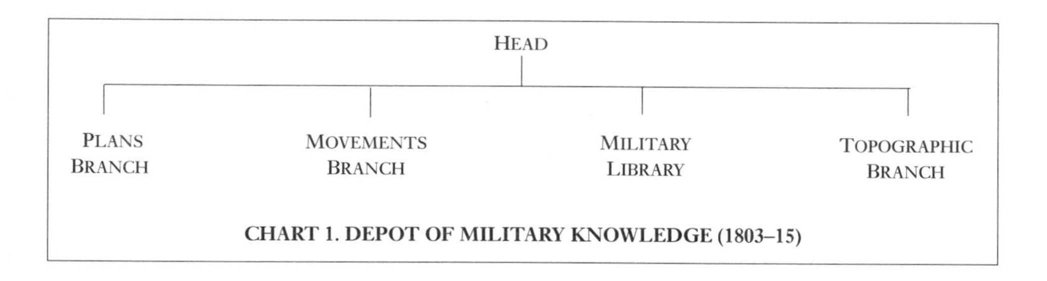

CHART 1. DEPOT OF MILITARY KNOWLEDGE (1803–15)

Branch made the most progress, under the command of Colonel Lewis Lindenthal; the present Ministry of Defence Library is largely a memorial to his zeal, and even today contains many books bearing his mark.

Despite the signing of the Treaty of Amiens, however, Bonaparte had shown no intention of living peacefully within the enlarged boundaries of France. He interfered in Italy and Switzerland, and sent French expeditions to both the East and West Indies. French officers had been sent to Egypt and British merchants found French ports were still closed to their exports. Faced with these hostile actions, the British deferred their departure from Malta, and, after a stormy interview between Napoleon and the British Ambassador to France, diplomatic relations between the two countries were broken off. Regarding renewed hostilities as inevitable, Britain declared war in 1803, the 'perpetual peace' having lasted just one year and fifty days.

Six weeks later, as a step towards the provision of tactical Intelligence in the event of an invasion of Britain, the government again sought to raise a Corps of Guides in the southern counties, the aim of this corps being to provide the Regular Army with reliable local knowledge of routes, tactical features and sources of water and food. Units were formed by Sussex and Kent in July 1803, and by Devon and Cornwall later in the year. However, as the Battle of Trafalgar removed the threat of invasion in 1805, the Kent and Sussex Guides were again rapidly disbanded, the Cornish unit converted to Yeomanry, and the Devon Guides became the Devon Guides Cavalry in 1812. The French Corps of Guides-Interpreters was no more successful, and was almost completely abolished in 1814.

While both the French and British Armies had accepted that it was a good idea to group those with talents for reconnaissance and scouting into one unit, neither Army had considered such work suitable for regular soldiers. The Regular Army therefore lacked the specialist units so essential for the collection of reliable tactical Intelligence. The name 'Corps of Guides', continued, however, and for the next hundred years was carried to the Crimea, India, Canada and South Africa, but throughout the nineteenth century, in the absence of any regular

British Army unit formed to gather tactical Intelligence, a Corps of Guides or its equivalent had to be raised to fill the gap.

The first instance occurred as early as 1809 in the Peninsular War: Sir George Murray, who had been in charge of the Plans Branch of the Depot of Military Knowledge, was posted as Quartermaster-General to the Army in the Peninsula, and realised, after Wellington's first battle against the French at Rolica, that there was a need for a pool of men who could speak the local language and knew the local area. He therefore decided to raise a unit of men possessing these qualifications and to call it the Corps of Guides. Wellington was impressed by their performance, and expanded both their numbers and their duties – which now included the roles of interrogators, agents and couriers – in November of that year. This change in role illustrates the gradual evolution of tactical Intelligence in the field from the original basic requirement, to be able to speak the local language and to know the local topography, to the responsibility for providing a genuine Intelligence service. As the war continued, so the usefulness of the Guides became more apparent, and the unit was increased in size from 50 to 80 privates in September 1811, and to 150 privates six months later. By 1813 the Guides had become an accepted part of the Field Army; but again, as the need for tactical Intelligence receded after the victory of Waterloo, they were not re-formed after that campaign.

With regard to strategic Intelligence, Wellington followed the example of Marlborough by personally organising his network of spies and agents, many of whom were British Army officers with knowledge of the local language and topography, and himself acting as Head of Intelligence. For the Waterloo campaign, however, he appointed a former agent and commander of the Corps of Guides, Major Colquhoun Grant of the 11th Foot, to be head of the newly formed Intelligence Department. This campaign was thus the first in which a British Army in the field had had an Intelligence Department, and no more suitable man to head it than Grant could have been found. A fluent speaker of Spanish and Portuguese, he had made many successful sorties into Spain during the Peninsular campaign, and had become an expert on the French order of battle there. He had been captured by the French and taken as a prisoner to France, but he escaped to Paris, disguised as an Irish officer in French service, where he assumed the identity of an American and managed to get reports to Wellington of the French Army's move to Russia. He eventually persuaded the owner of a French fishing boat to take him out to a blockading British ship, and four months after his capture, he was back in the Peninsula, again carrying out Intelligence work for Wellington, until the latter selected him to command the Corps of Guides and appointed him Head Intelligence Officer.

Grant, and others like him, had been carrying out Intelligence duties quite distinct from the normal reconnaissance and tactical Intelligence produced by infantry scouts and cavalry patrols; while the gaining of such information has always formed part of the duties of a cavalry force, there had grown a need for this information to be supplemented by clandestine means involving deeper penetration of the enemy lines. During both the nineteenth and twentieth centuries there has emerged a group of men, of which Colquhoun Grant was typical, with specialised local and language knowledge and exceptional self-reliance, who have crossed the fine dividing line between conventional reconnaissance and 'special Intelligence' and who have become employed full-time in gathering, collating and analysing information about the enemy.

There was not to be another Head of Intelligence in the Field Army until the 1870s. In London, even before the end of the Napoleonic War, interest in the Intelligence department, the Depot of Military Knowledge, had also begun to wane. It is ironic that the years 1815–54, during which Britain subjugated India and became the largest imperial power in the world, should be described by British historians as the period of the 'Great Peace', but it is in just such times, when the populace does not feel threatened, that government and populace become united on a policy of reducing expenditure on defence. There had been a strong aversion to the idea of a regular army in Britain since the dictatorship of Cromwell's Major-Generals and King James's later concentration of the Army outside London in order to intimidate the inhabitants, and this, combined with a strong desire for reduced taxation, was persuasive. The Duke of Wellington, by now Commander-in-Chief, actively discouraged reform of the Army, and this reluctance to accept change, coupled with the reluctance of the government and people to spend money on defence, resulted in the British Army of 1854 being totally unprepared for war. However, the Russian invasion of Turkey in that year and its destruction of the Turkish Navy led both Britain and France to a declaration of war on Russia and the dispatch of a joint expeditionary force, first to Bulgaria and then to the Crimean Peninsula. Because of the parlous state of the Depot of Military Knowledge and the lack of military interest in Intelligence, nothing was known of the country, its army or its defences; as the British commander later bitterly complained:

> The Crimea was as completely unknown country to the Chiefs of the Allied Armies as it had been to Jason and his Argonauts when they journeyed to the same place in search of the Golden Fleece . . . the nature, strength and resources of the enemy lay almost completely in the region of speculation.

The Crimean War, in many other respects also one of the most shameful in British military history, represented the nadir of British military Intelligence: with no relevant information available from London's Depot of Military Knowledge and with no Intelligence organisation under the hand of the commander in the field, his comment quoted above was more than justified. In fact, if Major Thomas Best Jervis, a prematurely retired officer of the Bombay Engineers on holiday in Belgium, had not fortuitously discovered a copy of a Russian General Staff map of the Crimea and another of an Austrian military map of Turkey in twenty-one large sheets, the British commanders would have had no better idea of the geography of the Crimea than could be gleaned from an atlas.

War having just been declared, Jervis realised the value of his find and hurried back to London, where he managed to obtain an audience with the Secretary of State for War. Although his budget would not permit the reproduction of the maps by the Army, the Secretary of State was sufficiently impressed of their value to assure Jervis that if he would reproduce them himself, the government would purchase from him as many as might be required for issue to commanders in the field. Jervis agreed to undertake the task, and with the help of an officer and a clerk on loan from the Board of Ordnance, produced within a few weeks an English version of the Crimea map in ten sheets. This was well received, and demand for copies was great; copies were passed to Britain's ally, France, and they so impressed the French Emperor that he invited Jervis to France and presented him with a large gold snuffbox. Jervis had been pestering the British Government throughout 1854 to establish an Intelligence organisation in London similar to the French Depôt de la Guerre; his success with the maps eventually led the government to acquiesce and to authorise, on 2 February 1855, the establishment, under the aegis of the War Department, of a Statistical and Topographical Office (see Chart 2), with Jervis, now promoted to Lieutenant-Colonel, as Director. With a staff of two officers, a military clerk and twenty-six civilian lithographers, the new department started work in a tumbledown coach-house and stable off Whitehall a few weeks later. It moved to

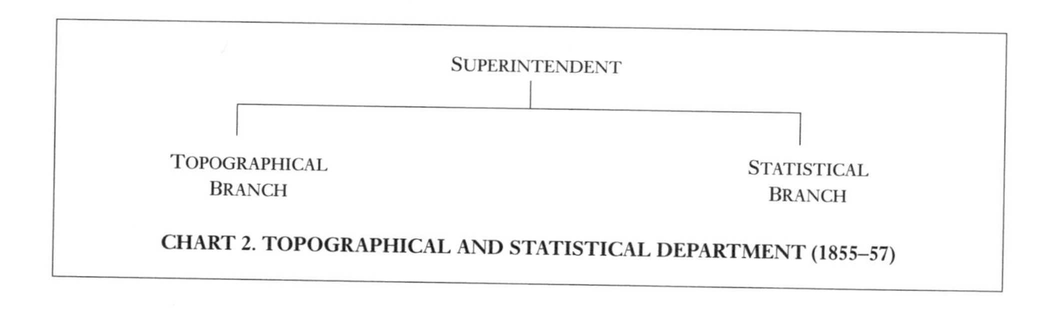

CHART 2. TOPOGRAPHICAL AND STATISTICAL DEPARTMENT (1855–57)

more suitable accommodation in 4 New Street, Spring Gardens, a site now occupied by the Admiralty, on 1 August 1856, remaining there until January 1874.

Jervis was a tireless, imaginative and determined Intelligence officer, who saw before his contemporaries the need for a central repository of Intelligence in London. The earlier Depot of Military Knowledge, founded in 1801, had been a similar idea, but this was almost dead by 1854; Jervis picked up the threads again and was instrumental in establishing what many people now see as the first step towards the creation of a British General Staff and the direct ancestor of the Joint Service Directorate of Intelligence in the present Ministry of Defence. Unfortunately, very little of either Jervis's enthusiasm or his product reached the Field Army training to win a war in the Crimea. Here, the general reaction to the collection of information about the enemy was summed up in the official history of the Crimean War in the statement: 'the gathering of knowledge by clandestine means was repulsive to the feelings of an English Gentleman'.

In everyone's mind there was a great deal of difference between tactical information obtained by reconnaissance and other overt means, and Intelligence which was obtained covertly and was classed as spying – one was fair, the other was not. As a result, no proper Intelligence organisation ever developed in the Crimea as it had done in the Peninsula; the nearest approach was the 'Head of Intelligence' at Lord Raglan's headquarters, the former British Vice-Consul at Kertch, Charles Cattley, who changed his name to Calvert for security reasons when the expeditionary force arrived at Eupatoria on 13 September 1854. In the absence of any military Intelligence officers or staff, Mr Calvert gradually assumed responsibility for all Intelligence duties and reported directly to the Commander-in-Chief. His duties included the control of Turkish and Tartar agents, interpreters and guides, and he worked in the Quartermaster-General's Department. In June 1855 he was put in charge of the newly formed Corps of Guides, but died three weeks later of cholera. His replacement, a Mr Jackson of the Foreign Office, arrived in the Crimea on 21 August 1855, just in time for the capture of Sebastopol and the virtual end of the war on 8 September.

Among other aspects of Intelligence which had been virtually ignored during the campaign, counter-Intelligence and security assumed a new importance. Not only did security of information not exist, but most people felt that it should not exist. The advent of the telegraph, however, meant that newspaper correspondents were present on the battlefield and able to transmit to their papers with little or no delay; they sent back not only graphic descriptions of the horrors of battle but also, by mixing with the officers, were able to make very accurate forecasts of future operations. This had the effect of exposing the incompetence of the high command to public gaze as well as having an adverse effect on morale at home. In addition, and of more immediate importance to the prosecution of the war in the field, it enabled the enemy to gain accurate and timely information of Allied intentions. The Tsar was reported as saying: 'We have no need of spies . . . we have *The Times*. The best means of communicating the outcome of events from Sebastopol to Moscow is via London.' Lord Raglan commented bitterly: 'The enemy need spend nothing under the heading of Secret Service . . . that enemy having at his command through the English press and from London to his headquarters by telegraph, every detail that can be required of the numbers, condition and equipment of his opponent's force.' Not only the despatches of newspaper correspondents were responsible for the constant breaches of security published in the British press; private letters home from British officers, servicemen and others were released to the press by their recipients in Britain, and these were subject to no form of censorship before despatch.

Thus in the Crimea campaign the British Army had been found wanting in all aspects of military Intelligence; non-existent at the start of the campaign, strategic, tactical and counter-Intelligence were only beginning to be developed by the end of the war. Thanks to the publicity given in the press to these weaknesses as a result of the appalling lack of security, however, the British public were aware of their Army's shortcomings and demanded improvement. When a Radical member of Parliament divided the Commons with his motion calling for a Select Committee to 'enquire into the conditions of our Army before Sebastopol and into the conduct of those Departments of the Government whose duty it has been to minister to the wants of that Army' on 29 January 1855, the government attempted to shift the blame on to the Army; the House was not impressed, the motion was carried by a two-thirds majority, and the government fell, as Gladstone put it, 'with such a whack that you could hear their heads thump as they struck the ground'. This was neither the first nor the last time that a government had been brought down in war for failing to prepare in peacetime.

The resulting Roebuck Committee sat for several months, examining the causes of administrative failure, and eventually produced a three-volume report, the final conclusion of which was that the blame lay with the complete unpreparedness of the authorities, both political and military, for the waging of a sustained European war. This committee was followed by several others, each examining specific aspects of military life. Not unnaturally, one of these was the Topographical and Statistical Department in London, created by Colonel Jervis, which had been unable, by virtue of the lateness of its creation, to furnish much in the way of Intelligence to assist the campaign. The report concluded that:

> The Department was organised in a hurry and under severe pressure . . . No very definite instructions appear to have been given to Colonel Jervis with respect to the objects in view and the mode of pursuing them.

The War Department acted quickly on this report, and in October 1857 the department was organised to include the Ordnance Survey, under a new Director, Lieutenant-Colonel Henry James of the Royal Engineers, and was made a separate department of the War Office. Intelligence and maps go naturally together, and as the Royal Engineers have traditionally been responsible for surveying, it would seem natural for a Royal Engineers officer to be chosen to head the responsible department. Unfortunately, however, Colonel James was interested mainly in the then comparatively new art of reproducing maps by photography, and not at all in other aspects of Intelligence. The department became fully occupied with the production of maps and other artwork, such as the plates for a new issue of Dress Regulations and a series of illustrations of Army equipment relating to the Royal Artillery, to the exclusion of Intelligence concerning the composition and characteristics of foreign armies. By 1869, only twelve years after its much publicised rebirth, the Topographical and Statistical Department had reverted to the insignificance of its predecessors prior to the Crimean War. Once again there was nobody employed in Britain on the collection and collation of military Intelligence.

If it seems to the reader that undue emphasis has been placed on the Crimean War in this account it is because this period marked the low point of British military Intelligence; it is from the mistakes made in and prior to this campaign that the subsequent, and eventually highly successful, Intelligence organisations of later wars were evolved. In addition, the Crimean War marked the beginning of the ever-increasing acceleration in the development of the capability and range of weapons, communications and mobility. The introduction of the rifled gun, the steam tractor, the telegraph and heliograph, the Morse code and photography at this time affected profoundly and irreversibly the whole spectrum of strategic, tactical and counter-Intelligence. As usual, however, the lessons were not immediately learnt, despite the reorganisations resulting from the recommendations of the Roebuck Committee.

By 1870 the very existence of the Topographical and Statistical Department was in jeopardy: funds had been cut and staff reduced, with the result that its Intelligence value to the Army was non-existent. However, the siege of Paris by the Prussian Army made the British Government again look to its defences, and a spirit of reform once more swept through the War Office, this time in the person of Mr Edward Cardwell, the Secretary of State for War. As Prussian victory followed

Prussian victory, the Prime Minister began to press the War Office for current assessments of the Prussian Army; the Topographical and Statistical Department was unable to supply this information, however, being fully occupied with the production of maps, illustrations for Dress Regulations and other lithographs.

Luckily for the Army and the T & S Department, the right man appeared at the right time. Captain Charles Wilson, also a Royal Engineer, was posted to the department as Executive Officer of the Topographical Section. Wilson had led an adventurous career in the Army, having spent four years delineating the frontier between the United States and Canada and a further year surveying the city of Jerusalem, and it was as a result of this experience that he was so dismayed by what he found when he arrived at the T & S Department. After only a few months in the post, Wilson submitted a strongly worded memorandum complaining that the recommendations of the Roebuck Committee had not been implemented and that the working of the department was being seriously hampered by lack of funds. As a result of this memorandum, Cardwell set up a strong committee under Lord Northbrook, his Under-Secretary of State, to investigate the T & S Department. Wilson was appointed secretary and charged with drafting the committee's report. He presented the report on 30 April 1870, and although it was only two pages long, this paper, written by a junior officer of exceptional ability and foresight, marks a significant point in the development of British military Intelligence. Cardwell adopted it almost in its entirety, and it is the foundation on which the present British Defence Intelligence organisation has been built. He recommended that:

1. The Ordnance Survey should be split from the Topographical Section and should be a charge upon the Civil rather than the Army vote.
2. The Department should be divided into two sections, a Topographical Section and a Statistical Section.
3. The Topographical Section should produce maps and should collect maps and photographs of all foreign countries.
4. The Statistical Section should be sub-divided into:
   Section 'A', covering Austria, Russia, Sweden, Norway, Turkey, Greece and Asia.
   Section 'B', covering Prussia, Germany, Italy, Switzerland, Spain and Denmark.
   Section 'C', covering France, Great Britain, Belgium, the Netherlands and America.
   All three sub-sections would have the task of collecting and classifying information, rendering such information generally useful and translating such foreign works as may be deemed desirable.
5. A sum of money, say £250, should be inserted in the Estimates each year for the purchase of foreign books and newspapers.
6. All confidential and other War Office reports, the printed orders and circulars of

all Departments of the Army and all Parliamentary reports on Army matters should be sent to the Topographical Department as a matter of course.

7. All military attaché reports should be sent to the Topographical Department, and officers of the Department should be allowed to communicate with them in a semi-official manner. Attachés should send, every quarter, notices of new books and maps published in their country and collect all foreign army circulars and orders relating to equipment and organisation. Attachés should also be encouraged to criticise the workings of foreign army systems, and should be selected from officers who have passed through the Topographical Department or Staff College or who belong to the Artillery or Engineers.
8. Officers of the Topographical Department should be encouraged to travel and attend the Autumn manoeuvres on the Continent.
9. Information collected by the Sections should be made useful not only to the Secretary of State but also to the Army as a whole by publishing quarterly a list of all maps and books added to the Library during the quarter, and translations of interesting articles, on military matters in foreign periodicals. Secondly, a series of pamphlets descriptive of foreign armies and similar to those prepared by the Prussian Topographical Department should be prepared.

This report has been reproduced virtually in its entirety as it sets out clearly the basic requirements of an Intelligence organisation; the recommendations were accepted almost without change by a further committee under Lord Northbrook in January 1871, and thus laid the foundation for the Ministry of Defence Intelligence organisation as it is known today. Wilson was promoted to be the Director of the reorganised T. and S. Department (see Chart 3), with three officers to help him, and tasked to:

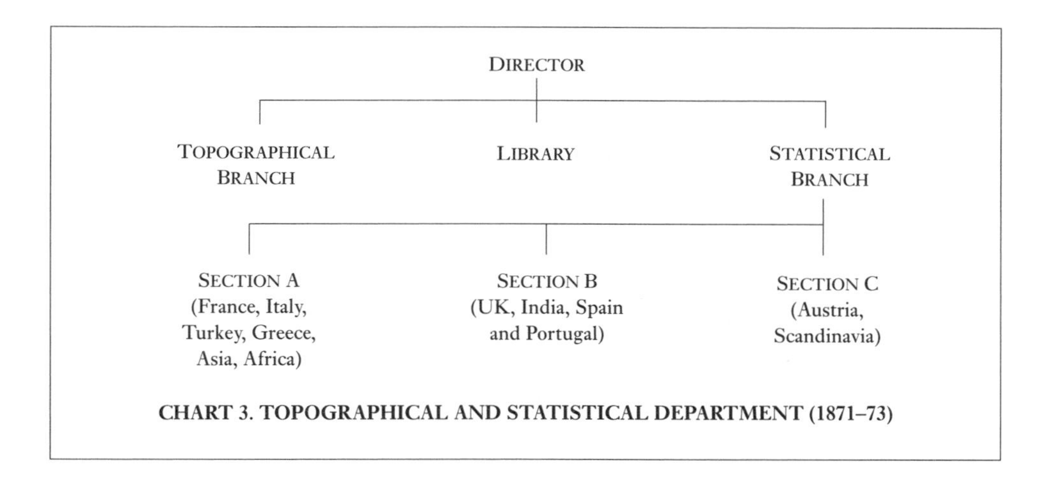

CHART 3. TOPOGRAPHICAL AND STATISTICAL DEPARTMENT (1871–73)

> . . . collect and classify all possible information relating to the strength, organisation and equipment of foreign armies, to keep themselves acquainted with the progress made by foreign countries in military art and science and to preserve the information in such a form that it can readily be consulted and made available for any purpose for which it may be required.

This brief is almost identical to that to which the current British Defence Intelligence organisation operates.

Wilson was not satisfied, however, and after a year's experience of the appointment, submitted another report to Cardwell, suggesting the need to have an officer of General rank to represent Intelligence interests and to present the Intelligence contribution to the Army High Command and to other government departments, this officer to be relieved of all command duties and to be free to study the military defence of the Empire and the preparation of the Army for war. This was the first time that the complementary nature of operations and Intelligence had been recognised, and formed the basis of the concept of the General Staff (Intelligence) chain of command and communication which later became standard in the British Army. Cardwell again accepted Wilson's recommendation, and on 24 February 1873 announced in the House of Commons the intention of the government to: 'establish an Intelligence Department with a Deputy Adjutant-General and to amalgamate with it the Topographical Department under the most excellent officer, Captain Wilson'. On 1 April 1873 Major-General Sir Patrick MacDougall was appointed to head a new organisation called the Intelligence Branch (see Chart 4), which, in addition to himself, was to consist of 1 major, 5 captains, 1 attached officer, 9 military and 10 civilian clerks; Wilson was promoted into the major's post.

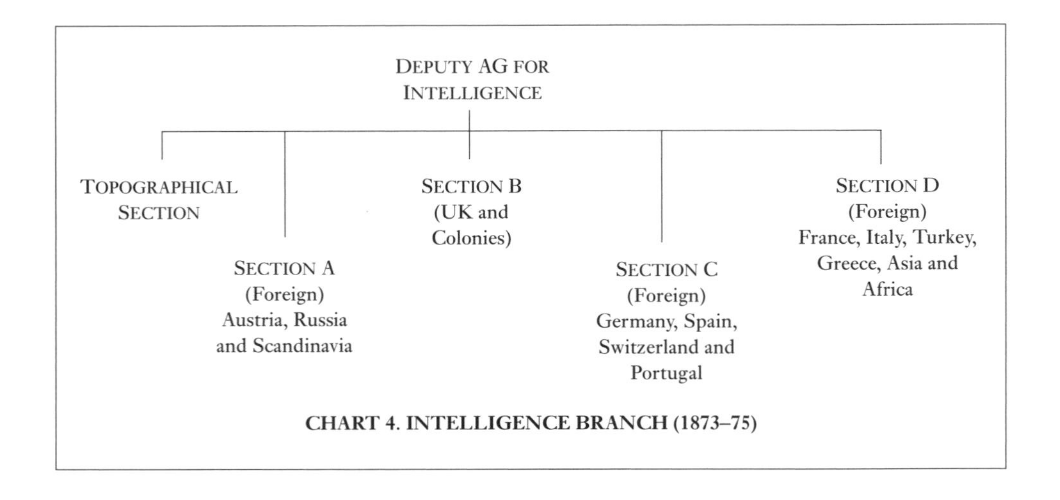

CHART 4. INTELLIGENCE BRANCH (1873–75)

Thus it was that some two hundred years after the birth of the regular British Army, Intelligence was at last recognised as being of sufficient importance to both have a function in time of peace and to become a separate branch of the Army command; 1 April 1873 is therefore memorable in the history of British military Intelligence, because since that date there has always been an Intelligence organisation in the British Army – of varying size, capability and influence, dependent upon personalities and available funds, but nevertheless in place and there to be built on as and when required.

However, the existence of an Intelligence Branch in London did nothing for either Wolseley in the Ashanti campaign of 1873, Chelmsford and Wolseley in the Zulu wars or other commanders in the various campaigns carried out in other parts of the world between 1873 and 1885. In each case, necessity dictated the formation and development of an Intelligence system which finally comprised field Intelligence units under the direct control of an Intelligence officer on the staff of the field force commander. As his Head of Intelligence for the Ashanti campaign, Wolseley had appointed the young and dashing Captain Redvers Buller of the Rifle Brigade, who quickly organised, from scratch, a highly successful network of agents and guides. In Zululand in 1878, however, Intelligence did not do so well; Lord Chelmsford took no Intelligence officer on his staff, relying instead upon a number of civilian political officers attached to each column to act as interpreters, employ guides and control spies. As civilians, the political officers were given scant recognition by the Army commanders, and Chelmsford's first campaign, in January and February 1879, was an ignominious failure. For the second campaign in March and April of that year, however, Chelmsford had the sense to appoint two military Intelligence officers, designated as such. With a well-organised field Intelligence service, his second campaign was successful, thanks to timely and accurate information.

In 1874 the Intelligence Branch in London had been removed from the Adjutant-General's Department of the War Office to that of the Quartermaster-General, a return to the practice of the eighteenth and the first half of the nineteenth centuries, and as such, a retrograde step. In January of that year the branch had moved from its cramped accommodation in Spring Gardens to Adair House in St James's Square so that it could be nearer to the War Office, then located in Pall Mall (see Chart 5). By 1882 the concept of the Intelligence Branch in London had become accepted and its contribution to both the War Office and the Government had been recognised. In 1884 the branch moved again, to 'two fine old houses' at 16 and 18 Queen Anne's Gate, giving considerably more room than Adair House, and this remained the home of War Office Intelligence until 1901.

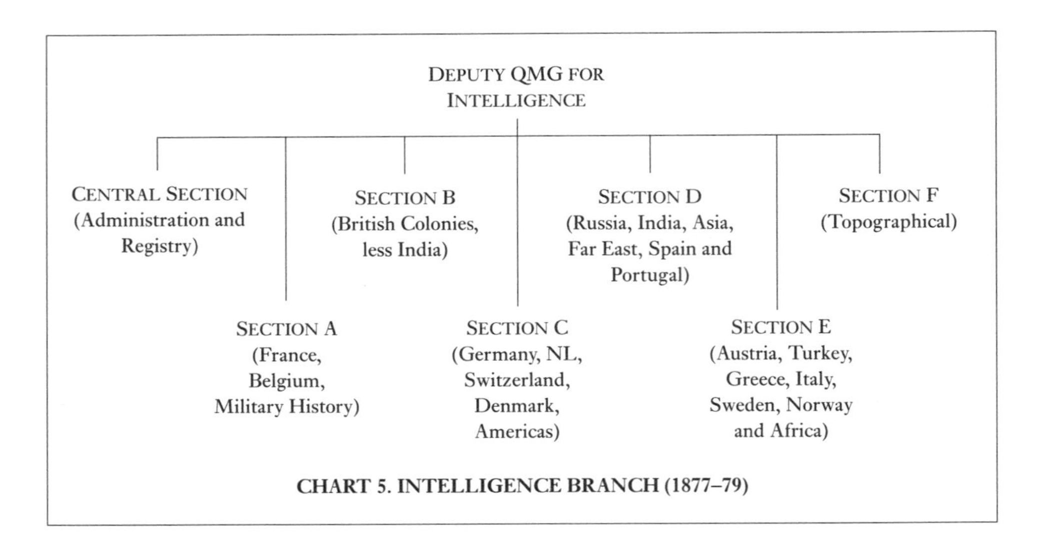

CHART 5. INTELLIGENCE BRANCH (1877–79)

From its establishment in 1873 until the outbreak of the First World War in 1914, the Intelligence Branch reached its lowest point in terms of efficacy, prestige and morale in 1885. This was due partly to a certain loss of direction after the departure of General Sir Patrick MacDougall for Canada in 1878 and his replacement by Major-General Sir Archibald Allison, and partly to the practice then prevalent of taking officers from the Intelligence Branch when overseas campaigns started. When fighting broke out in the Middle East, Allison and four of the majors serving in the branch left for Egypt, and it was left to deal with its first large-scale conflict under a gallant, but not outstanding, second-in-command. His staff officers were constantly leaving for operational service, and in the last Suakin expedition in 1885, four out of six of his majors were sent out to form the Intelligence Department for the expedition. However, the withdrawal of troops from the Sudan marked a significant turning-point for the branch because, for the first time, several officers who had previously served in the branch were posted back into it; foremost among these was Major-General Henry Brackenbury, who filled the vacant post of Head of Intelligence.

In the five years during which General Brackenbury headed the branch, it matured and developed to become once more an integral and important part of the War Office. On 1 June 1887, Brackenbury's title of Deputy Quartermaster-General for Intelligence was changed to Director of Military Intelligence (DMI), a title which was to remain unchanged until 1901. At the same time the Intelligence Branch was returned to the Adjutant-General's Department, where the product of the Intelligence staff could more easily be linked with the operational requirement. When Brackenbury was promoted to Lieutenant-General in 1888, the status of the branch was raised and it became the Intelligence Division (see Chart 6), with responsibilities as follows:

DMI – Lieutenant-General Brackenbury
DMI's Staff – two warrant officers and one confidential clerk
Sections A–E inclusive – country sections, each of one major, one captain and one military clerk
Section F – with same staff as other sections, dealing with compilation and production of maps
Library – with one librarian and two military clerks
Map Room – with curator and assistant
Drawing Office – with seven draughtsmen and three printers
Store Room – one warrant officer and one military clerk

This reorganisation expanded on that instigated in 1873 by Wilson, retaining the division into 'country sections', but rationalising the allocation of countries to sections and expanding the number of sections. That this system was sound in principle is shown by the fact that it was retained in the Directorate of Military Intelligence until 1965.

As well as reorganising the division, General Brackenbury took great care in selecting the officers who would serve in it. The majority had already served successfully in at least one Intelligence appointment, as had Brackenbury himself, and it was because the Intelligence Division was so well commanded and staffed that it became increasingly a source of advice not only to the Commander-in-Chief, but also to the Foreign Office.

Brackenbury had also established a close liaison with the Director of Naval Intelligence, established an interchange of information with the Colonial, India and

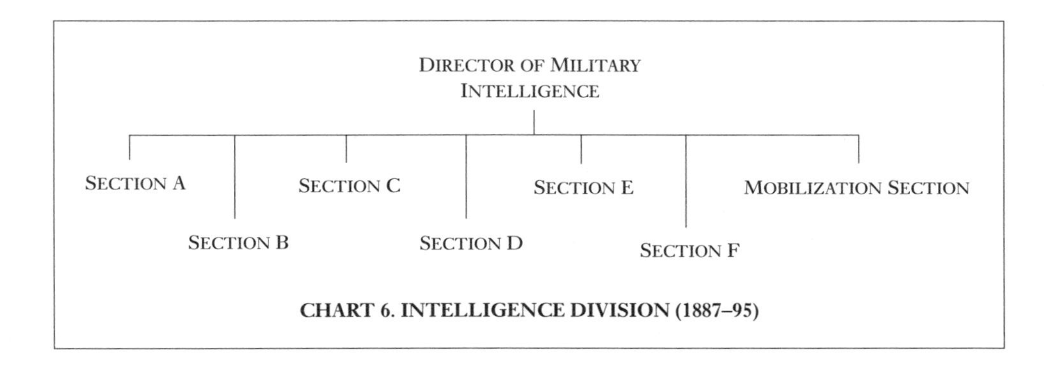

CHART 6. INTELLIGENCE DIVISION (1887–95)

Foreign Offices and tentatively with the Cabinet, and been instrumental in getting Intelligence officers established on the staffs of generals commanding overseas garrisons. In addition, he had begun the practice suggested by Charles Wilson many years earlier of circulating foreign military information to other departments of the War Office, and had established the principle that the Director of Military Intelligence should be consulted on all military matters concerning foreign countries. Brackenbury finished his five-year term as DMI in 1891, and left behind him an efficient and highly respected military Intelligence machine (see Chart 7). Under his successor, however, the division again entered the doldrums for a time.

Major-General E.F. Chapman, who assumed Brackenbury's mantle as DMI on 1 April 1891, had spent all his Army service in India; all his staff appointments there had been in the Quartermaster-General's Department, finally ending up as QMG in Bengal prior to his return to the UK to take up his appointment as DMI at the War Office. He had been selected for the appointment as there was fear of a Russian invasion of India, in which case his Indian experience would have been invaluable. In the event, however, the next five years saw successive crises in Europe and Africa rather than India. Chapman's tour of duty as DMI ended in March 1896, his successor being Colonel Sir John Ardagh, who was promoted to Major-General on taking up the appointment.

Ardagh was the last of the four men who, in the nineteenth century, share the credit for creating an efficient and universally respected Intelligence organisation in the War Office. Yet another member of the 'Wolseley Ring', that clique of officers who had served successfully with Lord Wolseley, now the Commander-

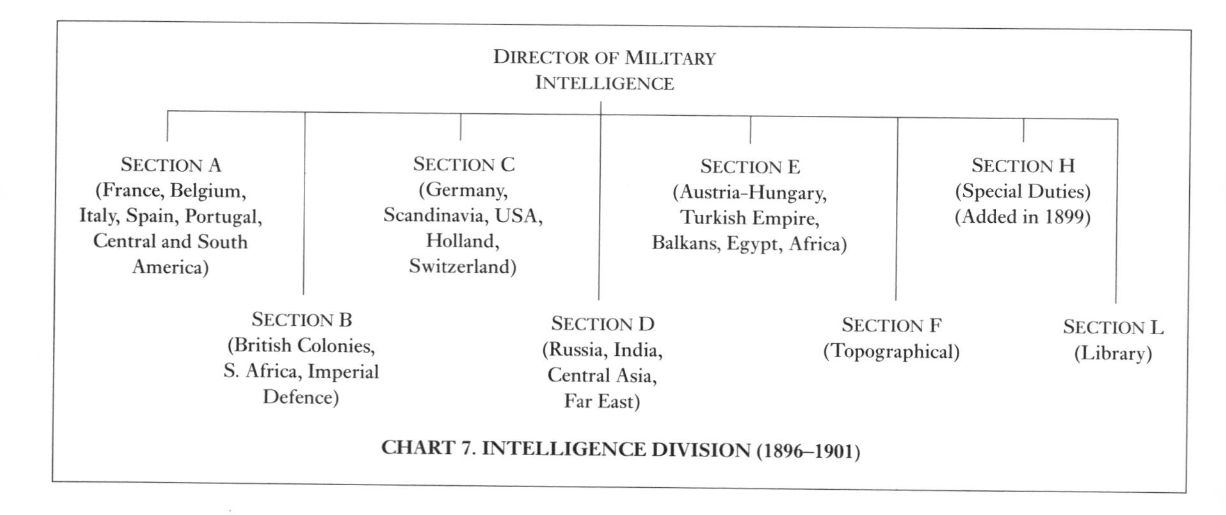

CHART 7. INTELLIGENCE DIVISION (1896–1901)

in-Chief, Ardagh had previous experience of Intelligence as well as diplomatic appointments and was well respected in the Foreign Office. He was also a personal friend of the Secretary of State for War, Lord Lansdowne, his former master in India, as well as of the Adjutant-General (Sir Redvers Buller), the Quartermaster-General (Sir Evelyn Wood) and the Director-General of Ordnance (Sir Henry Brackenbury), so that the Intelligence Division could be assured of friends at court should the need arise.

Ardagh's only disadvantage was his 'acceptability'; during the first three years of his tour as DMI no fewer than thirty small wars or expeditions were undertaken by British troops while, at the same time, he was constantly required to attend meetings of various committees as well as conferences on frontier disputes. In addition, despite all his other commitments, he was sent to The Hague in 1899 as military adviser to a peace conference, where he spent two exhausting months defending British interests by day while trying each night to keep in touch with the War Office, the Intelligence Division and Downing Street by letter. When the conference ended in July 1899 he returned to England and immediately collapsed from fever and exhaustion; as a consequence, he was away from work for a further three months. War with South Africa was declared in October of that year, but for five months before the biggest conflict since the Crimea, the Director of Military Intelligence was away from his desk. The head of the Colonial Section, which dealt with South Africa, had been posted to Natal as Intelligence Officer in September, so when war broke out, a lowly staff captain was in charge of this all-important section.

With South Africa's declaration of war on the UK, the pigeons started to come home to roost. The Secretary of State complained: 'The Government had as little expectation of war with the Orange Free State as they had of war with Switzerland.' The Commander-in-Chief added: 'We find the enemy who declared war against us is much more powerful than we expected.' Both were using phraseology bearing a strong similarity to that used by their respective predecessors at the beginning of the Crimean War forty-five years earlier. From other less highly placed people came complaints that the armament and strength of the Boers greatly exceeded expectations, that the theatre of war was unknown territory to the troops and that the provision of maps, essential to the successful conduct of operations, had been totally neglected. After three years of bitter criticism of the Intelligence Division by both Army and public, the division was formally put on trial before a Royal Commission under Lord Elgin, charged that:

1. It had failed to assess correctly the numerical strength of the Boers.
2. It was ignorant of their armament, especially their artillery.

3. It had failed to fathom the Boers' offensive designs on Natal.
4. No warnings as to the above had been given to the government.
5. British troops had been left unfurnished with maps and were without topographical information.

It may seem paradoxical that an Intelligence organisation so highly thought of, not only by the War Office but also by the government generally, should have been arraigned before a Royal Commission and charged with delinquency and dereliction of duty, but it must be remembered that the UK had been humiliated in South Africa and the public was looking for a scapegoat. Both within and outside Parliament, General Ardagh was personally accused of a neglect thought by many people to be little short of treason; Ardagh remained silent, however, and it was not until four years later, in 1903, that the Elgin Commission's report exonerating Ardagh and the Intelligence Division was issued.

The commission discovered that contrary to previously held beliefs, the Intelligence Division had in fact issued a succession of reports emphasising the likelihood of war with South Africa and warning that such a war would be both costly and bloody. As early as October 1896, General Ardagh had submitted a paper to the Commander-in-Chief which showed that the South African Republic was spending some £2,350,000 a year on military preparations, and that 'this large expenditure can have no other explanation than an anticipation of war, or an intention of aggression against this country'. On 5 April 1897 Mr Chamberlain had expressed his acknowledgement of 'the most valuable reports submitted by the Director of Military Intelligence as to the importations of vast quantities of munitions of war into the Transvaal'. In a memorandum prepared by the Intelligence Division on 21 September 1898 a remarkably accurate estimate of the effective strengths of the Armies of both the Transvaal and her sister republic was given, together with the statement:

> The Transvaal has, during the last two years, made military preparations on a scale which can only be intended to meet the contingency of a contest with the UK. These preparations continue and . . . may culminate in war at very short notice. At the outbreak of such a war we should, at first, be in a decided numerical inferiority . . . At least a month or six weeks must elapse before any appreciable reinforcements could arrive from England or India. The problem would therefore be a difficult one, and its difficulty will be enhanced by the fact that any mistakes or lack of finances at the outset would seriously affect subsequent operations.

Further memoranda submitted to the Commander-in-Chief on 7 June and 8 August 1899 laid stress on the probability of the active cooperation of the Orange Free State with the Transvaal in the event of war, and gave a revised estimate of 34,000 for the main Republic Army strength at the outbreak of war. In addition, a handbook on South Africa, classified 'Secret', was issued in April 1898 and declassified, revised and updated in June 1899. In 1903 this book was examined in minute detail by a hostile commission, aided by the priceless gift of hindsight, providing the ultimate test for any Intelligence staff; the result, however, was a remarkable vindication of the Intelligence Division's foresight, as the following table shows.

Item	Number reported in Handbook	Actual Number in Sept. 1899
Field guns in Transvaal	83	71
Ditto in Orange Free State	24	28
Machine-guns	34	27
Rifles	64,950	70,091
Rifle ammunition	23 million+ 10 million on order	33 million

Having demonstrated that the Intelligence division had in fact warned both the War Office and the government of enemy intentions and strengths, the Elgin Committee next attempted to discover what action had resulted from these warnings. Here, however, the trail became somewhat blurred, although it was found that a number of documents issued by the DMI had not been shown to the Cabinet, and that so strong had been the political desire to avoid talk of war, other memoranda had been deliberately altered before cirulation.

Almost overnight, attacks on the DMI and the Intelligence Division ceased and they were now praised in the press as 'the quiet backroom boys who had worked so diligently and successfully to predict the outbreak of war'. Nevertheless, the division had not been faultless; poor Intelligence can lose battles, but good Intelligence cannot, on its own, win them. The division had failed to persuade its superiors to take the action which their reports called for; that this was largely due to the organisation of the War Office did not entirely exonerate the DMI and his staff.

As in previous wars, the organisation for the gathering of tactical Intelligence in the field had been virtually non-existent at the outbreak of war; the fact that there was, and had been for some years, an efficient Intelligence Division in the War Office had had no effect upon the Field Army, and the lack of any briefing of the Army commanders by the Intelligence Division prior to their embarkation for

South Africa had not helped their appreciation of the situation which awaited their arrival there. This lack of briefing, it was found by the Elgin Commission, had been due not to any deficiency on the part of the Intelligence Division, but rather to the fact that the Secretary of State for War had told General Buller, whom he had appointed as Commander-in-Chief of the Expeditionary Force, not to discuss the forthcoming operation with the DMI, 'as the appointment is strictly confidential'. In addition, the two Intelligence officers stationed in South Africa at the outbreak of war each had other staff appointments, and as both subsequently admitted to the commission, 'as war became more and more likely, so their other duties became increasingly onerous and thus the time they could give to their Intelligence responsibilities less and less'.

In South Africa, as previously in so many other theatres of war in which the British Army had been involved, an Intelligence organisation had to be built up virtually from scratch. The first step was again to form locally enlisted volunteers with knowledge of the country and the local language into Intelligence-collecting and reconnaissance units, under the command of ten officers sent by the War Office to South Africa in July 1899 on 'special service'. These units, naturally enough from previous experience, were known as the Corps of Guides, but when General Buller arrived in Capetown in November 1899 with an Army Corps and all its staff and supporting services, he brought with him not one Intelligence Officer, while the Corps of Guides and nine of the ten officers on 'special service' were trapped in Ladysmith, Mafeking and Kimberley. There was no Intelligence staff awaiting him, and only one – the most junior – of the 'special service' officers was available.

Buller accordingly made this officer his Intelligence staff officer and selected as his Head of Intelligence a Natal farmer, the Hon. T.K. Murray, who had previously recruited the Corps of Guides then under siege in Ladysmith. As Buller wrote:

> The formation of the Intelligence Department was undertaken by the Honourable T.K. Murray who placed his thorough knowledge of the country and his unbounded energy at our service. He obtained for us a Corps of Guides whose services were invaluable, but all this work had to be begun from the beginning. The threads of the Intelligence Department that had been prepared being all in Ladysmith and inaccessible.

After the early defeats of 'Black Week', to which the lack of any kind of military Intelligence had undoubtedly contributed, the government decided that a new commander and staff would have to take over in South Africa, and selected Lord

Roberts. Before sailing on 23 December 1899, Roberts selected a small staff to accompany him, including General Kitchener from the Sudan as his Chief of Staff and Colonel G.F.R. Henderson from the Staff College to be the new Head of Intelligence. Henderson in his turn asked for his former pupil, Captain W. Robertson, from Queen Anne's Gate to be his Intelligence Officer. This team rapidly built on the organisation already started by Murray, and by the time the war ended in September 1900 there was a Director of Military Intelligence (South Africa) in command of a large and efficient Field Intelligence Department which combined for the first time in one organisation a headquarters Intelligence staff, field Intelligence officers and field units whose sole function was to gather Intelligence. The DMI (South Africa) was not satisfied that this organisation was yet as good as it could be, however, and in a paper dated July 1900, he proposed that:

1. All units which may have to move independently should possess a staff officer for Intelligence duties.
2. These officers should be allocated various grades of assistants, such as guides and interpreters, to assist them.
3. There should be a military counter-Intelligence unit within the Field Intelligence Department.
4. Press and private mail censorship should be carried out under the supervision of the Field Intelligence Department.

It is probable that these sound and eminently sensible proposals would have gone the way of many other reports from the by now rapidly shrinking army in South Africa had the Boers not obstinately refused to recognise that they had lost the war. They changed their tactics to commando-style raids on British military installations and their extended supply lines with considerable success, inflicting many casualties and humiliating defeats on their British enemy. It soon became clear that to defeat these tactics it was essential to combine good Intelligence with swift retaliatory action; the DMI's proposals to improve the Intelligence organisation were therefore quickly examined and implemented, with the result that the British Army had more Intelligence officers than ever before in its history. From a mere 10 in July 1899, their number had increased to 132, with 2,320 white soldiers and a host of native scouts, by the end of 1901.

To help gain additional Intelligence, balloons were issued to the Intelligence officers of the various columns, carrier pigeons were issued to scouts, Boer newspapers and captured documents were translated in special Intelligence translating cells, and the heliograph messages sent by the Boers were intercepted by small parties of signallers formed for the purpose in the first use of signal Intelligence (SIGINT), later to produce such dramatic results in both world wars. At the War Office, a new Section H was added (see Chart 7) to the Intelligence Division to take over responsibility for cable censorship, and in conjunction with Scotland Yard, the surveillance of suspected persons. The division had moved from Queen Anne's Gate to Winchester House, St James's Square, in 1901, to be nearer to the offices of the Commander-in-Chief in Pall Mall.

When the war finally ended, the standard of British military Intelligence, both in the Field Army in South Africa and in the War Office, had reached an all-time high, but this state had not easily been reached. The organisation in the field had been built up piecemeal, both as a reaction to the various threats as they arose and also in order to exploit new sources of Intelligence as they were thought of. In its final form, however, the basic organisation was sound and functional, and it has served as a model for all British field armies since the First World War. The British Army had finally had to acknowledge that Intelligence staff are essential parts of field armies and their component formations and units, as well as of the headquarters staff in London, in peacetime as well as in war.

The Intelligence Division in London, however, although functioning well, was staffed almost entirely by reserve officers, as most regular officers were serving 6,000 miles away in South Africa; the South African War had absorbed not only the whole of the Regular Army but also most of the Volunteer Army as well, leaving the UK denuded of troops in the face of an increasingly hostile, aggressive and well-armed Europe. A series of high-level committees was appointed, with the aims of reviewing the permanent establishment of the Mobilisation and Intelligence Department and of analysing, very critically, the good and bad points arising out of the recent war, in order to avoid repetition of the mistakes made and

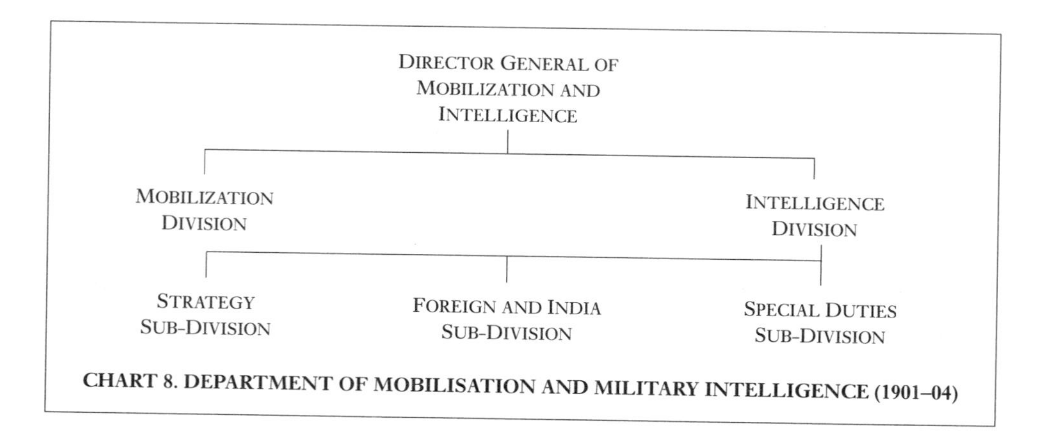

CHART 8. DEPARTMENT OF MOBILISATION AND MILITARY INTELLIGENCE (1901–04)

to be the better prepared for war in Europe, should it occur. The two main recommendations of Lord Esher's Committee when it issued its report in 1904 were immediately accepted and implemented. The first recommendation was that the office of Commander-in-Chief, for so long and so frustratingly occupied by the Duke of Cambridge, should be abolished after nearly two-and-a-half centuries. The second recommendation was the formation, at long last, of a General Staff in this new organisation; the Mobilisation and Intelligence Department would again be split into its component parts, Intelligence to become part of the Military Operations Directorate and Mobilisation to come under the Director of Military Training. It was also decided that the Intelligence function should be advisory only, the executive decisions being the prerogative of the General Staff.

This was the last major reorganisation resulting from the Boer War, although within the Military Operations (MO) Directorate itself there was a continual reorganisation of sections. Initially there were four (see Chart 9), each headed by a colonel:

MO 1 – Strategic, covering Imperial Defence and the strategical distribution of the Army
MO 2 – Foreign Intelligence
MO 3 – Administration and Special Duties (such as counter-Intelligence and censorship)
MO 4 – Topographical Section

In 1907 two new sections were formed (see Chart 10): MO 5 took over the functions of 'Special Duties' from MO 3, and MO 6 was created to collect and

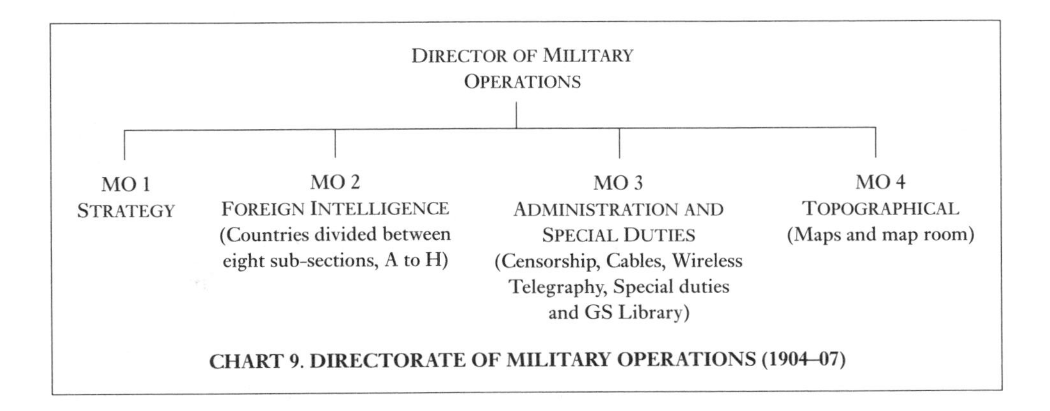

CHART 9. DIRECTORATE OF MILITARY OPERATIONS (1904–07)

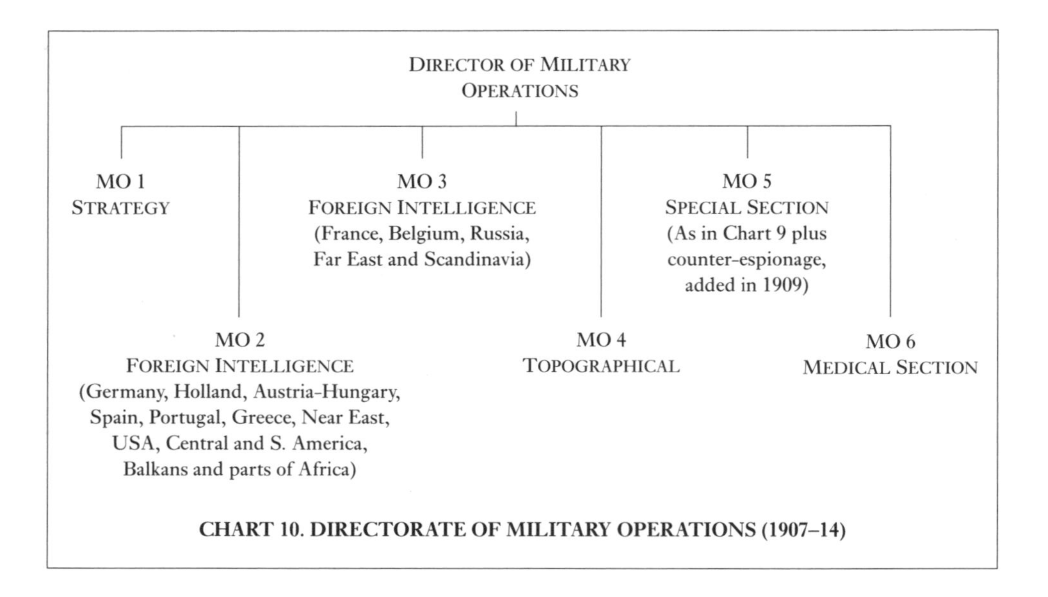

CHART 10. DIRECTORATE OF MILITARY OPERATIONS (1907–14)

collate medical Intelligence; prior to the 1904 reorganisation, 'Special Duties' had been the responsibility of Section H of the Intelligence Division.

In November 1906 the MO Directorate moved from Winchester House in St James's Square to the then new War Office Building (now known as the Old War Office Building, or OWOB) in Whitehall. In the final reorganisation of the MO Directorate before the outbreak of war in August 1914, MO 2 assumed responsibility for Intelligence on European countries and MO 3 for Asia, the Americas and the Far East. MO 5 added administration and the General Staff Library to its responsibilities as well as, in 1909, the Special Intelligence Bureau (later to be known as MI 5, or the Security Service, and MI 6, or the Secret Intelligence Service), consisting of a Home Section (later MI 5) under Captain Vernon Kell, of the South Staffordshire Regiment, with responsibility for counter-espionage, and a Foreign Section (later SIS, or MI 6) with responsibility for espionage overseas. Thus, with responsibility for Intelligence, counter-Intelligence and operational planning, the Director of Military Operations (DMO) had now become a very influential person in Whitehall, and the Intelligence Branch had a direct channel through him to the Chief of the Imperial General Staff (CIGS). Intelligence had at last found its rightful place in the War Office hierarchy.

The war clouds were beginning to gather over Europe, however, and spy fever began increasingly to grip the UK from 1909 onwards, fuelled by the writings of William Le Queux with the assistance of Lord Northcliffe's *Daily Mail*. Le Queux was the son of a French father and English mother, educated partly in the UK and partly on the Continent, who became a journalist and war correspondent for the *Daily Mail.* As a result of his travels he developed a fascination for espionage which, when coupled with his conviction that every country in Europe, especially Germany, had designs on the UK, gave him an almost paranoid fixation about German spies in the country, preparing for '*Der Tag*' (the day of invasion) for which the War Office and the British public were woefully, if not wilfully, unprepared. He wrote several novels on the subject, most of which became best-sellers, and there is no doubt that they helped to convince a large proportion of the British population of the dangers posed by German spies in the country; many of those so convinced were soldiers and civil servants, some of whom testified to, and others served on, Lord Esher's sub-committee of the Committee for Imperial Defence which met in 1909 to consider the question of foreign espionage in the UK. There is no doubt that Germany had been building up its navy since the turn of the century, and this was the basis on which Le Queux had built his fantasies.

On the other hand, the Germans were convinced that the UK would not be able to tolerate a rival on the high seas and was likely to launch a surprise attack on the German fleet in harbour. Particularly after two Royal Navy officers on SIS duty, Captain Brandon and Lieutenant Trench, were arrested in May 1910 while reconnoitring the German coast and sentenced to four years in prison, spy fever started to gain a hold in Germany. It was fuelled by a German 'Le Queux', General F. von Bernhardt, who published a book in 1912 entitled *Germany and the Next War*, and the German public became almost as obsessed with spies as the British were. The story, probably apocryphal, is told of a lady's maid who was strip-searched on leaving Germany, and the woman police officer carrying out the search excitedly reporting that the maid had secret writing on her bottom; she was arrested, the writing photographed and the photographs sent to German military Intelligence. It transpired that on the train to the frontier, the maid had gone to the lavatory and had covered the seat with newspaper before sitting down, for reasons of hygiene; the 'secret writing' was from that day's *Frankfurter Zeitung*!

The DMO and his staff were convinced by now that war with Germany was inevitable: the British 'Handbook on the German Army' was continually reviewed and kept up to date, German Field Service Regulations were translated and issued widely, and handbooks on roads and billeting facilities in northern France and Belgium were prepared and issued. There was no criticism in 1914, as there had been in 1900, that the Intelligence staff in London had failed to warn those in authority of the coming war, or had failed to plan for it.

The improvement of Intelligence collection in the field, recommended by the Esher Committee in 1903, was a different matter, however, and by 1914 it was still not considered necessary to raise in peacetime a specialist Intelligence-collecting unit; the next best thing was to compile a list of linguists and experts on various aspects of life in Europe, and this was commenced by MO 5 in 1913. As a result, on 5 August 1914, only eight hours after the UK's ultimatum to Germany had expired, some fifty university lecturers, journalists, businessmen and others in various parts of the world received a telegram asking them to join a new unit called the Intelligence Corps; three weeks later they moved to France, graded as 2nd Lieutenants (Interpreters) or as Agents First Class, having received virtually no training and with no idea of their role. After being allocated either a horse or a motor-cycle they were assigned to various headquarters whose commanders also had no idea at the time of the role that these odd characters were supposed to fill. These bewildered men represented the product of some 250 years of British Army experience in Intelligence in the field, but four years later, they and their successors had built up a fine reputation for painstaking, imaginative and professional Intelligence work in their peculiar skills of providing local knowledge, controlling agents, taking and interpreting aerial photographs, translating documents, interrogating prisoners, intercepting signals, censorship and counter-espionage security.

At the outbreak of war in August 1914 the War Office had an efficient Military Operations and Intelligence Directorate in place, which had maintained up-to-date information on the Armies of the Central Powers as well as having made detailed plans for its own duties and organisation in the event of war with Germany. With so many Field Intelligence Officers earmarked to join the British Expeditionary Force (BEF) in France on the outbreak of war, British military Intelligence can be said to have been better prepared for war than ever before in peacetime. The directorate had made excellent use of the 'planning years' immediately preceding the outbreak of war in Europe, when idealistic members of the government had laid the dead hand of pacifism on reform of the armed services and expenditure on them; they were called 'planning years' because the government would allow no actual expansion of the Army unless and until war was declared. Despite this restriction and the best efforts of the politicians, the nucleus of an Intelligence organisation capable of collecting and collating both strategic and tactical Intelligence was in existence.

In the final reorganisation before August 1914, MO 2 was responsible for Intelligence on countries in Europe (except France), the Middle East and the Americas, MO 3 was responsible for France, Russia, Scandinavia and the Far East, MO 4 was responsible for topographical matters, MO 5 for Special Intelligence, the General Staff Library and Directorate administration, and MO 6 for medical Intelligence. Their task was laid down in an exhaustive brief, not very different from that of today's Ministry of Defence Intelligence staff:

> The collection, collation and dissemination of information regarding the organisation, equipment, training and tactics, personalities, order of battle, morale and education of the armies of foreign countries, their possessions and mandated territories. The consideration of political, strategical, geographical and topographical questions concerning them from a military point of view, as well as matters of policy which may arise concerning such countries.

MO 6 was disbanded on mobilisation, its staff being returned to duty with the Royal Army Medical Corps, but ten days after the declaration of war, MO 7 was created, to deal with press censorship and public relations matters. In April 1915 MO 6 was re-formed, this time to deal with enemy ciphers, the espionage service (SIS) and the drafting of Intelligence despatches for the General Headquarters of the BEF. Together with MO 5, MO 7, the newly formed MO 8 (cable censorship) and MO 9 (postal censorship) it was placed in the Directorate of Special Intelligence under its newly appointed Director, Brigadier-General G.K. Cockerill.

If British military Intelligence was prepared for war as never before in peacetime, what it was not prepared for was war as never before. This war was the first in which aviation and aerial photography, the internal combustion and compression ignition engines, wireless telegraphy, poison gas, the tank, flame warfare and the submarine were to be used on a large scale, and warfare was never to be the same again. The Allies' plans had taken into account the greater range of reconnaissance which the aeroplane permitted, as well as the greater ground mobility afforded by the internal combustion engine. What neither the British nor the French Intelligence services had thought likely was the German plan of attack, the Schlieffen Plan, whereby the German forces swung through neutral Belgium round the northern flank of the strong French defensive line extending south from Luxemburg to Switzerland, in an attempt to conclude the campaign in the west within three weeks. Had it achieved this, Germany could then have devoted all its resources to the defeat of Russia on the Eastern Front. It was this violation of Belgium's neutrality which led to the UK's declaration of war, in fulfilment of its treaty obligations to Belgium.

The Allies had also been reckoning on a short war in the west: based on their Plan 17, the French aimed to stop the German attack dead by a move against its expected centre, thus achieving a breakthrough which would both paralyse the enemy's communications in Lorraine and split apart the wings of its attack. However, it must be stated that at the outbreak of war, official British circles had no knowledge of the contents of Plan 17, although the whole of the BEF planning, and indeed the *entente cordiale* between the UK and France, had been based on the premise that the BEF would fight beside the French Army in the event of war with Germany. Thus it was that the BEF was committed to supporting a French disaster; as soon as battle was joined, the French offensive plan collapsed against the weight and subtlety of the Schlieffen Plan, and the tragic mistakes and flaws in French strategy were plain for all to see.

Within only a few months of the arrival of the BEF in France, the best-trained, best-organised and best-equipped British Field Army ever to embark for war was bogged down in static trench warfare, very different from the war of movement for which it had been trained and equipped. The Intelligence Corps of fifty linguists and experts on Europe so hurriedly recruited to accompany the BEF had a chaotic introduction to life in field Intelligence. The head of Intelligence at British GHQ was Colonel G.M.W. Macdonogh, who had previously been the head of MO 5, the Special Intelligence and Administration section of the MO Directorate at the War Office. His original intention had been that the Intelligence Corps should comprise a Mounted Section (the mounts for which had already been requisitioned from the Grafton Hunt), a Motor-Cycle Section and a Dismounted Section, in addition to its headquarters. Once in France, however, it was soon decided that all Intelligence Corps officers needed motor-cycles, but the lack of driving experience of many of the Intelligence officers coupled with their bravado proved to be a dangerous and sometimes deadly combination. The Intelligence Branch at GHQ was organised into four departments, of which I(a) dealt with operational Intelligence, I(b) with security and secret service work, I(c) with censorship, and I(x) with personnel and administration.

The British High Command in France paid little heed to the reports of its Intelligence officers in the early months of the war. The Commander-in-Chief and his operations staff treated the French Intelligence reports of the German sweep through Belgium with similar scepticism, the reason in both cases being the preconceived ideas of the respective Commanders-in-Chief and their operations staffs. It was not unnatural that until the Intelligence staffs had proved the accuracy and worth of their information, their reports should be treated with reserve, but it is no use having a dog and barking oneself, and commanders need to keep an open mind, receptive to ideas other than their own, if they are to be successful. This is particularly true when the information coming in is the result of personal observation by experienced military personnel – in this case the crews of the four squadrons of reconnaissance aircraft of the Royal Flying Corps which had assembled at Maubeuge by 15 August 1914.

The majority, and the most valuable, of the Intelligence received during the mobile early phase of the war came for the first time from the air. On 20 August 1914, for example, the RFC observed a column of enemy troops, stretching as far as the eye could see, passing through Louvain, and on the following afternoon reconnaissance sorties reported a large body of cavalry, infantry and artillery south-east of Nivelles. This latter report was confirmed by an Intelligence officer who was in Nivelles when the cavalry arrived, who managed to escape by car. Based on these and other reports, Macdonogh correctly deduced that a German column of all arms was advancing rapidly from Brussels on Mons, but his appreciation was airily dismissed by Operations Branch as being somewhat exaggerated.

By 21 August, some of the Intelligence Corps officers had been assigned to special duties, such as interrogation, cipher work, photography and issuing passes; however, the majority in those early days were given little idea of what their duties were, and spent most of their time as dispatch riders or liaison officers on their motor-cycles. There was a certain amount of suspicion of the green-tabbed Intelligence Corps officer on the part of the troops: he had a marked reserve coupled with an insatiable curiosity, two characteristics which tend to be resented by British soldiers, which led them to suspect that the officer was more interested in reporting on the state of the unit he was visiting than in gleaning information about the enemy.

By December 1914 the Western Front had stabilised into a continuous and immobile line of trenches from the North Sea coast in the north to the Swiss frontier in the south. Under these circumstances, novel to the British Army at the time, there was obviously no scope for the cavalry to reconnoitre enemy positions or to exploit a breakthrough, its traditional roles; the only alternatives were, for close reconnaissance, the infantry patrol, mounted from the British trenches, with the twin aims of assessing the strength and layout of the enemy trenches and capturing prisoners and documents with a view to identifying the enemy units, and if possible, their immediate future plans. For long-range reconnaissance, the RFC had initially provided the only means, but once the German troop movements behind their lines started to be carried out by train, they were much less easy to follow and analyse than the earlier movements by road through Belgium and northern France. Aerial reconnaissance could only detect abnormal collections or movements of rolling stock; it could not tell whether troops were entraining or detraining, whether or not the trains were empty, in which direction the trains were moving or what units were involved.

To obtain this information it was necessary to organise covert networks of train-watchers behind the enemy lines. These were organised by the I(b) section of GHQ Intelligence Branch, headed initially by Major Walter Kirke. During the war, British military Intelligence employed about 6,000 agents in this capacity on the Western Front. Some were sent through or round the German lines, but most were French or Belgian civilians living locally. Of these, about a hundred were caught and executed and nearly seven hundred imprisoned by the Germans. Throughout the static phase of the war, this type of Intelligence, together with prisoner interrogation and examination of captured documents, formed the bulk of Intelligence work in the battle area; it was vital information, from which the enemy Order of Battle (OB) could be built up. This OB information in turn had a direct effect on the operations and movement of British forces, and it therefore became the first objective of the British secret Intelligence effort.

To organise a voluntary network of watchers was one thing; to get the agents into position, to get their orders to them and to get their reports back from them was another, with a solid line of trenches, some 350 miles long, between the train-watching agents and their Intelligence Corps controllers. The only viable alternatives were for communication either through the lines or round them at each end, and great was the ingenuity in solving these problems displayed by the officers of the Intelligence Corps during the next four years. At first, agents were landed behind the German lines by aircraft of the RFC. In 1917, however, as a result of General Trenchard's decision that this method was too expensive in terms of aircraft and pilots, dropping agents from aircraft by means of the 'Guardian Angel' parachute was substituted; again, restrictions placed on this method by the RFC, limiting its use to a fifteen mile-deep zone behind the German front line, by the weather and by the phases of the moon, finally led the I(b) staff at GHQ to favour landing agents from free balloon. Although this method was also weather- and wind-dependent, it at least had the advantage of silence.

After unsuccessful trials of various methods of communicating directly across the front line, British GHQ came to the conclusion that pigeons offered the best solution, and very large numbers were used; agents took with them the pigeons for their first communications, and further consignments were dropped to them from aircraft at agreed places and times as necessary. However, owing to pilots' difficulty in correctly identifying the exact dropping zone at night and the possibility of the agent being unable to keep the rendezvous, these operations were not very successful, despite the dropping of many consignments of pigeons.

Better results were obtained by communication round the neutral flanks of the enemy trench system, through Holland in the north and Switzerland in the south. Of the two, Holland seemed at first to be the better bet, partly because it was more accessible from the UK, and partly because it covered the rear of those

German formations opposing the British sector of the front, but Intelligence reports sent by this route took three weeks to reach GHQ.

In September 1917, first steps were taken by GHQ to set up a train-spotting network based on the important rail centre of Luxemburg, reporting via Switzerland to Captain The Hon. G.J.G. Bruce, who had previously been in charge of the Paris office of Major Cameron's network. This started to operate in June 1918, and soon became the best train-watching network at that time, operating successfully right up to the occupation of Luxemburg by the Americans at the conclusion of hostilities. Reports from this network took only five days to reach GHQ, compared to the minimum of three weeks taken by reports from the networks in Holland.

At a conference between the Allies on 22 November 1914, it had been decided to form a Joint Intelligence Bureau at Folkestone which would contain British, French and Belgian offices, working together but each running its own separate Intelligence operations. The British agents were recruited from the thousands of Belgian refugees who had flooded into northern France ahead of the advancing German Armies; they were returned to Belgium by a circuitous route, first crossing the Channel to England, thence to Holland on the Folkestone–Flushing ferry, and finally over the Dutch–Belgian frontier. The British bureau was established in a house on the sea-front at Folkestone, with a Captain Cecil Cameron in charge; by the spring of 1915 he was running, on behalf of GHQ at St Omer, one of two successful networks providing tactical Intelligence from behind the German lines in Belgium. The other network, started at the suggestion of a Captain Payne Best of the Intelligence Corps (of whom more will be heard in the Second World War), was run from an office in Basil Street, London, by a Major Ernest Wallinger, an artillery officer who had been wounded at Le Cateau, with Best as his second-in-command. The first network was known by the abbreviation CF (Cameron, Folkestone), the second by WL (Wallinger, London). A third network, known as the T network, was run from the War Office in London. The information from the two GHQ networks was fed forward to Major Kirke, second-in-command of the GHQ Intelligence Branch and in charge of the I(b) section, where it was collated with other information and disseminated to subordinate formations and units in the form of Intelligence summaries.

The unexpected solidification of the Western Front and the resulting necessity for GHQ to organise agent networks through Holland and Switzerland for the collection of tactical Intelligence soon led to clashes between GHQ and the Secret Intelligence Service (SIS); the latter's charter was for the gathering of strategic Intelligence of all types from all parts of the world. The SIS was now operating under the umbrella of the Admiralty from premises in London's Northumberland Avenue, with Commander Mansfield Smith-Cumming, RN, as its head; it had been separated from its sister Security Service, MO 5 of the War Office, and got off to a shaky start, feeling its lack of trained Intelligence officers and agents compared to the sophisticated networks then being operated by both the Army and the Royal Navy. The problems caused by the collision in Holland and Switzerland between the tactical networks run by GHQ and the strategic networks of the SIS were never completely solved during the war.

In addition to running covert Intelligence collection networks, the GHQ Intelligence Branch in France was responsible for frustrating German clandestine Intelligence-gathering activities behind the British lines, and for this purpose several members of MO 5, the Security Service, were posted to the BEF; in addition, a number of experienced officers from the police Special Branch were drafted into the Security Service and commissioned into the Intelligence Corps for counter-espionage duties in France. The Special Branch contingent was led by Detective-Inspector Martin Clancy and was based at the British GHQ at St Omer; one of the earliest to arrive there, Detective-Sergeant Daniel Maclaughlin, became the branch's first casualty when, as bodyguard to Lord Kitchener, Secretary of State for War, he died with him when the ship on which they were sailing to Russia was sunk in June 1916.

Bearing in mind the success achieved by SIGINT during the Boer War, GHQ at St Omer had established a listening and cipher-breaking section under a linguist, Captain Oswald Hitchings, to tap into German military communications. However, in contrast to the war at sea, where SIGINT was more important than that from agents (Human Intelligence – HUMINT), the reverse was true on the Western Front, particularly during the static phase. In the trenches, SIGINT consisted mainly of intercepted telephone messages but, even after the introduction of French listening devices into the British organisation, the results from telephone tapping were only modest. The Germans, on the other hand, appeared to have much greater success in the interception of British field telephone communications, due largely to the lack of discretion or any idea of the principles of security on the part of many, particularly some of the more senior, British officers.

It was a different story with the interception of German radio messages, however, where rather more success attended British efforts. British wireless sections with time on their hands had discovered that the Germans were generating a considerable amount of wireless traffic. When the contents of the intercepted messages were compared with locations and call-signs picked up by the British radio direction-finding (DF) station near Abbeville in January 1915, it was found that certain stations and their call-signs could be tied to identifiable units and formations. By analysing the radio traffic, GHQ was often able to identify units and their movements. Delighted with this initial success, GHQ moved the DF station base to the Calais–Amiens line, thereby greatly increasing both its range and its accuracy; they also provided it with direct landline communications to GHQ, which had then moved to Montreuil on 30 March 1916.

The potential of SIGINT was not lost on the Intelligence staff at the War Office, which at the beginning of 1916 had undergone a reorganisation at the behest of Lord Kitchener, the Secretary of State for War. At about the same time, Sir John French had been replaced by Sir Douglas Haig as Commander-in-Chief of the BEF in France. Haig had selected Lieutenant-Colonel (later Brigadier-General) John Charteris as his Brigadier-General, General Staff (Intelligence) at GHQ, thus releasing Brigadier-General (later Lieutenant-General Sir) G.M.W. Macdonogh to become the new Director of Military Intelligence (DMI) at the War Office on 3 January 1916.

With the reintroduction in December 1915 of the post of DMI, Kitchener had reverted to the title used from 1887 to 1901 and which lasted until the reorganisation of Defence Intelligence in 1965. It was in Kitchener's reorganisation that the various sections of the directorate were given the prefix 'MI' followed by a number, of which MI 5 (the Security Service) and MI 6 (the Secret Intelligence Service – SIS) are the most well known outside British Intelligence circles. At this time, however, MI 1 was the Secretariat Section, responsible for secret Intelligence as well as for administration and clerical services for the whole Directorate; MI 1(a) undertook the latter duties, while MI 1(b) coordinated secret Intelligence, investigated enemy ciphers and dealt with wireless telegraphy policy. MI 1(c), located in Northumberland Avenue and later to become MI 6, was the Foreign Section of Special Intelligence, responsible for the collection of secret Intelligence overseas, and MI 1(d) dealt with the production of Intelligence summaries.

Two other sections of the directorate were the 'Country Sections', following the system which had prevailed since 1871, whatever the title of the War Office department responsible for the collation and dissemination of Intelligence. MI 2 was the most important of the Country Sections until February 1917, MI 2(c) having responsibility for Intelligence concerning Germany, Austria-Hungary, Switzerland, the Netherlands and Luxemburg, MI 2(b) for the Ottoman Empire, and MI 2(a) for Spain, Portugal, Italy, the Balkans, the USA and the Americas. MI 3a covered France and Belgium, MI 3(b) covered the Russian Empire and Scandinavia, and MI 3(c) was responsible for the Far East. In February 1917, MI 2(c) handed over responsibility for all its countries to MI 3, taking in exchange the latter's responsibility for Russia and the Far East. MI 4 was responsible for the preparation, storage and issue of maps and geographical material, and for the General Staff Library. MI 5 was formed out of MO 5 and that part of MI 1(b) which dealt with counter-espionage, and was enlarged into four sub-sections also covering the Military Permit Office, civilian passenger traffic to and from the UK, restrictions on aliens in the UK, and military records of aliens. MI 6, however, was not the MI 6 which we know today – it dealt with trade policy, international law, traffic in arms, the Defence of the Realm Act (DORA), submarine cables, censorship stamps and British ciphers, as well as some of the administrative functions formerly carried out by MI 1(b). The other sections formed within the directorate were:

MI 7 – press control, press propaganda and military translation bureau
MI 8 – censorship of cables, trade and radio
MI 9 – postal censorship

In July 1916 a new and most important Section, MI 1(c), was formed to take over all wireless telegraphy duties, including direction-finding. A year later MI 10 was created, with the task of dealing with foreign military attachés and military missions. MI 1(g) was formed in September 1918 to coordinate security of information and deception, and in November 1918, owing to the collapse of Russia, a new Section, MIR, was formed to deal with Russia, the Caucasus, Asia and the Far East, including liaison with the General Staff at Army HQ in India (see Chart 11). The collapse of Russia after the Bolshevik Revolution of October 1917 meant that British military Intelligence now had a wider focus; not only did it mean the transfer of the German troops from the Eastern to the Western Front, with its Intelligence implications, but there were also to be attempts to shore up the White Russian resistance and overthrow the Bolsheviks by means of military missions and reinforcements. In addition there was the possibility of the Russian Revolution spreading to Western Europe and the British Isles, requiring the Secret Intelligence Service to acquire sources in the Russian revolutionary movement and the Security Service to monitor closely the British Communist Party and Russian Intelligence agents within the UK.

By the end of the war in November 1918, the Directorate of Military Intelligence was functioning as a well-oiled machine, with its satellite field Intelligence organisations in every theatre of war. Of these, that of the BEF in France was obviously the largest and the most important. Those in other theatres varied in size, that in the Egyptian Expeditionary Force (EEF) being headed by a

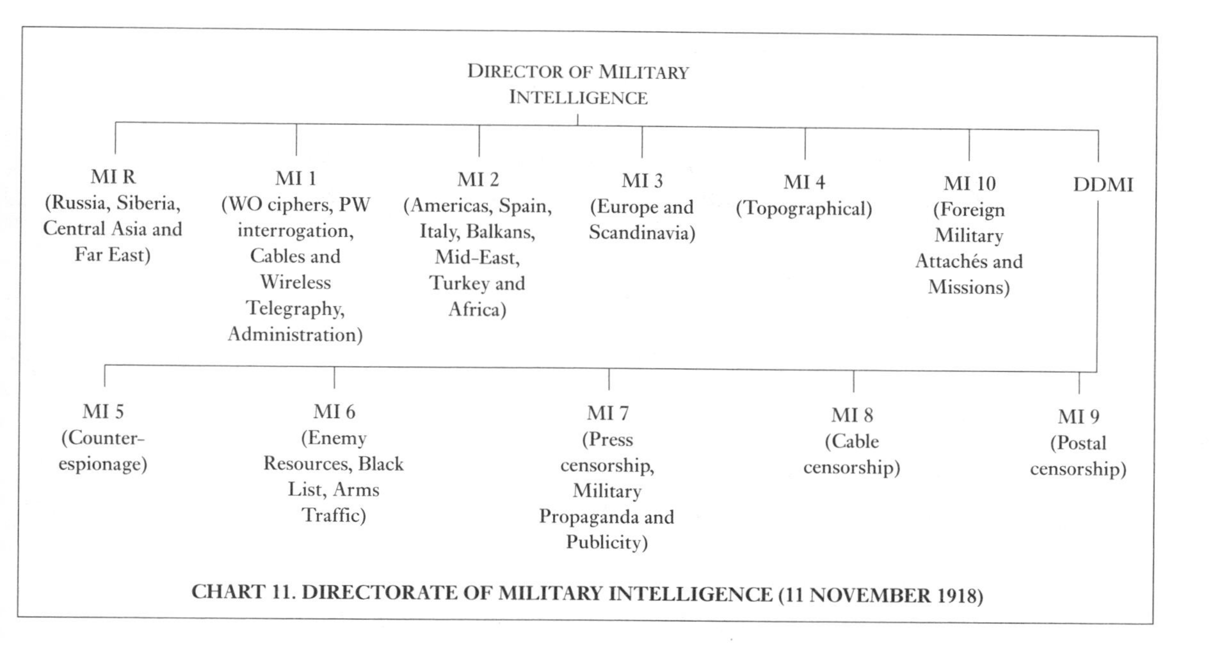

CHART 11. DIRECTORATE OF MILITARY INTELLIGENCE (11 NOVEMBER 1918)

Brigadier-General, and that in the British Salonika Army by a Lieutenant-Colonel. Neither the British Force in Italy nor the Mediterranean Expeditionary Force (MEF) at Gallipoli had separate Intelligence staffs, Intelligence being handled by the Operations Branch of the HQ in these cases.

On the whole, British military Intelligence had a very good record in the First World War; its successes greatly outnumbered its failures. Among the former was its consistent ability to read the German order of battle accurately throughout the campaign in France, and its precise prediction of the place and timing of the last great German offensive against Gough's Fifth Army in March 1918. Its failures were due more often to its reports being either disbelieved or ignored than to its information being incorrect. This was especially true during the tenure as head of the GHQ BEF Intelligence Branch of Brigadier-General Charteris; Charteris tended to withhold from Haig information which might have depressed Haig, or which ran counter to his own views. This is unforgiveable in an Intelligence officer, who must bring to the job a mind completely free from preconception and bias. For example, in November 1917, before the Battle of Cambrai, Charteris failed to show Haig Intelligence reports which indicated that German divisions had newly arrived from the Eastern Front, as he himself did not believe them. The result was that Haig was unprepared for the devastating German counter-attack which reversed the earlier British success. Charteris was sacked soon afterwards and replaced by Brigadier-General E.W. Cox, the former head of MI 3 in the War Office, with beneficial effect not only upon the use made of Intelligence by GHQ but also upon relations between the War Office and GHQ.

As Intelligence failures, some people have cited the surprise occasioned by the German introduction of poison gas on 22 April 1915, but this was not so much a failure of Intelligence as a failure, particularly on the part of the French, to take notice of the circumstantial evidence with which they had been presented on 14 April by a prisoner who actually had a respirator in his possession, as well as describing in detail the gas cylinders being set up in the German trenches and their method of discharge. Other prisoners, captured in March, had also given details of gas-cylinder stockpiling, and this information had appeared in an Intelligence bulletin of the French Tenth Army published on 30 March. Several other examples of Intelligence ignored were provided by the French, but few by the British.

British military tactical and strategic Intelligence can thus be said to have performed well in the First World War, thanks largely to the framework laid by the professional soldiers in the 'planning years' preceding it and the brilliance of many of the amateurs recruited into the organisation during the war. It has been said that Intelligence is too important to leave to amateurs, but the strange military conception that any officer, whether or not trained in Intelligence, is capable of filling satisfactorily an Intelligence staff post is very far from the truth. The individualist with original ideas and the initiative to put them into effect, with a logical and enquiring mind, a breadth of outlook and fluency in one or more foreign languages was regarded with suspicion by fellow professional officers; but these are just the characteristics required in a good Intelligence officer, and were more likely to be found among the amateurs of Kitchener's conscripts or those volunteering to serve for the duration of the emergency than among professional officers, in whom these characteristics had been suppressed, where they had existed, by the Army tradition of unquestioned acceptance of orders.

The wartime records of the covert Intelligence agencies MI 1(c) and MI 5 were very different. Of the two, the counter-espionage efforts of the Security Service were very much the more successful, although they attracted little attention or glamour. MI 5 expanded from a strength of a mere 19 officers (civilians and policemen) at the outbreak of war to a total of nearly 850 by the war's end. The heart of its organisation and an enormous contributor to its wartime success against espionage and subversion in the UK was its card index, the basis of which was Colonel Vernon Kell's pre-war register of aliens resident in the UK; this was rapidly expanded during the war to include suspect British and other nationals. The most important contribution, however, came from cable and postal censorship, particularly of communications to and from neutral countries.

The German military Intelligence organisation was known generally as the Nachrichtendienst des Heeres (ND), and later, within the Army, as Section IIIb; like most military Intelligence agencies, however, it was starved of funds in peacetime and relied very largely upon overt sources for its information. Its prime targets between the Russo–Japanese War in 1905 and the outbreak of the First World War in 1914 were Imperial Russia and its ally, France; the UK was considered to be a naval threat and therefore the responsibility of the German Navy's Intelligence branch. Because this branch was as starved of funds as the ND, the latter was preparing, at the outbreak of war, to expand its sources in the UK, but the declaration of war prevented this.

MI 5, having no powers of arrest, worked closely with the police Special Branch, itself only 114 strong, in arranging for the arrest of the 21 known or suspected German spies in the UK at the outbreak of war and the others detected during the war. More than 30 *bona fide* enemy agents were arrested during the war, but after the arrest of 7 more in June 1915, no further attempts were made by the Germans to establish a resident spy network in the UK. Of those agents who were arrested and charged with espionage on Germany's behalf, 21 were sentenced to death; of these, 14 were executed and 7 had their sentences commuted to penal servitude. One, a woman, escaped execution, much to Kell's fury; he protested, arguing that it set a precedent which would be taken advantage of by the German Secret Service, whose head, Gustav Steinhauer, would flood the UK with women agents as a result. The German agent network in the UK had as its hub a barber's shop on the Caledonian Road in Islington, north London, used by Steinhauer as a 'post-box' to communicate with his agents, but MI 5 discovered this, intercepted the barber's mail and closed the shop down at the outbreak of war, arresting all the agents at the same time. The woman whose reprieve had so angered Kell was a Dane, Eva de Bournonville. Her reports were sent on the back of letters to British prisoners of war, marked so that the German Intelligence Service would intercept them. Kell described her as 'a woman of good class and strikingly good education'.

The most successful of MI 5's operations in the First World War was perhaps the capture of Gustav Müller, who sent his reports home in the form of advertisements in the 'Personal' column of the *Daily Telegraph*. MI 5's suspicions were aroused by these messages, and they managed to decipher one which offered information on an arms shipment to Italy in return for payment of £120. Müller was subsequently arrested, interrogated, tried and shot, but advertisements purporting to come from him continued to appear for months after his death at the instigation of MI 5, who knew his code and system. The false Intelligence purporting to emanate from him was considered so good by his masters in Germany that they gave him a pay rise.

With the failure of their attempts to insert resident agents into the United Kingdom, the Germans took to relying instead on using neutral nationals visiting the UK on real or pretended business. This system brought them no more success than its predecessor; thanks to censorship and the all-important card index, MI 5 detected all of them, and by mid-1917, Germany appears to have given up its attempts to penetrate the UK. This was just as well, as the shock waves caused in London by the Russian Revolution meant that MI 5 had thenceforward to turn its attention away from German and towards Russian attempts to breach British security and to stir up the British working classes to revolution.

The Secret Intelligence Service, or MI 1(c) as it was then known, which had responsibility for gathering secret strategic Intelligence of all categories from all parts of the world, had relatively little success. In France it had been attempting to gather secret tactical military Intelligence in competition with the well-established and well-organised Intelligence organisation of GHQ. In other countries it lacked sources as well as reliable personnel. There were several reasons for this; the Chief, Mansfield Smith-Cumming, or 'C' as he was known within his organisation, had been out of action for some months early in the war after a car accident in which the driver, his son, had been killed, with the result that his operations had to be run by MO 5 in the War Office. In addition, SIS had only recently been brought under War Office control from the Admiralty, although funded by the Foreign Office Secret Vote; it moved again, to come under the Foreign Office umbrella, in 1917. Finally, Cumming's own lifestyle bordered on the flamboyant, and he had tended to recruit men of similar temperament and style into his organisation; some of these men were confidence tricksters and fraudsters, several were temperamentally unsound, and many had only the most rudimentary idea of security, with the result that they were easily detected by opposing counter-espionage services. Nevertheless, in the military field an undoubted SIS success was the network known as La Dame Blanche ('The White Lady'), the largest and most successful covert tactical military Intelligence network in France, and one which was still operational at the end of the war in November 1918. During its existence, more than a thousand civilians had been recruited and organised into some fifty train-watching posts, of whom only forty-five had been arrested and only one executed by the Germans. In addition, MI 1(c) had Directors of Intelligence in all the main theatres of war, the largest establishment being in Cairo, as well as representatives in Washington, New York, Russia, Switzerland and Holland. However, the alarm with which the Russian Revolution was viewed in London caused SIS to change its priorities away from the tactical to the strategic, from the military to the political, and from Germany to Russia.

How had the German Intelligence services fared against the Allies in the First World War? Prior to the outbreak of war, starved of funds, they had relied very largely on overt sources of information, such as provided by their service attachés, diplomatic and consular representatives, business visitors and the foreign press. When war came, however, the head of the ND, Major Nicolai, was allocated virtually unlimited funds with which to expand his service, but as he pointed out in his memoirs in 1925, this did not make up for his government's pre-war neglect of Intelligence, which resulted in his having neither trained men nor foreign bases from which to operate. Of the agents resident in the UK when war broke out or who were infiltrated into the country during the war, all were found on capture to have been ill-trained and badly prepared, and most were inadequate personalities. Had they not been caught, their Intelligence product would have been of little value to the Germans, as their access to reliable sources of a sufficiently high level was limited if not non-existent. Most were not German nationals, and most of the information they gathered was readily available in newspapers which could find their way into German hands via Holland. The assessment of Germany's secret Intelligence achievements against the UK in the First World War must therefore be that it achieved little. The successes of military Intelligence units in the field tell a different story, however, particularly on the Western Front. There can be no doubt that the tactical Intelligence derived from wire-tapping, prisoners of war, air photography and train-watchers was as good as that achieved by the Allies.

With the ending of the 'war to end war', British military Intelligence rapidly wound down; Intelligence posts in Army units were either left unfilled or their incumbents misemployed on other tasks, while the Intelligence Corps lasted, in greatly reduced size, only until the British Army on the Rhine was recalled in 1929. As in previous times of peace, the peacetime Intelligence organisation was to be starved of both money and affection.

CHAPTER 2

British Military Intelligence, 1919–45

As in previous times of peace, no sooner had the British Intelligence organisations been reorganised on to a peacetime basis than they suffered a Treasury economy drive which, between 1919 and 1922, reduced the SIS budget, for example, from £240,000 annually to a mere £90,000. With the changed Intelligence priorities, SIS had been given the exclusive control of British espionage which it still enjoys; the cryptographers of MI 1(b) and (e) were amalgamated with those of the Admiralty's Room 40 in 1919 to form the Government Code and Cipher School (GC & CS).

In 1921, control of GC & CS passed to the Foreign Office, which also had control of SIS, but both were neglected by the Foreign Office, which made little effort to win them adequate budgets and refused to concern itself with recruitment. This was unfortunate to say the least as, in the inter-war years, many SIS recruits were deficient in quality, due largely to Smith-Cumming restricting recruitment to men with minds uncontaminated by a university education, in a perhaps misguided attempt to preserve the service from penetration by Bolsheviks. As a result, Soviet Intelligence services were able to tap these resources several years before their British counterparts did, and were subsequently able to infiltrate several of their recruits into both SIS and the Security Service. H.A.R. ('Kim') Philby was one such; talent-spotted for the Soviets while at Cambridge University in 1932, recruited by them in Austria in 1933, and later given the assignment of penetrating British Intelligence. He succeeded in his assignment so well that he served SIS for some thirty years in increasingly senior posts. In fact, he was being groomed by Stewart Menzies, CSS at the time, to succeed him as 'C'. Had it not been for his discovery and subsequent flight to the Soviet Union in January 1963, he would very probably have been so appointed.

Within the War Office, a similar lack of interest in Intelligence resulted in not a single handbook on a foreign Army, military report on a foreign country or summary of the military resources of a foreign country being produced between 1920 and

1939. This contrasted spectacularly with the period 1904–14, during which every foreign Army and every undeveloped country in which operations might be expected to take place had been covered by such publications. The only Intelligence publications produced by the War Office in the period up to 1939 were two editions of the *Manual of Military Intelligence*; however, the country sections did at least maintain their collation files. In 1922, the Operations and the Intelligence Directorates were again combined into a Directorate of Military Operations and Intelligence (DMO & I), consisting of three Operations sections and five Intelligence sections. With this reorganisation, the DMO & I was restored to its position as the senior of the General Staff Directorates. This organisation remained virtually unchanged until 1940, the Intelligence part of the combined directorate comprising:

MI 1 – translations and administration
MI 2 and MI 3 – country sections
MI 4 – maps
MI 5 – security
Military representative from the Commonwealth of Australia

The main preoccupation of tactical military Intelligence in the field between the wars was imperial policing in the colonies and mandated territories, together with duties in aid of the Civil Power in Ireland. For the Security Service and SIS, the most urgent tasks after the First World War were the thwarting both of Bolshevism at home and abroad and of Sinn Fein terrorism in Ireland and the mainland. The threat presented by Bolshevism from 1918 to 1920 is felt by some to have been exaggerated, but this feeling ignores the vacuum of instability left in Europe by the collapse of Germany and the undoubted aim of the revolutionaries to spread Bolshevism as quickly as possible, first to Holland and Switzerland and then to

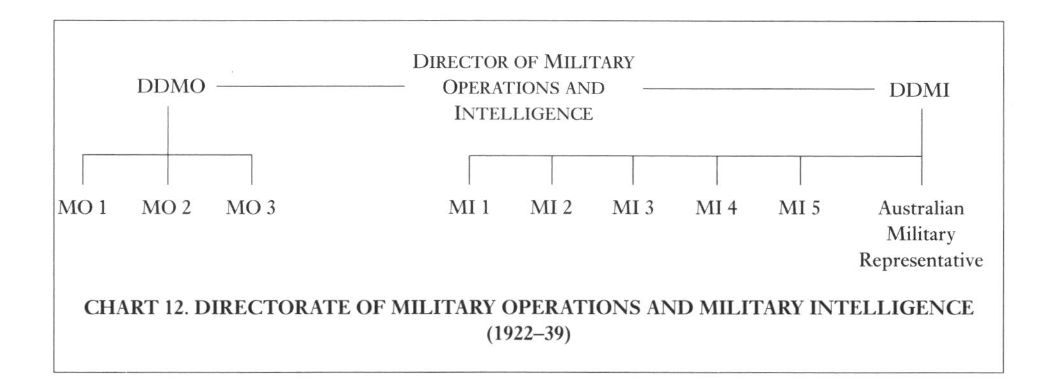

CHART 12. DIRECTORATE OF MILITARY OPERATIONS AND MILITARY INTELLIGENCE (1922–39)

Germany, France, Italy and the United Kingdom. In its attempt to thwart the Bolsheviks in Russia, the SIS failed lamentably to gain Intelligence, despite the valiant and sometimes flamboyant efforts of agents such as Sir Robert Bruce Lockhart, Paul Dukes and Sidney Reilly; in fact, until compromised by the Cabinet in an appalling breach of security in 1927, the most fruitful source of Intelligence on Russia was the GC & CS, whose code-breakers had managed to intercept and decode the diplomatic telegrams and radio messages of the Soviet Government.

It was not that MI 1(c)'s operations in Russia, limited as they were, were not carried out by brave men, neither were they entirely lacking in tactical success, but they failed strategically, partly through the reluctance of the Cabinet to allow military intervention on more than a token scale. Sidney Reilly was possibly the most remarkable of the colourful series of agents inserted into Russia by Smith-Cumming after the Bolshevik Revolution; a born gambler and inveterate womaniser, immaculately clothed and with an aura of power, he arrived in Moscow in May 1918, briefed by 'C' to make a personal assessment of Lenin. Reilly had been born Sigmund Rosenblum, the illegitimate son of a Jewish doctor, in Odessa. After emigrating to Brazil, he then moved to London, where he married a widow named Margaret Reilly Callaghan and changed his name to Sidney Reilly. He then moved to New York, where he was established by the outbreak of war and had bigamously married his second wife, Nadine. He had also met the New York representatives of 'C'. He joined the Royal Flying Corps, but was transferred to SIS in March 1918; three years later, after various adventures in Russia (for which he was awarded the Military Cross) at great expense to His Majesty's Government and with little Intelligence to show for it, Reilly came under suspicion of having come too much under the influence of either the White Russians whose cause he had been promoting or of the Soviet counter-espionage organisation, the OGPU. He dropped into relative obscurity, and his death, reported in *The Times* on 15 December 1925, is shrouded in mystery. His disappearance ended, for some years, the Russian ventures of SIS, although his feats of daring earned him the title 'Ace of Spies'.

In Ireland, too, the story was one of almost constant failure, due partly to amateurish bungling and partly to an almost complete lack of coordination between Dublin and London. During the war, the British Intelligence effort in Ireland had been directed at German rather than Irish Nationalist intrigue, due to underestimation of the military potential of Sinn Fein and gross overestimation of German influence on the Nationalist unrest. In addition, after the war the military Intelligence organisation in Ireland was cut back, that of the Royal Navy was closed down, the Intelligence assessments provided by the Royal Irish

Constabulary (RIC) were not reliable, and the British coordinator of Intelligence was not replaced when he returned to the UK in 1919. British Intelligence in Ireland was not only inefficient but was also insecure; it had been penetrated by the Irish Republican Army (IRA), which had managed to infiltrate four agents into the headquarters of the RIC and the Dublin Metropolitan Police (DMP), while British Intelligence was unable to recruit informers within the IRA due to the latter's increasingly brutal action against any informers discovered within the organisation. Thanks to the agents within the RIC and DMP, the IRA squad of expert gunmen, specially formed for the purpose in September 1919, was able to murder British agents and informers at will, and the British Intelligence organisation became almost impotent. Neither was there a well-organised counter-espionage team available in Ireland.

The chief of SIS, Sir Mansfield Smith-Cumming, died in June 1925 at the time of a dispute between the Army and other service Intelligence organisations on the one hand and the Foreign Office on the other, concerning the latter's monopoly of Intelligence emanating from GC & CS. His death afforded the opportunity of a compromise, with the appointment of his successor, Rear-Admiral Hugh ('Quex') Sinclair. Sinclair was appointed not only as Chief of the Secret Service (CSS or 'C') but also as Director of GC & CS. Alastair Denniston, while remaining as head of GC & CS – an appointment he was to hold until 1942 – now reported to CSS. Until 1925, SIS and GC & CS had occupied separate London headquarters in Melbury Road and Queen's Gate respectively; in June of that year, however, they moved to adjacent offices in Broadway Buildings, an office block at 54 Broadway, opposite St James's Park Underground station in Westminster, while 'C' had a flat in Queen Anne's Gate, immediately behind 54 Broadway, and connected to it. While he sought to preserve the utmost secrecy concerning his new address, Sinclair, like his predecessor, was not the most security-minded of men, and his address was soon known, at least to London taxi-drivers, given away by his distinctive open Lancia car, which was often parked outside. The SIS remained under Foreign Office control and was funded from the Foreign Office Secret Vote, but it retained a military Intelligence title as MI 6; it was made exclusively responsible for British espionage on a national as well as an inter-service basis, with the Air Ministry, the Home Office, the India Office and the Colonial Office being added to a list of customers which already included the Foreign Office, the War Office and the Admiralty. Its overseas representatives operated under the official cover afforded by the Passport Control organisation, attached to British embassies, legations and consulates.

It is a truism that if you want peace, you must be prepared for war. The British Government had neglected to follow this advice before many previous wars, and had paid the penalty; it did so again before the outbreak of the Second World War in 1939. This neglect applied as much to the Intelligence organisations as to rearmament, despite the urgent need, from 1935 onwards, for more and better Intelligence concerning Germany. Preoccupation with the USSR had partially blinded the British Government to the growing German problem after Hitler's accession to power, and as a result its Intelligence resources had been concentrated very largely on the Soviet Union. In addition, steps to coordinate the work of the several independent Intelligence organisations, particularly those of the three armed services and the Foreign Office, had not been taken because of the reluctance of these departments to surrender control of their own organisations for the acquisition, interpretation and use of information bearing upon their work to inter-departmental bodies. The Foreign Office in particular, having no branch of its own specifically charged with the Intelligence function, displayed the least interest in the problem; after all, the entire Foreign Office organisation, including its diplomatic missions overseas, was engaged in the collection, collation, interpretation and dissemination of Intelligence on foreign countries, even if this was categorised as 'information' rather than 'Intelligence' and mainly political in content. It had no interest in sharing this Intelligence and its resulting conclusions with the service ministries.

However, pressures were building up on the service ministries to collaborate with one another and with the Foreign Office on Intelligence matters. In the autumn of 1935, the Deputy Chiefs of Staff reported:

> The Intelligence which it is now necessary to cover in time of peace in order to be properly prepared for the eventuality of war with any Great Power has been almost immeasurably extended and complicated by reason of:
> (1) The extent to which modern war involves the whole resources of the nation.
> (2) The vast extension of the zone of operations brought about by the advance of aviation.

In response to these pressures, the Joint Intelligence Sub-Committee (JIC) of the Chiefs of Staff Committee was formed in June 1936, replacing the Inter-Service Intelligence Committee (ISIC) formed only six months earlier. The JIC acted as the channel through which the Joint Planning Staff obtained Intelligence on all matters on which more than one service might have something to contribute, and at once established itself as a valuable part of the Intelligence organisation. After some initial reluctance, the Foreign Office started to attend meetings after January 1939, and provided the permanent chairman after the reorganisation which took place in July of that year.

This reorganisation gave the JIC the form in which it remained for the duration of the Second World War; it consisted of the Directors (or their deputies) of the three Service Intelligence Directorates and a Counsellor from the Foreign Office, and it was tasked, among other things, to:

(i) Assess and coordinate Intelligence received from abroad, to ensure that any Government action required was based on the most suitable and carefully coordinated information obtainable.
(ii) Consider any further measures thought necessary to improve the efficient working of the Intelligence organisation of the country as a whole.

For the previous twenty years this concept had been evolving slowly and haphazardly in response to events, but once in place it functioned very well.

If there had been insufficient military or any other Intelligence activity in the UK before 1939, after the outbreak of war changes in organisation and increases in establishments came thick and fast. The War Office Directorate of Military Intelligence was greatly expanded, as were the other Service Intelligence Directorates, and the Ministry of Economic Warfare (MEW) was established, with its own Intelligence branch, to assess enemy industrial and raw material capacity and output. Also formed at this time was the Political Warfare Executive (PWE), charged with the task of analysing enemy propaganda and compiling a digest of foreign press and radio output for circulation to all departments. The Combined Services Detailed Interrogation Centre (CSDIC), which undertook the detailed interrogation of enemy prisoners of war and was the responsibility of a new branch of the Directorate of Military Intelligence, MI 9, came into being in March 1940 as part of a general enlargement of the Directorate. Other changes at this time (see Chart 13) included:

1. A DDMI (Organisation), responsible for:
   MI 1 – administration
   MI 4 – geographical section
   MI 6 – special duties (SIS)
   MI 8 – radio intercept ('Y'), signals security and secret communications
   MI 9 – POW interrogation
   MIL – liaison
   MIR – research (guerrilla warfare, under DMI).

2. A DDMI (Information), responsible for:
   MI 2 – country section, dealing with the Middle and Far East, Scandinavia, USA, USSR, and Central and South America.
   MI 3 – country section, dealing with Europe, except the USSR and Baltic Provinces
   MI 10 – technical Intelligence (all countries)
   MI(JIC) – liaison between DMI and JIC
3. A Director of Defence Security Intelligence (Maj.-Gen. Vernon Kell) with a Deputy Director, responsible for:
   MI 5 – Security Service

The creation of MI 8 was soon followed by that of MI 10, to cover technical Intelligence; technical Intelligence collation and dissemination had previously been considered the responsibility of the two 'country' sections in the MI Directorate, each of which had one Major on its staff to deal with it. However, the rate of development of weapons and military equipment world-wide far exceeded the capacity of two Majors to keep up, particularly as neither had any technical training. The Intelligence on German weapons and equipment taken over by MI 10 from MI 3, for example, was laughable in its inadequacy, and amounted to nothing more than one incomplete photograph album with a minimum of technical data.

MI 10 comprised three sub-sections:

MI 10(a) – armoured fighting vehicles, artillery and infantry weapons
MI 10(b) – engineering equipment and soft-skinned vehicles
MI 10(c) – roads, railways, bridges, inland waterways, electricity and other utilities, oil storage and resources, liaison with MEW on enemy industries and land war potential

These sub-divisions and duties remained substantially the same until the end of the Second World War, although in 1944 MI 10(c) also assumed responsibility in the MI Directorate for scientific Intelligence, covering such aspects as guided weapons, and chemical and biological warfare; these subjects were hived off to a new branch, MI 16, formed in 1945 to cover all aspects of scientific military Intelligence. MI 10 was also responsible for liaison between the War Office and the Ministry of Economic Warfare (MEW), then occupying Lansdowne House in Berkeley Square, on such matters as estimates of German production of tanks and other military weapons and equipment.

The next most important change to occur in the organisation of the MI Directorate in the War Office was the creation in May 1940 of MI 14 out of the sub-section MI 3(b); MI 3 had been charged with the collection and collation of military Intelligence on all the countries of Continental Europe, but it was felt that the war against Germany required the setting up of a branch specialising in Intelligence on the German Army. Later that year two other new branches were created: MI 11 to deal with military security and field censorship, and MI 12 for liaison with the censorship organisation; both, together with MI 5, were subordinated to the DDMI (Security). Major-General Sir Vernon Kell, who had been the Director-General of the Security Service for the past thirty years, had been retired in June 1940 and been replaced by Sir David Petrie, who occupied the post of DDMI(S) as a local Brigadier, and had been recalled from semi-retirement in November 1940 to fill it.

With these changes, the organisation for the collation, evaluation and dissemination of strategic military Intelligence during the Second World War was largely in place, with good liaison established with the other strategic Intelligence-producing agencies in London and with the JIC, functioning well under its Foreign Office chairman Victor Cavendish-Bentinck (later to be the Duke of Portland) as the coordinating channel to the Joint Planning Staff.

As regards tactical military Intelligence, the BEF in Belgium had its own DMI and Intelligence staff at GHQ, as well as Intelligence staffs in the HQs of its subordinate formations and Intelligence Officers in all units. The same was true of other overseas and UK commands. The Intelligence Corps had been re-formed in July 1940 after having been disbanded in 1929, and there had been considerable urgency attaching to its recruitment of suitable personnel; an Intelligence Corps Depot was formed, together with a Training Centre at Matlock in Derbyshire to give specialised training in field Intelligence, field security, POW interrogation and photo interpretation. Officers of the corps were selected by members of DMI's staff; a special sub-section of the directorate, MI 1X, had been set up in September 1939 to coordinate the selection, training and posting of Intelligence Corps officers, and found itself supplying not only the Army but also SIS, MI 5 and later the Special Operations Executive (SOE) with recruits.

The mention of SOE needs explanation in a book dealing with military Intelligence. The organisation was formed under the aegis of the Ministry of Economic Warfare, largely at the suggestion of its Minister, Hugh Dalton, on 16 July 1940, with the aim, in the words of Winston Churchill, of 'setting Europe ablaze'. Regular warfare having failed, irregular warfare was to redeem the situation, and SOE was tasked to do so by means of sabotage and subversion in the occupied territories of Europe. The idea was not new, only the organisation to carry it out; prior to this date, the Naval Intelligence Department (NID), SIS and the Directorate of Military Intelligence had all been involved in various schemes for sabotage, particularly in the Balkans in the hope of denying Romanian oil to Germany. In the MI Directorate, the branch concerned was MIR, and in the SIS, Section D. 'C' had undoubtedly hoped that the task of controlling and coordinating this work would fall to SIS and its enlarged Section D, and there is no doubt that he did not take kindly to this encroachment on his virtual monopoly of covert operations abroad. There was resentment at having to share scarce transport resources with the new organisation, as well as the likelihood of a conflict of interest arising between sabotage and Intelligence-collection. Nevertheless, 'C' fought a successful battle to run SOE's radio communications, which SIS did until 1942. The military head of SOE was Brigadier (later Major-General Sir) Colin McVean Gubbins, who had previously served in MIR as a Major.

SOE started out in three rooms in the St Ermin's Hotel in Caxton Street, moving to 64 Baker Street, and later expanding into five other large buildings in the same street. Apart from the jealousy of SIS, SOE also had to cope with suspicion from the War Office and the Foreign Office as well as penetration by German counter-Intelligence, and especially in France, by Communists who used the organisation and the weapons which it so conveniently supplied to settle old scores with rivals and collaborators.

Sabotage behind enemy lines was also carried out by all-military units such as the Long Range Desert Group in the Western Desert, and the Special Air Service (SAS), but these were used on military targets, were under military control and are not to be confused with SOE's networks of mixed civilian and military personnel run from the United Kingdom. The SAS had been formed in the Western Desert in 1941, with the aim of harrying enemy military lines of communication; in this, later in the war, it often collaborated with local partisans in Greece, Italy, France, Norway and the Far East, for example.

The MEW in Lansdowne House, Berkeley Square, had Intelligence interests other than the by-products of its sabotage organisation; it had an Intelligence Department, which became the Enemy and Occupied Territories Department after the fall of France in 1940 and, in 1941, the Enemy Branch. This department was responsible for the production of Intelligence concerning enemy financial transactions, raw materials, availability of shipping, and weapon, vehicle and aircraft production in both Germany and its occupied territories. Unfortunately, the relationship between Economic Warfare Intelligence (EWI) and the service Intelligence departments had not been formally defined when MEW came into being. Its purpose was to keep under constant observation the enemy's economic potential for making war, with a view to assisting other more specialised branches of the Intelligence organisation in London, but the service ministries retained their right to receive, and process for themselves, economic Intelligence which concerned them; they did not take kindly to the idea of surrendering this right to a new and inexperienced ministry at a time when the importance of Intelligence was greatly increased by the outbreak of war. The JIC was not competent to adjudicate between the competing papers on economic questions concerning Germany produced by the War Office, Air Ministry and MEW in late 1939 and early 1940; it was not until May 1940 that MEW was finally given a seat on the JIC.

The War Office MI Directorate was especially concerned with Germany's tank production; before the war, this estimation had been left to MEW's predecessor, and it continued to be the responsibity of EWI after its formation, although information on this subject at this time was so poor that no good estimates could be made. It was even more difficult to assess Germany's tank output than its aircraft production, due to the wide dispersion of production of both tanks themselves and their components. Lacking adequate factual knowledge not only of the firms involved in tank production but also of the types of tank being produced in 1940, EWI could only fall back on guesswork based upon British factory requirements of floor space, steel and workforce for producing similar sizes of tank; these 'guestimates', based on false assumptions of a steep increase in German tank production following the outbreak of war and errors in calculating the numbers of tanks in German armoured formations, led the War Office to overestimate grossly the rate of increase of German tank stocks in the first six months of the war. In March 1940 they were believed to total 5,800; for June 1940, a total of 7–8,000 of all types was estimated. Even the lower figure of 7,000 implied production of more than 2,000 tanks in the ten months from September 1939 to the following June – the actual figure was later found to have been 755! The output of all types for the whole of 1940 was only 1,458, a monthly rate of only 121. New methods of calculating enemy tank production, involving the analysis of tank and component serial numbers and code markings, in conjunction with the US Embassy in London, led in 1943 to very much more accurate estimates of production for 1941, 1942 and 1943. This more accurate analysis was, of course, also greatly helped by the large sample of markings obtained from vehicles captured in the Middle East; none had been available after the BEF's abortive campaign in France in 1940.

In December 1940 it was decided to create an organisation to look at the course of the war from the enemy's point of view; this was originally known as the Future Operations (Enemy) Section (FOES), but this was disbanded in March 1941 and replaced by the Axis Planning Section (APS). The APS in turn evolved into the Joint Intelligence Staff (JIS), an inner committee of the JIC. By the spring of 1941 progress was also being made towards the acceptance by the ministries concerned of the principle of central, inter-service assessment of strategic Intelligence, as well as central control of various other inter-service organisations such as the Inter-Service Topographical Department (ISTD), the Inter-Service Cipher and W/T Security Committee and the Intelligence Section (Operations) (IS(O)), an inter-service organisation established in an attempt to collate the Intelligence required for operational planning.

Of the covert Intelligence producers, the biggest changes took place in the Government Code and Cipher School, whose move to Broadway under the aegis of CSS in June 1926 was mentioned in Chapter 1. In 1928 a committee known as the 'Y' Committee was formed to coordinate the activities of the various service radio intercept stations, of which the War Office contributed the No. 2 Wireless Company at Sarafand in Palestine and, after 1930, further stations at Shanghai, in China, and Cherat on the Indian north-west frontier. While Soviet traffic was the main preoccupation of GC & CS in the first half of the 1930s, with Japanese Far East traffic running it a close second, the outbreak of the Spanish Civil War brought a great increase in radio traffic from the Iberian Peninsula. Interception of this traffic was carried out by a secret Army station near Chatham and a naval station near Winchester, with direct landlines to Broadway. In 1937 the 'Y' Committee also arranged for three further intercept stations to be built, staffed by Foreign Office personnel, to concentrate on German and Italian diplomatic traffic. On the horizon, however, a significant problem for GC & CS was beginning to appear – the prospect of the widespread introduction of automatic electro-mechanical enciphering and deciphering machines into the German armed forces.

Probably as the result of the publication of various books describing the successes of the Admiralty's Room 40 intercept and decryption organisation during the First World War, in 1926 the German Navy had started equipping its ships with a version of a widely available machine known by the commercial name of 'Enigma'; the German Army had started to use a military version two years later. In 1926 the British Government had also given active consideration to the introduction of similar machines for sensitive communications, and a working party deliberated for eight years before recommending that a version of the Enigma with an additional 'Type X' attachment should be procured by the Air Ministry and distributed to both the RAF and the Army. In the opinion of all the GC & CS specialists, both the Enigma and the Type X attachment, if properly used, were immune to cryptanalytical attack, if only because the number of cipher permutations was beyond the capacity of the unassisted human brain to unravel and there was no machine available at that time which could do the job. In fact, although there were very many British and US successes in breaking Enigma codes during the Second World War, many remained unbroken throughout the war. By the end of 1935, the Germans had produced sufficient quantities of Enigma machines to equip not only the three armed services but also nearly every other government department and agency; German radio traffic using Enigma-encoded messages was being intercepted by stations in the United Kingdom and also by the French and the Poles, but not, at this time, being deciphered by any of them.

In May 1938, after the *Anschluss*, when war with Germany seemed inevitable, three developments occurred in GC & CS which were to have a profound effect on its wartime performance: first, an alternative headquarters was purchased at Bletchley Park in Hertfordshire, on the correct assumption that London would be a target for enemy air attack; second, a German Section was established at Broadway, and Treasury approval was given to 'C's contingency plan for a large emergency increase in establishment; and finally, authority was given by 'C' for a meeting at Broadway between French and British experts, as a direct result of which contact between the Polish Cipher Bureau and GC & CS was established in January of the following year. The Poles had made more progress in the decryption of German Enigma material than either the British or the French, and were the direct means of opening the way for the later successes of GC & CS, which were to make such a difference to the Allies' prosecution of the war.

At a further meeting at the end of July 1939, the Poles revealed that they had managed to construct duplicates of the German Enigma machines and were prepared to let London and Paris have one each. These were delivered in August 1939, in time for the move of GC & CS to Bletchley Park, where signs at the gates showed it to be the location of the Government Communications Bureau, and in time for its rapid expansion into a unit employing some 200 'boffins', as the already selected personnel started reporting to their wartime place of duty.

At this time, GC & CS was organised into a Communications Security Section under the Deputy Director, which dealt with the security of the UK's own codes, a Diplomatic Section (by far the largest) comprising geographically orientated country sub-sections, the three service sections and, most recently formed, the Commercial Section; the customer most interested in this latter section's output was the MEW's Intelligence Department. The Diplomatic Section had broken the diplomatic codes of many neutral countries, as well as those of Italy.

The Director of GC & CS, Admiral Sinclair, who was also 'C' of SIS, died on 4 November 1939; he was succeeded by his SIS deputy, Stewart Menzies, who was knighted for his work in 1943 and remained as 'C' until 1951. Because of the very great wartime expansion of GC & CS, his appointment was upgraded in 1944.

By May 1940 the code-breakers at Bletchley Park had succeeded in breaking one of the Luftwaffe operational versions of the Enigma machine cipher, and from that point were able to read most of the Luftwaffe Enigma traffic until the end of the war. The prospect of similarly breaking the Wehrmacht, Kriegsmarine, Army and other operational German machine codes posed the question of how best to make use of the high-grade Intelligence arising from this traffic. It was obviously essential to keep from the Germans the fact that their supposedly secure codes were being broken, and this implied that the recipients of this Intelligence should be specially indoctrinated as to the source, and their numbers kept to an absolute minimum. Apart from Winston Churchill, who had taken a special interest in Intelligence matters in both the Boer War and the First World War, at the Prime Minister's insistence the number of recipients was drastically reduced to some thirty of those most closely concerned with the direction of the war; of these thirty, only six of thirty-five Cabinet Ministers were included. To give the impression that the material had originated from a spy rather than from SIGINT, the Intelligence resulting from the decrypts was given the source code-word 'Boniface' as well as the security classification 'Most Secret'. Churchill insisted on seeing the decrypts in their original form, with nothing deleted; he took such an interest in the operation that he had a special buff-coloured box for decrypts, and the day's 'product' was sent to him daily from Broadway, often brought by 'C' personally.

In the first sixteen months of the war, GC & CS had expanded fourfold; this expansion, and the very careful selection of recruits to the organisation, enabled it to break the German Navy Enigma in 1941, and that of the German Army in 1942. The result was that high-grade, accurate political and strategic military Intelligence was available to the Allied war planners and the fighting services for the rest of the war of a quality and quantity far outstripping that provided by the agent Intelligence from SIS, prisoners of war, air reconnaissance and other sources. As we have seen, however, high grade Intelligence is no good unless it is believed, and 'Boniface' was at first just not believed; the SIS was held in very low esteem in Whitehall at this time, partly because of the Venlo fiasco (described later in this chapter), partly because they had no credible agents and partly because their military appreciations had proved worthless. The credibility of the 'Boniface' reports was not helped either by the non-military terminology and sometimes downright inaccurate translations used in the simplified translated texts distributed to the service Intelligence directorates. There were too few GC & CS staff with service experience, and Menzies ('C') was anxious not to risk compromising his golden egg-layer by enlarging the circle of indoctrinated recipients. This had to be done, however, if full use was to be made of this source, and arrangements were made for summaries of SIGINT to be passed to the BEF GHQ in Belgium via Special Liaison Units (SLUs) attached to GHQ; these SLUs would be responsible for showing the material to those authorised to receive it, and for destroying it immediately thereafter.

As the 'Boniface' material gradually began to prove its reliability, steps were taken to expand into the Middle East, and in 1941 the foundations were laid for an organisation known as the Combined Bureau Middle East (CBME), which was to combine cryptographic with intercept work and traffic analysis. It was also to supply the local MI 5 and MI 6 offices – known as Security Intelligence Middle East (SIME) and Inter-Services Liaison Department (ISLD) respectively – with SIGINT of interest to them. Expansion into other theatres of war followed, but as the war moved away from the Middle East, CBME was closed down in March 1944. In the spring of 1943, formal agreement was reached with the USA for GC & CS to co-operate with its equivalents in the US Navy and War Departments, and US representatives were completely integrated into GC & CS.

By 1943 the Enigma material was known by the code-name 'Ultra', and was being distributed on a wider but still very restricted scale. In 1943 the staff of GC & CS had just about doubled from 2,095 to 5,052, and in 1944 it further increased to 7,725, of whom 4,350 were from the armed services. It reached its peak in January 1945, when it employed a total of nearly 9,000 people. Its output as well as its staff increased throughout this period, reaching its wartime peak in April 1945 with the decryption of 3,400,000 cipher groups; it broke more than fifty new Enigma codes from June 1943 to June 1944, compared to half this number in the previous twelve months. By 1945, GC & CS had changed its name to Government Communications Headquarters (GCHQ) and moved from Bletchley Park, first to Eastcote and thence, in the 1950s, to Cheltenham.

The 'Y' Board, which was responsible for SIGINT policy to the JIC, was renamed the Signal Intelligence Board in October 1943, and at the same time absorbed the 'Y' Committee; it was also given a new charter, in which SIGINT was defined as consisting of:

Interception
Cryptanalysis
Traffic analysis (TA)
Special Intelligence resulting from these processes

It was from this point that the term 'Signal Intelligence' (later abbreviated to SIGINT) replaced 'Y' in the Intelligence vocabulary as the generic term, 'Y' from that time being limited to interception, the breaking of low-grade tactical codes and direction-finding.

If it seems to the reader that an excessive amount of space in a book dealing with military Intelligence has been devoted to the GC & CS, it is because the SIGINT it produced was already, by April 1942, the single most important source of Intelligence, according to a survey conducted by the JIC at that time. It was followed, a long way behind, by air photo-reconnaissance (PR), but this was highly weather-dependent and could rarely be devoted to one task for long. The agents of MI 6, on the other hand, were very far down the list, as regards both quantity and quality; despite the glamorous image of the secret agent presented in works of fiction, based largely on the exploits of one or two outrageous examples such as Sidney Reilly and Paul Dukes. Secret agents in the Second World War never supplied more than 5 per cent of the information received by the War Office Directorate of Military Intelligence and its subordinate organisations in overseas commands.

In technical military Intelligence, whose requirements differ from those of other categories of military Intelligence, POW interrogation and captured documents, photographs and equipment played a somewhat larger part than SIGINT in the evaluation of current and future enemy weapons. In tactical and economic Intelligence also, SIGINT played only a minor part, particularly in north-west Europe, where much of the enemy's communications were by landline; tactical Intelligence required a quicker response than was generally possible from the sometimes lengthy decryption process, and in this field, POW interrogation and captured documents, particularly from the spring of 1943 onwards, military attaché reports from neutral countries, air photo-reconnaissance, Army 'Y' and SOE agents provided the bulk of tactical order of battle Intelligence. Reports in the enemy press and on the radio as well as unclassified German and neutral publications obtained from neutral countries provided the bulk of the input to MEW's EWI department regarding the German economy.

Having looked in detail at one covert producer of military Intelligence, let us examine the wartime performance of the other two, MI 5 and MI 6. We left MI 5, the Security Service, between the two world wars, preoccupied with attempting to counter both Bolshevik penetration of the trade unions and their attempts to subvert both the government and the IRA, both in Ireland and in mainland Britain, having had a very successful campaign against German agents there during the First World War. At the outbreak of the Second World War, MI 5 had an influx of new recruits from the universities, some provided by MI 1X, some by the Intelligence Corps and some recruited direct; many of these were unimpressed with the leadership of the Director, Sir Vernon Kell, who had been in the department for thirty years, was aged sixty-nine and was in failing health, and his deputy since 1917, Sir Eric Holt-Wilson.

In 1939 Kell was determined to repeat his success of 1914 against German agents in the UK by eliminating, in one move, the Abwehr networks operating there, and proposed to use the Aliens' Registration Act to do so. A large number of enemy aliens were registered in the country, and there were some 400 suspects on MI 5's own list. In September 1939, all were ordered to report to their local police stations for processing. This processing was carried out by a series of one-man tribunals, with 120 specially and secretly selected judges and King's Counsels who judged the cases of individual aliens. This system allowed many Abwehr agents to be taken into custody without arousing their suspicions that they had been identified as possible spies, and without the need for Special Branch to carry out individual arrests. These aliens were sorted into one of three categories: Category A were immediately placed in detention; Category B were subject to certain restrictions, and Category C, the vast majority, were allowed complete freedom.

With the ending of the 'phoney war' in 1940, and the consequent threat of a German invasion of the UK, the situation changed drastically; the government therefore extended internment in May 1940 to all German and Austrian males in Category B between the ages of sixteen and sixty, and in June 1940 to all females of the same nationalities and ages. At the end of June 1940 all Category C males were also ordered to report, and with this measure, Kell was reasonably confident that many of the Abwehr's networks had been closed down. Confirmation that this was the case was given by a double agent whose network was the only one left working after the mass internments of 1940.

The headquarters of MI 5 was now in St James's Street in London, while its registry, transport department and card index had been moved to Wormwood Scrubs for safety. After these were bombed during the Battle of Britain, the administrative offices were moved to Blenheim Palace in Oxfordshire. At the end of the war the headquarters moved to Leconfield House in Curzon Street, London; its overt address was a suite of rooms at Room 055, on the ground floor of the War Office Building in Whitehall. The counter-subversion 'B' Division operated in conditions of great secrecy under Maxwell Knight, its head since 1924, from Dolphin Square.

But Kell was no expert in administration, and the bureaucracy of the greatly enlarged MI 5 left much to be desired; his famous card index of suspected subversives was vast and ramshackle, and MI 5's failure to deal with a largely imaginary 'fifth column' had not impressed Churchill. Accordingly, in May 1940 he instituted the Security Executive, with Lord Swinton, the former Air

Minister, as its first chairman, to deal with what he called the 'overlaps and underlaps' between the various organisations dealing with counter-espionage and counter-subversion in the country; the executive was especially to find out whether or not there was a 'fifth column' in the UK, and if so, to eliminate it. From the beginning, Swinton took an especial interest in the organisation and administration of MI 5, which he was not slow to criticise; the famous card index also received the attention of a business machines expert brought in by Swinton for the purpose. Despite the apparent early success against the Abwehr in the UK, Kell was burnt out, and the last straw was probably the clumsy search of the German Embassy in London, then in the care of the Swiss, which he organised in the first week of June 1940; the Swiss complained, and Kell and his deputy, Holt-Wilson, were dismissed on 10 June. Care was needed in the selection of their replacements, but in the mean time 'Jasper' Harker stood in as acting Director-General. Although he was not judged suitable to be the permanent incumbent, he was selected as deputy to the new Director-General, Sir David Petrie, when the latter was appointed to the post in November 1940.

The witch-hunt for a non-existent 'fifth column' distracted MI 5 from their other tasks during the summer and autumn of 1940. However, with the UK virtually isolated from the Continent after the Dunkirk and Cherbourg evacuations it was relatively easy for MI 5 to keep the remaining routes of entry under close surveillance, and the Germans were therefore forced to resort to clandestine methods in attempting to insert their agents into the country. From September to November 1940 more than twenty-five agents were landed in the UK, either by parachute or by boat; all were easily caught by MI 5 thanks to their poorly forged documents and their inadequate training and equipment. Many were 'turned' and operated against Germany in the brilliant Operation DOUBLE-CROSS run by 'B' Division of MI 5 under the supervision of the Twenty (XX, 'double-cross') Committee chaired by (Sir) J.C. Masterman. Among members of MI 5's 'B1' Section involved in this operation was (Sir) Anthony Blunt, who later turned out to have been a Soviet agent.

It is an astonishing fact that the German espionage system in the UK during the Second World War was run by the British. It was, of course, of inestimable value in the deception operations preceding Operation OVERLORD, the Allied invasion of north-west Europe in 1944. Of those German agents who would not co-operate in Operation DOUBLE-CROSS between the outbreak of war and the end of it, fifteen were hanged, the last at Pentonville on 12 July 1944, and one shot by firing-squad; a seventeenth was very lucky to be reprieved.

With his arrangements for the internment of enemy aliens at the beginning of the war, Kell had achieved the quick success against German agents and potential agents that he had desired, and had repeated his triumph of the First World War. The successful 'turning' of the majority of the German agents landed clandestinely in the country during the war was another triumph, achieved by a greatly enlarged service under his successor, despite the inevitable lowering of morale which followed the shake-up of the service after Kell's dismissal. However, the broadening of the very tight pre-war recruiting base inevitably let in some potential security risks, such as homosexuals, covert members of the Communist Party and others, and this was to have an adverse effect on the security of the service and of MI 6 and other government departments, both during and after the war. In this connection, it is significant that a service that had been concentrating on the detection of Soviet and Communist Party of Great Britain attempts at espionage and subversion since the October Revolution of 1917 should have proved so unable to uncover the Communist-inspired traitors of the Cambridge spy ring (see Chapter 3) and others in MI 5, MI 6, GC & CS and the Foreign Office before, during and after the Second World War, yet on the outbreak of war was able immediately to uncover all German espionage agents in the country and to turn them against their German masters throughout the war. For this reason alone it seems more than probable that there was a highly placed Soviet agent, identity as yet unknown, in the MI 5 hierarchy who was able to frustrate any attempts at uncovering the Soviet spies in the British Intelligence community.

The pre-war record of MI 6 had been poor; it also started the war badly due to two misfortunes in November 1939. The first occurred on 4 November with the death from a malignant tumour of Admiral Sir Hugh Sinclair, 'C'; he was replaced on 28 November by his deputy, Major Stewart Menzies. The second blow occurred on 9 November, when the German Sicherheitsdienst (SD), their security service, kidnapped the SIS Head of Station in The Hague, as well as the Resident in The Hague of a secondary SIS network, the 'Z' organisation, in a well-planned 'sting' operation at Venlo, on the Dutch–German frontier.

The SIS Head of Station was a Major Richard Stevens, who was operating in The Hague under Passport Control cover from a house well known to the locals as the base for the British Secret Service; this house had received a certain notoriety in 1936, when Stevens's predecessor, Major Hugh Dalton, had committed suicide there after having been caught embezzling MI 6 funds. The 'Z' organisation was a parallel network of SIS representatives run by Claude Dansey of the SIS from offices in Bush House, Aldwych, and was composed of expatriate Britons settled in foreign communities and business executives working for British companies. The 'Z' Resident in The Hague was Captain Sigismund Payne Best, who ran a network of train-watchers throughout Holland with Major Wallinger in the First World War.

For some reason, difficult to understand at this remove, Dansey had instructed his network officers to disclose themselves to their local SIS Heads of Station upon the outbreak of war, and Best accordingly did so to Stevens. The Passport Control organisation was already a fairly thin cover for SIS at this time, and by requiring his 'Z' Residents to disclose themselves to and to work with the SIS Heads of Station, Dansey was ensuring that if one's cover were to be 'blown', they both would be. This is what happened in The Hague; Stevens and Best provided the Germans with detailed information about both MI 5 and MI 6 after their capture, as was discovered after the war when they underwent detailed interrogation by those organisations. Both admitted under interrogation that they had co-operated with the SD, but surprisingly, no further action was taken against them. How detailed the information they had imparted to their captors had been was revealed some twenty years after their capture, when a summary of what they had revealed, prepared by the German security service (RSHA) in readiness for the invasion of the UK, was discovered among German records. This document revealed detailed knowledge of the organisation, personnel and their code numbers, locations and functions of both services, including the 'Z' network, and was annotated with the name of the source of each piece of information.

This blow, together with the German occupation of most of Europe, ensured that MI 6 had virtually to start from scratch again in building up a covert Intelligence organisation. This in turn meant that the quality of its agent Intelligence was poor for much of the war; it was not until after the summer of 1943 that SIS started to produce worthwhile HUMINT on the V-Weapon sites in northern France and generally throughout Europe, due largely to their co-operation with the Polish and other European secret services. Had 'C' not had the foresight to gain control of GC & CS when he did, and had the latter's code-breakers not made their lucky breakthrough in 1940, it is open to question whether Menzies and SIS could have survived.

Another example of SIS foresight had been the joint funding with the French in March 1939 of a programme of covert aerial photography of Germany which produced a mass of useful information. This was not well received by the RAF, which did not at that time appreciate the need for a specialist photo-reconnaissance unit; this specialist unit was at first run by SIS, but was later handed over to the RAF. It was the precursor of the many wartime RAF PR squadrons and air photo interpretation units which provided so much valuable Intelligence during the war. It will be remembered that after SIGINT, PR was found by the JIC to have been the second most valuable source of military Intelligence during the Second World War. Thus SIS was perhaps already seeing the writing on the wall and preparing for the decline in value of the human agent in covert Intelligence which had been noticeable during the war and is likely to increase as technology advances.

No account of British military Intelligence in the two world wars would be complete without some mention of deception – an Intelligence function so often essential to the gaining of surprise in both tactical and strategic operations. At the outbreak of the Second World War, deception policy had been one of the responsibilities of the Inter-Service Security Board; this responsibility was transferred in early 1941 to a small Deception Staff within the Joint Planning Staff, and four months later, to a larger organisation, under Colonel John H Bevan, known as the London Controlling Section (LCS). Meanwhile, in the Middle East an organisation under the command of a Colonel Dudley Clark and known as 'A' Force had been established at the end of 1940 by General Wavell for the purpose of organising and carrying out offensive deception. 'A' Force comprised three units of company strength, specially trained in the operation of visual deception devices, as well as numerous agents in the Middle East and in African countries. The company-sized units made and used large numbers of dummy tanks, guns, lorries and other military equipment, which were deployed to conceal real troop movements and concentrations in conjunction with fake radio traffic. Wavell had been on General Allenby's staff in Palestine during the First World War, and had been a great admirer of his use of deception, especially in the attack on Beersheba in October 1917, when he had used the 'dead officer with blood-stained plans' ploy with great success.

There were many successful uses of deception by the Allies during the Second World War, particularly in the Middle East, but the biggest and most outstandingly successful was Operation FORTITUDE/BODYGUARD, the deception operation for the Allied invasion of north-west Europe, Operation OVERLORD, in June 1944. This was a bold scheme designed to convince the Germans that the main Allied landings would be in the Pas de Calais area some six weeks after the landings in Normandy, and that the latter were merely a diversion; for this purpose a notional First US Army Group (FUSAG) was created in East Anglia and South-East England under the command of General George S. Patton Jr.

Extensive and complicated radio networks were set up, operated by a US signals battalion, to simulate the traffic of an army group in training and in operations; use was made of the DOUBLE-CROSS agent networks to plant false information in the minds of the German Intelligence officers and concentrations of dummy tanks, guns, tents and landing craft were built up in the notional concentration areas. Misleading lighting schemes were employed to decoy German PR aircraft away from genuine concentrations of landing craft, and a sustained and concentrated bombing campaign of the Pas de Calais and communications leading inland from it was initiated. The enemy reaction to this series of deception schemes was almost exactly as planned: the German High Command believed that the landings in Normandy were a diversion, and as late as 25 June 1944, von Rundstedt stated in his weekly report that the US Army Group assembled in south-east England, though ready to embark, had still not been committed by the Allies.

At the receiving end of all the raw Intelligence provided by the covert organisations and by the theatres of war in the shape of POW interrogation reports, captured documents and captured equipment, the War Office MI Directorate had got its basic organisation more or less correct by the end of 1941, and the changes made from then until the war's end were mainly in the nature of fine tuning. In the summer of 1941, for example, MI 3 took over from MI 2 responsibility for the USSR, Eastern Europe and Scandinavia. It was thus covering all Europe, with the exception of Germany and German-occupied territories, which were covered by MI 14. In December 1941 MI 19 was established, to be responsible for enemy POWs; MI 9, however, retained its responsibility for the organisation of POW escape routes and for the debriefing of returning British POWs. MI 17 was formed in April 1943 to act as the DMI's secretariat, and absorbed both MI(JIC) and MI(Co-ord), previously responsible for coordinating the work of the Intelligence and Operations Directorates; it also contained a sub-section for the distribution of SIGINT summaries within the War Office. In July 1943 MI 15 was created to collate and distribute all Intelligence on German air defences as an inter-service and inter-Allied organisation; this had previously been done by MI 14, which was now able to concentrate on the German order of battle, organisation and personality Intelligence.

Three new deputy directors were also appointed: DDMI(PW) was established in 1941 to take charge of MI 9 and MI 19; DDMI(F) was appointed in March 1942 to be the MI Directorate representative at SIS HQ, and DDMI(Y) was appointed in the spring of 1943 to control the work of MI 8 and Signals 4, with responsibility to both DMI and the Director of Signals. DDMI(Y) was also the War Office representative on the 'Y' Committee, and acted as the communication channel between DMI and GC & CS. Three further deputy directors were appointed in 1944: the first, for planning, was DDMI(P), to whom MI 17 and IS(O) were subordinated; the others were DDMI(Germany), to take charge of MI 14 and MI 15, and DDMI(Censorship). The Military Intelligence Research Section (MIRS) was an Anglo-American section formed in 1943, under MI 14, to coordinate Intelligence on the German Army from captured documents. In 1945 MI 16 was formed to take over responsibility for scientific Intelligence from MI 10(c), and with MI 10, was grouped

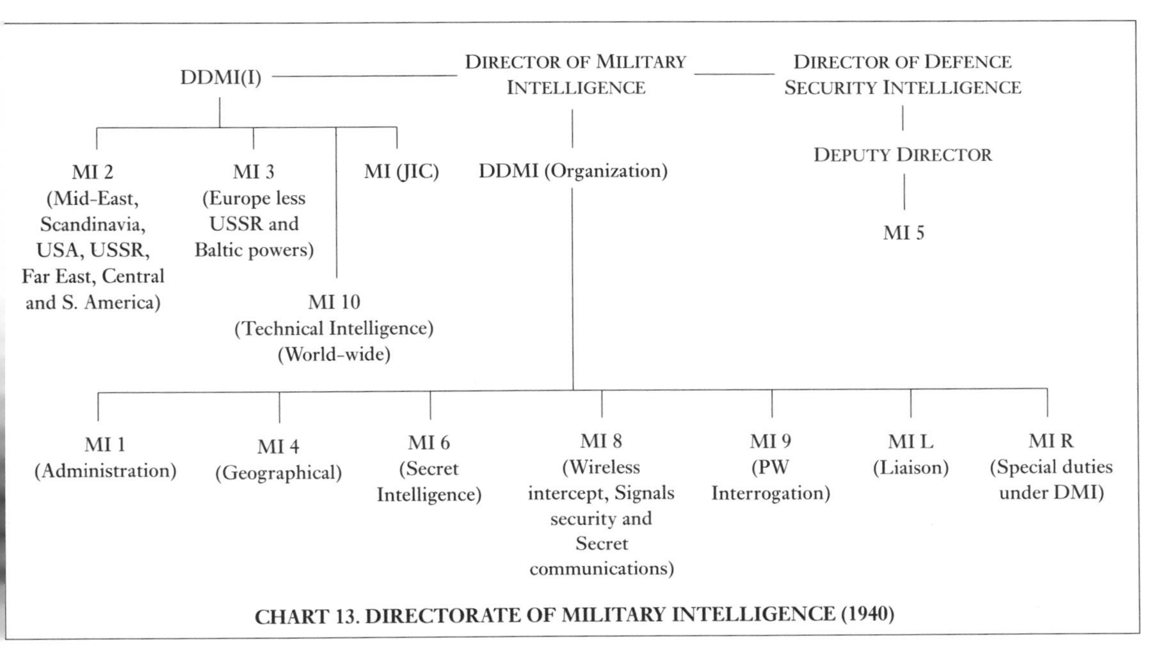

CHART 13. DIRECTORATE OF MILITARY INTELLIGENCE (1940)

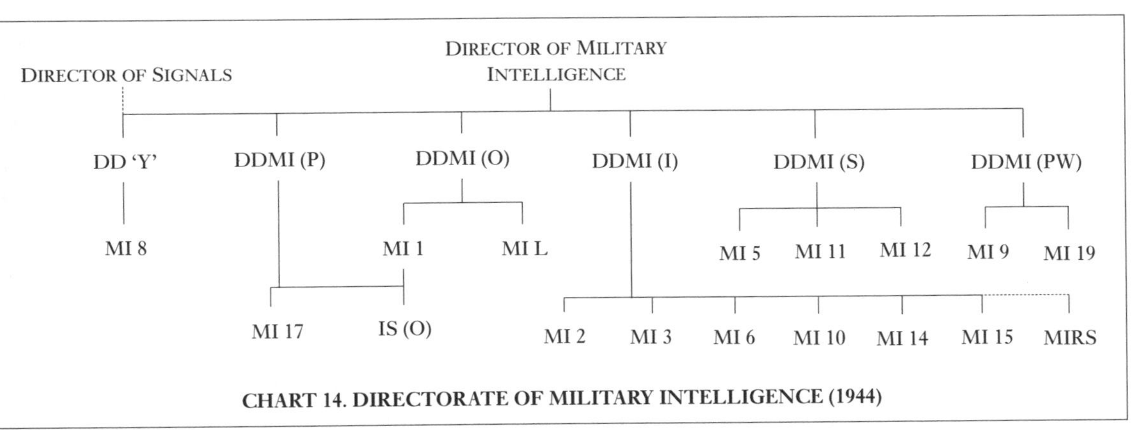

CHART 14. DIRECTORATE OF MILITARY INTELLIGENCE (1944)

under the DDMI(I & P), which had assumed the functions of DDMI(Information) and DDMI(Planning). These changes are illustrated in Charts 13 and 14.

During the war it had been increasingly borne in upon British military Intelligence, and on the Intelligence Directorates of the Royal Navy and Royal Air Force, that little cooperation would be received or could be expected from Soviet military Intelligence; despite the assistance given to the Soviets by the British in all aspects of their fight against the German invaders, including the warning (based on Ultra sources, but rejected by Stalin) of the German intention to invade the Soviet Union in June 1941, this was not reciprocated, and any information that was given by the Soviet military was suspect. Particularly from 1943 onwards, with the Soviet-inspired campaign in the UK for the opening of a second front at a time when the opening of a second front in Europe would have been quite beyond the capacity of the British Armed Forces, it became increasingly clear that Stalin's paranoia, coupled with the Russians' natural and in-born suspicion of foreigners, would not only prevent Soviet cooperation with the Western Allies, but probably foreshadowed an actively anti-British and anti-American attitude. It therefore seemed prudent to the Service Intelligence Directorates, as the outcome of the war became increasingly clear, to take a greater interest in the organisation, personalities and equipment of the Red Army. The only information on Red Army equipment then available to MI 10 came from captured German Intelligence documents, apart from the shipment to the UK from the USSR in 1943 of a brand-new T-34 medium and KV-1 heavy tank, complete with spares and ammunition.

A breakthrough came with the German surrender, however, when the Intelligence collation files and handbooks on the Red Army compiled and maintained by the German Intelligence organisation Fremde Heer (Ost) (Foreign Armies (East)) fell into British hands; these compendious files contained all the information on the Red Army and its equipment that had been collected by the Germans since the invasion of the Soviet Union in June 1941, and comprised POW interrogation reports, captured Soviet documents, photographs and sketches, and gave as good a picture of the state of the Red Army as could be wished. They formed a sound basis on which to build the MI Directorate's own files during the Cold War which followed the ending of the Second World War, and MI 3, which was to deal with the Soviet Union and the Warsaw Pact countries, was built up as a result, as MI 4 and MI 14 were amalgamated and run down.

In stark contrast to the lack of cooperation from the USSR, the exchange of information between British and US Intelligence agencies had been virtually complete, especially after the BRUSA agreement on the exchange of Intelligence was signed in 1943. Whilst initially of most benefit to the United States, whose Intelligence agencies were initially small, untrained and lacking experience, by the end of the war British military Intelligence agencies were deriving equal benefit from the exchange.

At the end of the Second World War, the Allies formed the Allied Control Commission for Germany (CCG) and the Allied Commission for Austria (ACA); both countries were divided into four zones, one per occupying power, and their capitals, Berlin and Vienna, were similarly divided into sectors. The national components of these commissions were responsible for the running and civilian administration of their zone or sector of occupation; for instance, the British component of the CCG was known as the Control Commission for Germany (British Element) (CCG(BE)). This was organised into a series of divisions, one of which was the Intelligence Division, with its headquarters at Hereford and headed by Major-General Sir Kenneth Strong, who had been head of General Eisenhower's Intelligence staff at SHAEF HQ during the north-west Europe campaign. One of the main preoccupations of this division immediately after the war was the organisation of agent networks in the Soviet Zone. These produced mainly low-grade information of Soviet troop movements, rather like the train-watching networks in France run by Wallinger and Cameron in the First World War.

By 1947, in the post-war rundown of the Directorate of Military Intelligence, there were only three deputy directors (see Chart 15); these were:

DDMI (Information) – controlling MI(JIS), MI 2, MI 3, MI 4 (now responsible for Germany), MI 10 and MI 16
DDMI (Organisation & Security) – controlling MI 1, MI 7, MIL, MI 9/19 & MI 11
DDMI (Y) – controlling MI 8

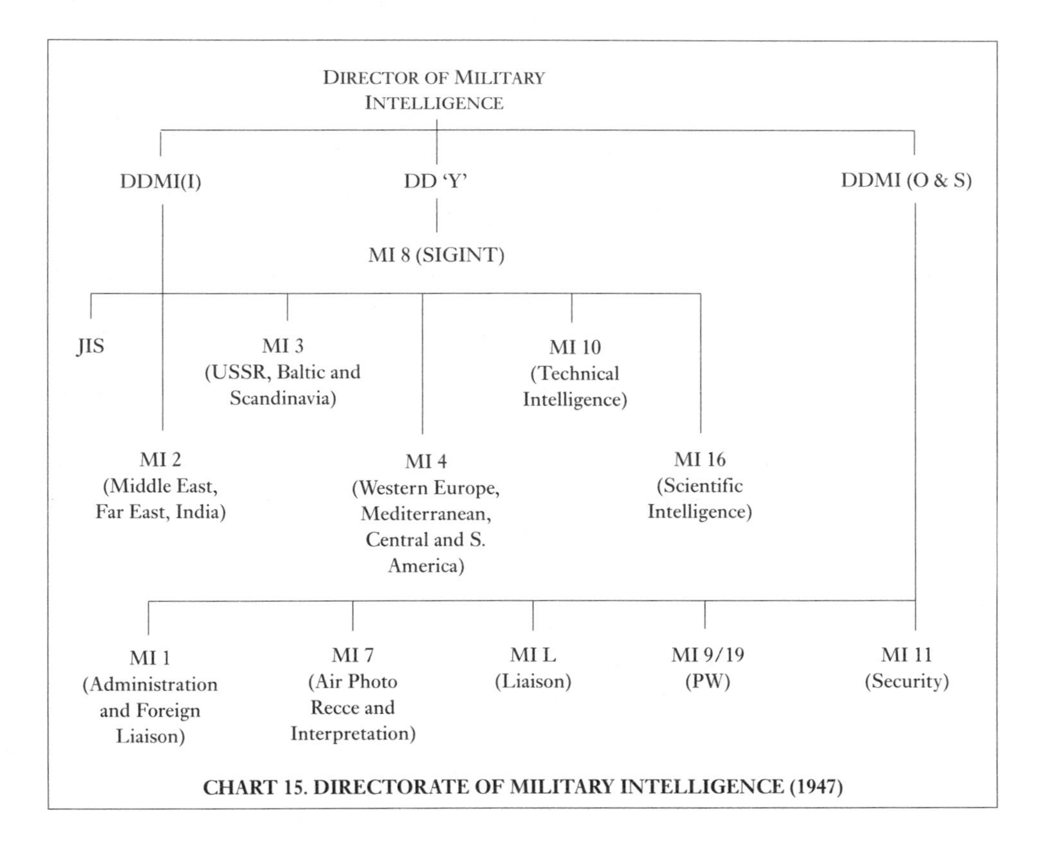

CHART 15. DIRECTORATE OF MILITARY INTELLIGENCE (1947)

One other Intelligence development immediately after the war's end was the formation in late 1945 of the Joint Intelligence Bureau, located at first in Bryanston Square, London, in a terrace of late Georgian town houses which had been crudely converted into one house by knocking through the doorways between the houses to make a rabbit warren of poky and ill-lit passages and offices. It had been found during the latter stages of the Second World War that scientific Intelligence, with its more general interest and application, tended to be of interest to more than one service: for instance, MI 16 and ADI(Science), the War Office and Air Ministry scientific Intelligence branches, were overlapping in their work on the German V-weapons. Accordingly, when the Ministry of Economic Warfare was disbanded at the end of the war it was felt that scientific and economic Intelligence might, together with some other types of Intelligence of joint Service interest, be more beneficiently and conveniently dealt with by a new joint-service organisation; the Joint Intelligence Bureau was created for the purpose, and represented a first attempt at the unified handling and analysis of Intelligence needed by more than one government department, and a first step towards the integration of Intelligence analysis. It was not liked by the services, many of whose senior personnel felt it to be a threat to the traditional single-service Intelligence organisations. Service technical and scientific Intelligence branches were co-located at Bryanston Square in 1946 with the other branches of the JIB, but this first attempt at unification was not successful, and was abandoned a few months later, when the technical Intelligence branches were returned to their respective ministries.

Two documents obtained in 1940 had enabled the War Office MI Directorate to recover from what would otherwise have been a parlous Intelligence situation until the Ultra material came on stream. The first was captured from the staff car of the liaison officer to the Commander-in-Chief of German Army Group B on 25 May 1940, and enabled MI 3 for the first time to build up an authoritative picture of the German Army's order of battle. Other captured documents, together with POW interrogation, German Press and radio reports and some of the Ultra material permitted them to keep this picture up to date throughout the rest of the war, particularly after 1943. At this time the flow of documents became so large that MIRS was formed to cope with the cataloguing, translation and dissemination of the material.

The second document was sent anonymously to the British Embassy in Oslo, and gave technical information on German rocket, proximity fuse and other weapon research and development; because of its anonymity, not much credence was placed initially in the document's accuracy or credibility, but as the war progressed and the forecasts of the document were increasingly fulfilled, it was increasingly accepted as reliable.

As in the First World War, British military Intelligence in the Second World War was extremely efficient and successful: the enemy's order of battle, weapons and equipment and production of war materiel were accurately estimated, its industry accurately located and its strategy accurately predicted. With one notable – although, as it turned out, not disastrous – exception, British failures to react correctly to enemy actions were not due to failures of Intelligence to predict these actions, but rather to failure of commanders to accept the accuracy of the Intelligence they were given. The exception was the production and stockpiling by the Germans of not one but three different types of nerve gas, of which British Intelligence remained completely unaware throughout the war; luckily, the Germans did not use it.

The German Intelligence organisation in the Second World War was better prepared than it had been in the First World War. The principal German Intelligence service from the outbreak of war was the Abwehr, which together with the Amtsgruppe Ausland formed the Amt Auslandsnachrichten und Abwehr, one of the directorates of the Oberkommando der Wehrmacht (OKW), which was the military staff of the Commander-in-Chief of the Armed Forces. The Abwehr was the secret Intelligence service of the High Command, while the Amtsgruppe Ausland coordinated the attaché sections of the service ministries, which collected Intelligence by overt and lawful means. The Abwehr owed its name to the Treaty of Versailles, which stipulated that Germany could not possess an offensive espionage service, but could have a counter-espionage and security organisation; when Germany organised an espionage service in contravention of the treaty, it did so under cover of security, and continued to use the term Abwehr ('defence') to include both offensive and defensive functions.

The Abwehr was composed mainly of officers of the old Imperial Army and Navy, officers of the First World War recalled from the reserve, and officers of the post-First World War Reichswehr. As with the British clandestine services, the Abwehr was essentially the Chief's private army, largely recruited through personal contact. The Chief when war broke out was Admiral Wilhelm Canaris, appointed in 1935 at the age of forty-seven; he came from a middle-class evangelical family of Lombard origin, but Germanised for 200 years. He reported to Keitel, the head of the OKW, through whom he had access to Hitler.

The Abwehr was organised into four principal *Abteilungen* ('departments'); Abt I was responsible for espionage and was roughly equivalent to SIS, Abt II for sabotage and subversion performing the functions of SOE and PWE, Abt III for counter-espionage and protective security, equivalent to MI 5 and Section V of SIS. The fourth Abteilung, Abt Z, was a general administrative department serving the whole organisation. When war broke out, the headquarters of the Abwehr, comprising some 650 all ranks, was located at Tirpitzufer 72, Berlin, near the OKW. On paper its organisation looked impressive, but the reality was rather different: central control was weak, and a British report of 1944 remarked that the Abwehr had the appearance not of a single large Intelligence service, but of a loose association of many small ones, competing and sometimes conflicting with one another.

The Sicherheitsdienst was a part of the Reichsführer SS (RFSS), developed by the Nazi Party as its own Intelligence service, and recognised in 1936 as an Intelligence organisation of the Nazi Party and the State. In 1936 Heinrich Himmler, the Reichsführer SS, became Chief of the German Police, which was divided into two categories, the Ordnungspolizei (ORPO) and the Sicherheitspolizei (SIPO); the latter comprised the Kriminalpolizei (Kripo) and the Geheime Staatspolizei (Gestapo), and was placed under Reinhardt Heydrich, who was already head of the SD. After Heydrich's assassination in 1942, Kaltenbrunner succeeded him, after a gap of some months. The RSHA was organised into seven departments, of which only Amt III, Amt IV and Amt VI were of counter-Intelligence interest; Amt III directed the activities of the SD within Germany, its task being to ensure that 'the state of the people is sound and no harmful tendencies emerge', Amt IV was responsible for executive action, and Amt VI was the SD in its capacity as a secret foreign political Intelligence service.

There was a clear possibility of overlap between Abt III of the Abwehr and Amt IV of the RSHA, and between the Abwehr's Abt I and the RSHA's Amt VI. At the outbreak of war, an agreement reached in 1936 between Canaris and Heydrich known as 'The Ten Commandments' governed relations between the Abwehr and the RSHA; this laid down that on the offensive side, the Abwehr should concern itself purely with military Intelligence and pass to the SD any political Intelligence which it might acquire, while the SD would reciprocate by passing to the Abwehr any military Intelligence which came its way. On the defensive side, the agreement recognised that counter-espionage was the responsibility of the Abwehr (although dependent on the Gestapo for executive action), while political investigation was the responsibility of the RSHA.

The war gave the RSHA scope for steady expansion of its activities as a rival to the Abwehr. Its successful kidnapping of the two SIS officers, Best and Stevens, at Venlo in December 1939 by Amt IV, masterminded by Walter Schellenberg, gave impetus to its ambitions. Amt VI, on the other hand, was a minor department at the outbreak of war; Himmler aimed to have a foreign Intelligence service of his own, but until 1942 the RSHA lacked suitable personnel for this type of work. In 1942 the picture changed with the appointment of the able and ambitious Schellenberg to head Amt VI; he had attracted favourable attention with his handling of the Venlo incident, had a clear idea of the weaknesses of the German Intelligence organisation, and aimed to create a single, unified Intelligence service. Under his direction there occurred a steady expansion of Amt VI's activities, with representation throughout both occupied and neutral Europe, in Turkey and in South America. In 1942 its representative in Vichy France was exceptionally well informed; its Rome representative correctly forecast the intentions of Marshal Badoglio (which the Abwehr conspicuously failed to do), and his information made possible the rescue of Mussolini by Otto Skorzeny, an officer in Amt VI. The *Cicero* case, in Turkey, in which the British Ambassador's valet, a German agent, was able to gain access to the documents in the ambassador's safe, was another Amt VI coup which added to its reputation.

The high reputation enjoyed by the Abwehr at the beginning of the war was based upon its having met the requirements placed upon it for the Polish campaign, the invasions of Norway and Denmark and the Blitzkrieg in the west. It successfully sabotaged the mobilisation of Yugoslav forces and prevented the destruction of its communications, while Canaris's special relationship with several key Spanish officers, including General Franco, meant that Spain, although a non-belligerent, was used by the Abwehr more or less as it chose as a base for Intelligence and sabotage operations. In addition, in conjunction with the Gestapo and radio intercept services, the Abwehr scored major successes against resistance movements in Western Europe; three of the most important Allied networks in France, the Interallié, Autogiro and Prosper networks, were completely penetrated in 1941, SOE operations in Belgium were badly damaged, and those in Holland were completely controlled for some twenty months. Soviet espionage rings in France, the Low Countries and Germany itself, the *Rote Kapelle* ('Red Orchestra'), were smashed and some two hundred of their members executed.

It was not until 1942, when it failed correctly to forecast the objective of the Allied Operation TORCH, that the reliability of the Abwehr started to be questioned; failure again to forecast Operation HUSKY, the invasion of Sicily in July 1943, and Marshal Badoglio's intentions after the fall of Mussolini added to the doubts. At the same time, in Germany the balance of power was moving against the General Staff and other conservative elements and in favour of the Nazi Party in general and Himmler in particular; this resulted in the rise of the SD at the Abwehr's expense, the latter rightly being suspected of having a defeatist attitude as well as harbouring elements actively disloyal to the Nazi

Party. In the first half of 1943, therefore, changes were made at the top of the Abwehr, but in February 1944 Hitler ordered the creation of a unified Intelligence service; with effect from 1 June 1944 a new organisation, the RSHA Militärisches Amt (Mil Amt), was formed, absorbing the remains of the Abwehr. However, the re-formed Intelligence service was no more successful than the earlier Abwehr, and it collapsed totally with the Wehrmacht at the end of the war; having been forbidden to visualise defeat, it had no contingency plans for survival or resistance, and Schellenberg and Skorzeny both surrendered.

CHAPTER 3

The Cold War: 1946–88

Victory in the Second World War had given the Soviet Union dominion over large swathes of territory in Europe and the Balkans, and had effectively expanded its frontiers westwards and southwards to include Poland, Hungary, Czechoslovakia, Romania, Bulgaria, Albania, Yugoslavia, the Baltic States, East Germany (the German Democratic Republic – DDR) and part of Austria. All these countries had Communist governments imposed, with their armed services supplied with Soviet weapons and equipment and organised on Soviet lines. Cooperation with the Western Allies was minimal at the end of the war, and decreased as time went on. Berlin was an island occupied by the four Allied powers within the Soviet zone of Germany, and access to it by the Western Allies from West Germany was constantly hindered by the Soviet authorities; this was a continuous source of friction between the USSR and the Western occupying powers, culminating in the blockade of Berlin by the Soviets in 1948–49. The Soviet attitude largely dictated the response of the Western Allies, which was to recognise the implied threat to their security and to step up their defence establishments and their Intelligence efforts against the Soviet Union and its satellites accordingly.

In contrast to the expansion of the Soviet empire, those of the UK, France and other European countries were shrinking, and doing so over a relatively short period, as former dominions and colonies were granted their independence. Communist influences had been at work there too, and many ended up with a Communist-led government after independence, or Communist-inspired riots and insurgency before it. The threat of Communism to the democracies of the West was very real for many years after the ending of the war, and several campaigns against it were waged by the UK, the USA, France and, in Korea, the United Nations forces. However, it was in Europe that the main threat lay, and it was in Europe, especially in Germany, that the main military Intelligence effort would be concentrated for the next few years.

One of the results of the increasing tension between the superpowers of East and West, the USSR and the USA, was the UKUSA agreement, signed in 1947, whereby the British and US Governments agreed to share their Intelligence product with each other. This agreement grew out of the earlier BRUSA agreement made in 1943 with similar aims, and encouraged the exchange not only of Intelligence, but also of Intelligence officers in their various agencies.

Another result, as the Soviets realised the extent of Western Intelligence operations and the drain of technicians and professional people resulting from line-crossers and defectors from East Germany, was the erection of what came to be known as the 'Iron Curtain' of barbed wire, minefields, watch-towers and other obstacles erected by the Soviet occupation authorities along the border between East and West Germany, which brought this channel of Intelligence to a virtual halt. In 1954 alone, more than 184,000 people had left East Germany for the West.

A third result was the signing of the Brussels Treaty in 1948: a military and economic pact of mutual assistance, by the UK, France, Holland, Belgium and Luxemburg. The Western European Union arose out of this pact, organising the defence aspects of the Treaty, and with Field-Marshal Sir Bernard Montgomery as its first head. These agreements finally led to the establishment of the North Atlantic Treaty Organisation (NATO) in 1949, a compendious organisation of Western democracies led by the USA and committed to mutual defence in the case of armed aggression against any signatory. Partly in response to the formation of NATO and partly in response to the proposed remilitarisation of West Germany in 1956, the USSR signed a similar mutual defence treaty, the Warsaw Pact, with its satellites in 1955, but this merely confirmed the status quo.

As part of the agreement setting up the post-war Control Commission for Germany, each of the Allied occupying powers was permitted to attach a military mission to the headquarters of the others. British, French and US missions to the HQs of their Western Allies, and vice versa, were more in the nature of liaison missions, but for the Allied missions to the Soviet HQ and Soviet missions to the HQs of the Western Allies, the position was very different. The British C-in-C's Mission to the Soviet HQ in Potsdam (BRIXMIS) was more like an enlarged military attaché staff, trained in the overt and covert collection of Intelligence by attending Soviet Army manoeuvres, photographing Soviet Army equipment and observing troop movements within the Group of Soviet Forces in Germany (GSFG). The Soviet C-in-C's mission to the BAOR HQ (known as SOXMIS in British Intelligence circles) firstly in Bad Öynhausen and later in Mönchengladbach, was similarly trained and employed, and was very persistent in its efforts. On one important British Army exercise in BAOR in 1956, from which all SOXMIS representatives were banned, the author had to arrest at pistol point one SOXMIS vehicle crew which had penetrated to the HQ of an armoured regiment at the heart of the exercise, and shepherd them out of the area with an armoured scout car escort.

The ending of the Second World War brought the usual post-war cutbacks and reductions in the UK's Intelligence agencies, although the Soviet harassment and aggressive Intelligence activity against the Western Allies meant that the reductions were less swingeing than had been the case after previous wars. In the War Office's MI Directorate the cuts were mainly limited to those branches concerned with Germany and Western Europe; those such as MI 3, which dealt with the USSR and its satellites, were strengthened, and the resulting reorganisation is shown in Chart 15. GCHQ (the former GC & CS) moved from Bletchley Park to Eastcote in the suburbs of London, and as it had done after the First World War, changed its priorities from German to Soviet communications. Its attack on Soviet diplomatic traffic enjoyed a certain success for a limited time, the material resulting from this being code-named 'Venona'.

SOE was wound up in 1946, and responsibility for covert action returned to MI 6, which formed a new branch to deal with it, and thus added to the administrative confusion resulting from changed priorities and the transition from hot war to Cold War. One example of this confusion occurred in the Middle East, where the SIS organisation had had the cover title of Inter-Service Liaison Department (ISLD). Concluding that this organisation's cover had been 'blown', SIS changed its title to Combined Research and Planning Office (CRPO); it was not until after several batches of mail addressed to CRPO, Middle East, had failed to arrive that the missing mail was discovered in the hands of a mystified sergeant in Jerusalem working in the Command Regimental Pay Office (also abbreviated CRPO), Middle East. Thanks largely to the wartime success of GCHQ with the Ultra material, however, SIS emerged from the war covered in the glory reflected from it; this masked its relative lack of success with other covert sources of Intelligence, and delayed the major overhaul the organisation needed in order to adapt to modern Cold War operations.

As had been the case in 1918, the Security Service, MI 5, came out of the Second World War with flying colours and in better shape than the SIS, very largely due to the successful rounding-up at the beginning of the war of German agents then resident in the UK and the success with which it caught all those subsequently trying to enter the country, 'turning' a majority of them and running them in the DOUBLE-CROSS operation. MI 5 was initially distrusted by many members of the 1945 Labour Government and the more Left-leaning members of the Labour Party, however, and this government mistrust led to an outsider, Sir Percy Sillitoe, a former Chief Constable, being appointed to head it over the heads of the several suitably qualified candidates from within the organisation when Sir David Petrie retired in 1946. As after the First World War, however, this mistrust gradually melted away in the face of blatant Communist espionage and attempts to cause industrial and civil unrest in the country, and the government made increasing use of the Security Service.

Within the UK, MI 5's attention was increasingly concentrated on the activities of the Soviet Embassy, Trade Organisation, news agency TASS, the Communist Party of Great Britain (CPGB) and its many front organisations. However, it was embarrassingly, conspicuously and suspiciously unsuccessful in uncovering the Soviet agents who had been working in MI 5, MI 6, GCHQ and the Foreign Office during and after the war, and who were eventually uncovered by Intelligence from Soviet defectors and the decrypting of Soviet radio communications between Moscow Centre and its outstations, rather than by the Security Service's own counter-espionage efforts. Outside the UK it was heavily involved in assisting the counter-insurgency campaigns in former colonies, particularly in Malaya, where the Communist Party had embarked upon a guerrilla war in 1948 which was to last until the Communist leader surrendered in 1955.

The threat posed by the USSR and the Communist movement to world peace, and the many resulting international crises and lesser wars, kept up the pressure both on the service departments (for change in the British armed services) and on the Treasury (for adequate funding of the armed services and the Intelligence agencies, which had been lacking after previous wars); the Korean War, the Berlin blockade, the Suez campaign, the Communist revolt in Malaya, the civil war and terrorism in Cyprus and the earmarking of forces for NATO, among other involvements, meant that the retreat into lethargy and *laissez-faire* which had been so characteristic of the British and their government after previous wars was prevented.

The ever-present threat from the USSR and the Warsaw Pact countries, together with the existence of NATO, eventually combined to force change upon the reluctant services, a change which finally came in 1964 with the creation of a single unified Defence Staff. The former Admiralty, War Office and Air Ministry were abolished and merged into the Ministry of Defence, housed in a large new building in Whitehall, the separate departments then becoming known as MOD(Navy), MOD(Army) and MOD(RAF) respectively. Their Intelligence organisations and the former JIB were also merged to form the Defence Intelligence Staff (DIS), and their individual branches were renumbered in the 'DI' series, so it is probably now inaccurate, albeit convenient, to continue to call the Security Service by its military Intelligence title of MI 5, and the SIS by the title of MI 6.

The first Director-General of Defence Intelligence was Sir Kenneth Strong, the former head of Eisenhower's SHAPE Intelligence organisation and later of JIB, now a civilian. His deputy, the Deputy Chief of Defence Staff (Intelligence), was to be a serving officer, and alternated between the three armed services. Under the Director-General were four directors, one of Service Intelligence, one of Scientific and Technical Intelligence, one of Economic and Logistic Intelligence and one of Management and Support Intelligence, as well as the Head of Defence Intelligence Staff (Central Secretariat). Under these, four Deputy Directors of Intelligence covered Administration and Security, Warsaw Pact Countries, countries in the rest of the world and, lastly, Intelligence Collection.

When the General Staff system was first, belatedly, introduced into the British Army in 1904, the Chief of the Imperial General Staff (CIGS) had under him three principal staff officers: the Adjutant-General (AG), responsible for administration of personnel ('A' matters); the Quartermaster-General (QMG), responsible for supply and quartering ('Q' matters), and the Master-General of the Ordnance (MGO), responsible for weapon and equipment design and procurement. The four operational branches, covering Operations, Intelligence, Training and Staff Duties, came under the CIGS and were responsible for 'G' matters. This division of responsibility between 'G', 'A' and 'Q' matters was followed at all headquarters down to, and including, unit level.

From brigade headquarters upwards, 'G' staff officers had the title of General Staff Officer, Grade 1, 2 or 3, 'Q' staff officers the title of Assistant or Deputy Assistant Quartermaster-General (AQMG or DAQMG) and 'A' staff officers the title of Assistant or Deputy Assistant Adjutant-General (AAG or DAAG). Intelligence branches at formation headquarters were known as General Staff (Intelligence), abbreviated to GS(I) or, later, G(Int). These titles were cumbersome and difficult for members of other NATO Army staffs (all of which were based upon the French staff nomenclature) to comprehend, so all these titles were changed in 1980, after much resistance from senior British Army officers, to conform to the system used by NATO. Under this change, which applied to all formation and command headquarters but not to the headquarters of the Ministry of Defence, all branches of these lower headquarters were deemed to be General Staff branches and given the initial 'G'. The former 'A' branch was given the number '1', Intelligence the number '2', Operations and Staff Duties the number '3' and 'Q' branch the number '4'. These were written as G1, G2, G3 and G4, while the staff officers serving in these branches were titled Staff Officer 1, 2 or 3 (SO1, SO2 or SO3), according to the rank of the appointment; Grade 1 officers were Lieutenant-Colonels, Grade 2 officers Majors, and Grade 3 officers Captains.

With this basic reorganisation the Army now had available in peacetime, possibly for the first time in British Army history, a large and well-organised strategic military Intelligence staff. It had taken at least a hundred years, with the examples of the Crimean War, the Boer War and the Second World War before them, for the British Government to recognise that the best insurance against the occurrence of war is to be prepared for it, and one of the most essential preparations is to know as much as possible about one's potential enemy. An early reminder of this came with the realisation that the sources of military Intelligence on the Soviet Union and its satellite countries available at the end of the war were extremely limited, particularly after the information from the German wartime Intelligence files had been assimilated.

One further indication of the importance attached to Intelligence, its collection, collation and dissemination by the British Army since the end of the Second World War was the unprecedented retention in the Regular Army of the Intelligence Corps in peacetime. With its headquarters and depot, together with the School of Service Intelligence, at Ashford in Kent, the Intelligence Corps is responsible for the selection and training of officers and NCOs to fill Intelligence appointments in the Army. Responsibility for the Corps within the General Staff of MoD(Army) lies with the Director of Military Operations (DMO), thus perpetuating the essential link between Operations and Intelligence originally forged in 1904. The Intelligence Corps embraces the training of interrogators, field security staff, Intelligence officers and NCOs in Intelligence staffs in commands and formations both at home and overseas and the training of military attachés. The interrogation function is of particular importance in wartime, and the Intelligence Corps provides the Army element in joint forward interrogation teams and in the Joint Services Specialised Interrogation Centre (JSSIC), the successor to the CSDIC of the Second World War.

Among the categories of information which a military Intelligence organisation needs to acquire about a foreign army are the following (not in order of priority):

1. Order of battle (OB or ORBAT)
2. Details of unit and formation organisations
3. Unit and formation identification markings
4. Weapon and equipment details
5. Mobilisation plans
6. Training state and readiness for war
7. Details of commanders and their characteristics
8. Details of land, sea and air defences, military airfields, ports, road, rail and telegraphic communications, topography, climate, endemic diseases, etc.

Of the information required by the military Intelligence organisation on a foreign country, at least 80 per cent is openly available in one form or another in a democracy. In the dictatorships of the Soviet Union and its satellite countries, however, this was definitely not the case. In these countries the press and radio were strictly controlled, and their content was therefore unreliable, while in the Soviet Union there were not even any reliable maps: after Stalin made the NKVD (the Soviet security organisation at the time) responsible for mapping the Soviet Union before the war, it became impossible to obtain an accurate map of either town or country – almost everything was changed, including the courses of roads and rivers, city districts and the location and outline of buildings, people could not recognise their motherland on the map, and tourists tried in vain to work out where they were. To obtain the necessary information, therefore, the British Intelligence agencies had to turn to covert sources, the responsibility for the provision of which lay with SIS and GCHQ. However, it seems that the former had no sources in the USSR, and precious few (and those only of a very low level) in East Germany or any of the Soviet satellites. However, as mentioned above, GCHQ was able for a time to decrypt some of the Soviet military and diplomatic traffic under the code-name 'Venona'.

The counter-espionage task of the Security Service in protecting British nuclear and other military weapon and organisational developments was especially difficult, due to the skill with which the USSR had recruited British residents as agents and had planted Soviet citizens as 'illegals' in the UK before, during and after the Second World War. MI 5's task was made more difficult both by the sympathy for the Soviet Union which had been engendered in the UK by its wartime exploits as one of the Allies and by the high level of 'trade-craft' employed by the Soviet agents and their controllers in going about their nefarious business.

The first real indication of the extent to which the Soviets were endeavouring to penetrate the arms industries, military research and development establishments and governments of their former Western allies came shortly after VJ-Day, when a cipher clerk to the Military Attaché in the Soviet Embassy in Ottawa, a Lieutenant Igor Gouzenko, defected to the Canadian authorities in 1945. Wishing to defect for ideological reasons, he left his office on 5 September with a collection of carefully selected documents from his own and other offices, and spent that evening and the whole of the next day trying unsuccessfully, with his family, to convince an Ottawa daily paper and Canadian officials that he was serious.

On the second night, when he and his family returned to their apartment, he noticed two men on the opposite side of the street, apparently keeping it under surveillance, so he approached his Canadian neighbours for help, one of them agreeing to put him and his family up for the night and the other cycling to the local police for help. The city police visited Gouzenko, and after hearing his story and those of his neighbours, maintained surveillance on the apartment block.

At about midnight they were investigating a report of intruders in the block when they discovered that the front door to Gouzenko's apartment had been broken and that four men were searching the apartment. From their documents, the men were found to come from the Soviet Embassy; the leader was the senior NKVD representative in the Embassy, with cover appointments as Consul and Second Secretary, while the others were the Assistant Air Attaché, a Lieutenant on the Military Attaché's staff and the NKVD cipher clerk. They all disappeared from the scene while the police were reporting to their HQ for instructions, but with this confirmation of Gouzenko's story, the RCMP placed a guard on the neighbour's apartment, where Gouzenko and his family remained for the rest of the night.

The following morning they were taken to the local office of the Royal Canadian Mounted Police (RCMP), where Gouzenko told his story, handed over his documents and asked to be taken into protective custody.

The Canadian Government appointed a Royal Commission to 'investigate the facts relating to and the circumstances surrounding, the communication, by public officials and others in positions of trust, of secret and confidential information to agents of a foreign power'. The Commission's report, published in June 1946, was a damning indictment of Soviet diplomats and their conduct in a friendly country. In addition to naming fourteen public officials and others, including Members of Parliament, in positions of trust who had disclosed secret and confidential information and a further five cover-names whose owners could not be identified, the Commission reported the following facts:

1. There exists in Canada a Fifth Column organised and directed by Russian agents in Canada and Russia.
2. Within the Fifth Column there are several spy rings.
3. We have been able to identify many of the members of one of these rings, namely that of which Colonel Zabotin [the Soviet Military Attaché in Ottawa] was the head in Canada.
4. Membership of Communist organisations or a sympathy towards Communist ideologies was the primary force which caused these agents to agree to do the acts referred to.
5. The persons named . . . were members of Colonel Zabotin's organisation . . .
7. There was an organisation whose duty it was to procure false Canadian passports and other citizenship documents for the use of agents . . .

8. Zabotin and his assistants were helping to supervise and finance the work of an organisation of agents operating in certain European countries . . .
9. Members of the staff of the Russian Embassy at Ottawa who were actively engaged in inadmissible espionage activities are named in Section II.

Several aspects of this story deserve comment. First, concerning the initial lack of belief or interest shown in Gouzenko's story by the Canadians, it must be remembered that in the war just ended, the USSR had been one of Canada's allies and there was a natural reluctance to believe ill of it on the part of people who had had no experience of dealing with it. Second, the fierce reaction of the staff of the Soviet Embassy to the defection of one of their members was typical of the implacable attitude of the Soviets to any act of disloyalty to the system, which was also notable in subsequent defections. In this connection, there was a typical official Soviet reaction the day after Gouzenko's defection, when the Canadian Department of External Affairs received a bare-faced note from the Soviet Embassy, reporting that Gouzenko was missing from his place of work together with a sum of money belonging to the Embassy, and asking the Canadian authorities to apprehend Gouzenko and hand him over to the Embassy for deportation as a criminal. Needless to say, the Canadians did no such thing, but instead removed him to a place of safety, where he was interrogated at great length, not only by the Canadians but also by the British and American covert Intelligence and counter-Intelligence organisations. It is significant that Zabotin returned to the Soviet Union on a visit in December 1945, from which he did not return.

Much valuable Intelligence was derived from Gouzenko over a lengthy period, as a result of which several Soviet spy rings were broken up. It was as a result of Gouzenko's information, for example, that the British atom spy, Dr Alan Nunn May, was arrested and convicted of espionage in 1946. Gouzenko was also the first to point the finger of suspicion towards – if not directly at – 'Kim' Philby, the long-time KGB agent in MI 6; unfortunately, the clue was too vague to allow certainty.

The mention of Philby here deserves clarification. The son of St John Philby, an orientalist and Indian civil servant, Harold Adrian Russell ('Kim') Philby was one of several undergraduates talent-spotted at Cambridge for the Soviets in the 1930s. An early convert to the Bolshevist ideology, he was recruited as a Soviet agent in 1934, with the specific long-term aim of penetrating the British Secret Intelligence Service. He managed to be recruited into the wartime SIS, where he served for some time as head of Section V, SIS's counter-espionage section. In this capacity he was well placed to safeguard Soviet Intelligence interests by alerting them to potential Soviet defectors and revealing SIS operations against Soviet targets, as well as the names of SIS personnel and agents. Before his final exposure as a Soviet 'mole' he was being groomed, by Stewart Menzies, 'C' of SIS, as his successor. This sorry tale of British wartime and post-war SIS recruiting and security vetting procedures (or lack of them) goes a long way towards explaining the reasons for SIS's long-time failure both to recruit worthwhile agents behind the Iron Curtain and to uncover other Soviet 'moles' in the organisation.

The Gouzenko case, the first instance of Soviet espionage to be discovered after the war, has been dealt with at length because of the effect it had in converting public opinion in Canada, the UK and the USA from a largely pro-Soviet stance to one of realisation that the Soviets were not to be trusted; this realisation was increasingly confirmed by subsequent revelations by Soviet defectors and in public trials of those caught by Western security services supplying classified information to Soviet agents. Several of these trials occurred in the UK, notably those of John Vassall, Harry Houghton and Ethel Gee, Peter and Helen Kroger, Gordon Lonsdale, Klaus Fuchs and George Blake, as well as the latter's escape from prison and subsequent defection to the USSR, and the defections to the Soviet Union of Donald Maclean, Guy Burgess and Kim Philby. There were also several cases of expulsion as *persona non grata* of many Soviet diplomats over the Cold War years, culminating in the mass expulsion of 105 of them in the autumn of 1971. (More will be told of these and other cases in Chapter 5.)

As far as military Intelligence was concerned, the Gouzenko case emphasised the ever-present danger of Soviet espionage in a peacetime environment, with consequent effects on military security. In the words of Lord Radcliffe in his 1962 report on security procedures in the public service: 'The biggest single risk to security at the present time is probably a general lack of conviction that any substantial threat exists.' This is still true to a certain extent, but the espionage threat to the United Kingdom from hostile Intelligence services, both within the UK and overseas, is nevertheless as great as or greater than ever. There is now also a significant threat from domestic and international subversive and terrorist organisations. The need for intelligent application of effective security measures is thus greater than ever. Within the Army, security is a command responsibility involving commanders and their staffs, units and formations at all levels, but while overall responsibility for security advice rests with military Intelligence, security is the business of everyone, not only security staffs and unit security officers.

Military security involves the security of personnel, of communications, of operations and of premises. Personnel security can never be one hundred per cent effective, but the system employed by the British Army, and by other government departments using classified information, gives reasonably reliable results when properly carried out; it involves a superficial look at the records of those people requiring access to information of low security classification (Normal Vetting – NV), a much more detailed investigation by trained security investigators of those personnel who require regular access to highly classified information (Positive Vetting – PV) and Developed Vetting (DV) for recruits to the Security Service, SIS and GCHQ. However, vetting can do no more than establish that at the time of vetting a person was or was not considered reliable. To be fully effective, the reliability of anyone having regular access to highly classified information or to sensitive installations must be kept under review by both that person's unit and the vetting authorities.

Allied to personnel security is security of information, and for this purpose information is classified into one of five security classifications:

1. Unclassified (UNCLAS) information may be made available to anybody, without restriction.
2. Restricted (RESTD) information may not be communicated to the press or to any person not authorised to receive it (until 1944 this classification was known as 'Not to be Published').
3. Confidential (CONFD).
4. Secret.
5. Top Secret (TOPSEC) (until 1944 known as 'Most Secret').

Information in the last three categories may not be disclosed to any person not cleared to receive it and who has no 'need to know'; hard-headed assessment of a person's need to know is one of the basic principles of sound information security, another being a person's 'need to hold' classified information in his or her files. Within the United Kingdom and in areas of British influence overseas, the overall responsibility for security lies with the Security Service (MI 5); within the Army it lies with the Director of Security (Army) in the MoD, who has representatives at the headquarters of commands both in the UK and overseas. The common objective of both is to frustrate the threat to the security of the United Kingdom and its armed services from espionage, subversion, sabotage or terrorism.

Staff Officers (Security) form part of the headquarters staffs of all army formations, on a scale determined by the size of the command and on local requirements. All units have a Security Officer, while security units of the Intelligence Corps, organised on a group, company or section basis, provide specialist security support both to units and to HQ staffs. Most theatres have an Intelligence and Security Group, commanded by a Lieutenant-Colonel of the

Intelligence Corps, in which all personnel are trained in Intelligence and security duties and procedures. A Security Company of the Intelligence Corps comprises a number of Security Sections, which can be deployed either to formation headquarters or on a geographical basis, according to need.

Intelligence Corps security units act in an advisory capacity only; they have no powers of arrest, and should they discover a breach of security, can only bring it to the attention of either the commander of the unit or formation concerned or to the Special Investigation Branch (SIB) of the Corps of Royal Military Police (CRMP). The SIB is the executive branch if arrest and interrogation of suspects is required, and its relationship to the Intelligence Corps security staff closely parallels that between the police Special Branch and the Security Service, MI 5, in the United Kingdom.

The security staff of the Army also plays a large part in any deception operation, one of the means of gaining surprise in military operations which was so brilliantly applied by the Allies at the time of the landings in Normandy in 1944. It may be practised at either strategic or tactical levels, or both, but to be convincing to the enemy it is essential that it be coordinated with information known or suspected to be already in the enemy's possession. All sources of information likely to be available to the enemy must be primed to tell the same story, or parts of the story, which when collated by the enemy Intelligence staffs will add up to the desired whole. One final function of military Intelligence in which security plays a major part is that of censorship of mail, cables, the media and trade, as well as with the corollary of censorship: propaganda.

The inadequacy of British offensive military Intelligence on the USSR was also soon made painfully clear at the Berlin Victory Parade in 1945. This caused MI 10, the branch of the MI Directorate in the War Office concerned with technical Intelligence, to realise just how inadequate British knowledge of Soviet weapon development then was: several examples of a completely new heavily armed Soviet heavy tank with an advanced armour layout of which British and American Intelligence had had no previous knowledge trundled past the saluting base, to the surprise and consternation of the Western Allies' military representatives in the audience. From the captured German Fremde Heer (Ost) files it was tentatively identified as the Iosef Stalin 3 (IS-3) heavy tank, informally known in the Red Army as '*Shchuka*' ('Pike'), but although immediately placed very high on the Intelligence requirements search list, it was some years before full information on its specification and performance became available, by which time it was being replaced by later designs. The SIS had been totally unable to provide this information from covert sources, but some confirmation of its name and performance was given to the then CIGS in the course of an official visit to the Soviet Union in 1947. A suggestion by the MI 10 tank desk officer, put up to the DMI and thence to the JIC, that an attempt should be made to capture a sample from a Soviet tank unit quartered conveniently close to the border of the British sector of Berlin was emphatically turned down by the Foreign Office.

The IS-3 was obviously better armed and better armoured than any tank then in the service of the Western powers, but the British Intelligence organisation set out to convince the Soviet authorities otherwise by parading two of the six specimens of an unsuccessful prototype 72-tonne British AFV named 'Tortoise' around the armoured regiments in BAOR. This was done in 1948, under conditions of seemingly tight security designed to be breached by Soviet agents. Meanwhile, design of a heavy tank capable of taking on the IS-3 on equal terms was put in hand; this tank was the 65-tonne 'Conqueror', which made its appearance in British service in the 1950s. Whether or not the elaborate deception plan was successful in bluffing Soviet Intelligence is not known – probably not, as their penetration of British organisations was so widespread.

The Soviet detonation of a nuclear device in August 1949 again emphasised the weakness of British and US strategic Intelligence on the USSR; although it had been known that the Soviets had for some years been engaged in nuclear research, and it was a fair bet that, since the detonation of the two US nuclear weapons over Japan in 1945, this research would have been devoted to the development of nuclear weapons, there had been no prior indication that they had reached the point of being able to generate a nuclear explosion. US and British Intelligence estimates had considered that this point was unlikely to be reached for several more years, again demonstrating the lack of access by SIS or US sources to reliable high-level information within the Soviet Union. Although the British Ministry of Defence now had an excellent strategic Intelligence evaluation and dissemination organisation, there was little or no strategic information on the Soviet Union coming in to the Defence Intelligence Staff to be evaluated. One reason for this parlous state of affairs was the existence of Soviet moles in MI 6 who, as we have seen, were able, until they were exposed, to nip in the bud any attempt to recruit agents in the USSR or its satellites, or in their armed services.

Apart from the USSR and its satellites, however, there was much else to occupy the Defence Intelligence Staff and its subordinate organisations in the military commands overseas. The twin problems of demobilisation and over-commitment facing the British Army after VJ-Day were the same as had faced the Army of 1919, but this time the demobilisation problem had been faced and solved. The Army's commitments after VJ-Day were very much greater than they had been after the

First World War, however. In Europe the Army was required to garrison not merely a bridgehead over the Rhine at Cologne, but the whole of a devastated northern Germany and part of Berlin, as well as a large part of Austria. In Italy too there was the problem of Trieste, being claimed by President Tito for Yugoslavia; at one time it appeared likely that British troops would have to fight Tito's partisans for possession of this city. Cyprus, Palestine, Egypt and Libya needed garrisons, while British troops became embroiled in the Greek civil war between Communists and Greek Government forces in 1946. India, agitating for independence, and Burma presented problems, as did the UK's other Far East dependencies, formerly under Japanese occupation and desperately requiring major reconstruction and stability. It was obvious that large overseas military garrisons would be required for the foreseeable future, and that it would be impossible to reduce the Army to its pre-war strength if these commitments were to be met.

With the granting of independence to India, and what became Pakistan, in 1947, after two hundred years the British Army was able to shed with relief a commitment which had become too difficult to fulfil. The burden of Greece was handed over to the Americans so that the British troops there could also be withdrawn, but the situation in Palestine proved more intractable. In 1945 the British Army had two divisions there, providing the strategic reserve for the Middle East, but in October of that year a Jewish bombing campaign against economic targets in the country together with large-scale rioting necessitated the strengthening of the garrison with reinforcements from BAOR. A very unpleasant counter-insurgency campaign ensued, of a type with which the British Army would become increasingly familiar in the post-war years. In November 1947 the United Nations eventually stepped in and partitioned the country between Arabs and Jews, and as the British mandate came to an end in May 1948, the British Army was finally able to withdraw to leave the state of Israel to fight its own battles for survival.

British relief was short-lived, however. No sooner had the withdrawal from Palestine been completed than trouble arose in Malaya with the killing by young Chinese of three rubber-estate managers there in June 1948. These attacks had been instigated by the Chinese-run Malayan Communist Party, which believed that the time was ripe for revolution; they marked the beginning of another counter-insurgency campaign which was to endure for twelve years, the jungle, together with the mountains running down the spine of the country, proving ideal terrorist terrain. The atrocities rapidly multiplied, and by March 1950 the Communists had killed some 850 civilians, 325 police and 150 soldiers for a loss of some 2,000 of their own men killed or captured; the Communist losses were immediately made up by new recruits from the Chinese supporters living in villages on the edge of the jungle, however.

After the assassination of Sir Hugh Gurney, the British High Commissioner, in October 1951, General (later Field-Marshal) Sir Gerald Templer was appointed as both High Commissioner and Director of Operations. Templer had Intelligence experience, having served as GSO I (Int) responsible for security and counter-espionage on the staff of General Mason MacFarlane, the DMI to the BEF in 1940, as well as himself serving as DMI in the War Office in the late 1940s. His Intelligence experience served him well here, and he immediately realised that the existing Intelligence organisation was inadequate to fight a successful counter-insurgency campaign (even his predecessor as Director of Operations, Lieutenant-General Sir Harold Briggs, admitted in 1950 that Intelligence was 'our Achilles heel') and took steps to reorganise and expand the organisation of his Special Branch, under the direction of senior MI 5 officers who also worked with him in the planning of operations against the insurgents.

His actions and leadership, combined with the close cooperation of the reorganised Special Branch and the Army's security forces, including the Special Air Service (SAS), reactivated for the purpose, turned the campaign in Malaya into what was probably the most successful counter-insurgency campaign of the post-war era. By the time the Communist leader, Chin Peng, emerged from the jungle to surrender in 1955 it was clear that the campaign was won. The Declaration of Independence for the renamed Malaysia issued in August 1957 was a further nail in the coffin of the terrorists, but it was not until three years later that they were finally chased across the Thai border and the campaign came to an end. It had been won by good Intelligence, swiftly and ruthlessly acted upon, together with an enlightened resettlement programme for the Chinese villages. The campaign was to prove a model for future British counter-insurgency campaigns elsewhere.

June 1948 also saw the imposition by the Soviets of the Berlin blockade as a result of the breakdown in negotiations between the Western Allies and the USSR over the future of Germany. It lasted for a year, and led directly to the formation of NATO, which aimed to discourage the Soviet Union from embarking upon any military expansion into Western Europe. The most likely Soviet objective in any such adventure was thought to be West Germany, so the occupation troops in BAOR had to be rapidly converted into an operational force; this meant the expansion of BAOR from two divisions to five, with the necessary logistic support to enable it to wage general war. This additional requirement for troops forced the government to increase the term of National Service from eighteen months to two years in 1950. It was just as well this had been done, as a further call on Army resources came in June 1950 with the outbreak of war in Korea; the quick deployment of United Nations forces called for a British contribution, which expanded from an initial two infantry battalions, sent from Hong Kong, to the equivalent of two brigades, which combined with units from Canada, Australia and New Zealand to form the Commonwealth Division.

The Korean War involved Communist China on the side of North Korea, after the latter's forces were driven back to the Yalu River; the combined Communist force pushed the UN forces back south of the 38th Parallel, and it was during this retreat that the British Vice-Consul in Seoul, one George Blake, was captured by the North Koreans and held captive for three years. He was an SIS officer, and is alleged to have been brutally interrogated and then recruited as a Soviet agent during his captivity. Upon his release, after the truce was signed at Panmunjon in July 1953, he was given recuperation leave by SIS after being debriefed, and was then posted to the SIS station in Berlin; there he conscientiously passed to his KGB case officer every document that ever crossed his desk, as well as giving him the names of at least forty SIS agents and giving away plans of an elaborate joint SIS/CIA operation to penetrate GSFG communications. He was found out in 1961, arrested, interrogated, charged and sentenced to forty years in prison, a sentence which reflected the appalling damage he had done to the UK and the SIS, only marginally less than that inflicted by Philby and the other members of his Cambridge spy ring.

In 1952 trouble also erupted in Kenya, where elements of the Kikuyu tribe were agitating for the return of so-called tribal lands. The Mau Mau, as the dissidents were known, were murdering increasing numbers of loyal Kikuyu tribespeople and European settlers, and troop reinforcements had to be flown in. These eventually amounted to two British brigades which, together with African troops, were employed on large-scale sweep operations against the Mau Mau, operating from the jungle. These tactics were relatively ineffective, however, until the security forces were concentrated in one area at a time, the police and military Intelligence staffs were integrated and a small War Cabinet was set up. The lessons learned in Malaya were again successfully applied here, and the Mau Mau rising was effectively suppressed by the spring of 1955.

While this campaign was winding down, another insurgency campaign was starting, this time in Cyprus. A movement calling itself the National Organisation of Cypriot Fighters (or EOKA – the abbreviation of its Greek title) and agitating for '*Enosis*' (the union of Cyprus with Greece) set off a series of bomb explosions in Nicosia in March 1955. To unite Cyprus with Greece would deny the British a base of strategic importance, as well as antagonising the large Turkish minority on the island, so the British garrison was strengthened. By January 1956 four brigades had been deployed on the island, and Field-Marshal Sir John Harding, who had commanded in Malaya at the time of the troubles there, was appointed Governor. Again the SAS were called in, and a number of large-scale operations was organised in the Troodos Mountains, where the EOKA bands under the leadership of a Colonel Grivas were based; although these resulted in a number of the bands being broken up, Grivas himself remained at large, and the operations against him had to be suspended in July 1956, when Colonel Nasser, Prime Minister of Egypt, announced that the Suez Canal was to be nationalised.

British troops had finally left Egypt only four months earlier, and Nasser's announcement took both the British and French Governments by surprise. It represented another failure of British strategic Intelligence-gathering. In a hurriedly planned operation in collusion with the French and Israeli Governments and against international (particularly US) opposition a force of corps strength under the command of General Sir Hugh Stockwell was cobbled together and landed, in conjunction with a French force, in the Canal Zone in November 1956. Suffering only a minimum of casualties, the combined force had achieved a cease-fire within twenty-four hours, and remained in occupation for two months until the United Nations took over.

After the Suez episode, the British Army resumed its campaign in Cyprus where it had left off, and by 1958 a virtual peace had been restored on the island. It was not until August 1960, however, after much negotiation with Greece, Turkey and the Cypriots, that the independent Republic of Cyprus was born, after eighty-two years of British rule, the UK retaining two Sovereign Base Areas and a number of radio and radar sites; a garrison was therefore still required there.

The British Army's overseas garrison commitments were reduced under the Macmillan Government's 'wind of change in Africa' policy, and colony after colony was granted its independence. This was just as well, as conscription in the UK was ended in 1960 and the resulting all-regular volunteer Army would have been too small to cope with the commitment. It nevertheless remained heavily committed overseas: when Iraq threatened Kuwait in 1961, for example, a hastily assembled brigade was rushed there and sweltered in the desert heat until October of that year.

In December of the following year an Indonesian revolt against the Sultan of Brunei was quickly crushed by another force of brigade strength, despatched from the 17th Division in Malaya. President Soekarno retaliated by sending parties of irregulars across the border into Sarawak and Sabah (formerly North

Borneo) to harass the authorities. In 1963, after the incorporation of Sarawak and Sabah into the Federation of Malaysia, Soekarno virtually declared open war by sending Indonesian troops across the border, and for the next three years the British Army was involved in another jungle campaign. The jungle skills of Malaya and Burma were quickly revived, but the Indonesian troops were more skilled in jungle fighting than the terrorists in Malaya, and the British commander, General Walter Walker, decided to take the war to the Indonesians in an operation of great secrecy code-named Operation CLARET. Patrols penetrated as much as ten miles into Indonesian territory and laid ambushes which were often highly successful; the SAS, operating in four-man patrols, spent months at a time on CLARET operations, befriending border villagers and sending back valuable Intelligence. A peace agreement was finally reached in 1966.

There was little time for congratulation, however. In 1964 trouble erupted again in Cyprus between Turkish and Greek Cypriots, necessitating the despatch from the UK of reinforcements until the UN took over the commitment of policing the line dividing the Turkish area from the Greek in March of that year. In the same year there was unrest in Aden, requiring the despatch of a brigade from Northern Ireland, where it had been assisting the Royal Ulster Constabulary in the border campaign of 1956–62. The Aden troubles lasted three years, until Aden achieved independence and the troops were withdrawn.

In 1969 the Irish problem again reared its head, as it had been doing at intervals for the previous three hundred years, when civil unrest beyond the capacity of the RUC to contain broke out on the streets of Belfast and Londonderry. British troops were deployed, not only from the mainland but also from BAOR, reaching a peak of more than 20,000 in 1972. It was soon found that many of the lessons learned in the counter-insurgency campaigns in Malaya and other theatres did not apply in Ulster, where the Army was operating under the watchful eyes of the media, and where, martial law not having been declared, soldiers operated under the law of the land, any infringement of which can lead to criminal charges.

New techniques such as controlling riots without the traditional use of aimed live ammunition, the application of strict rules of engagement, the use of baton rounds and the employment of 'snatch squads' against ringleaders had to be learnt, and the acquisition of accurate Intelligence by the use of the SAS, undercover agents and other covert means became, if possible, more important. At least there was no language problem this time. Although a cease-fire was called by the Provisional IRA in 1997 so that they could attend talks on the future of Northern Ireland, the troubles have been rumbling on since 1969, and at the time of writing, a solution seems as far away as ever.

Apart from minor involvements such as in Belize, where a small British force has been stationed to protect the country against a long-standing claim on it by Guatemala, in Cyprus, where a contingent continues to be supplied to the UN, in Zimbabwe, where a force was sent to supervise the Lancaster House Agreement in 1979, in the Lebanon, where a contingent was sent as part of the Multi-National Force in 1983–84, and in Bosnia, again as part of the UN force UNPROFOR from 1993, British garrisons remain in Cyprus, Gibraltar, Brunei and the Falkland Islands; that in Hong Kong was withdrawn in 1997 when the colony was handed back to China. Two other military campaigns of importance remain to be mentioned in this list of those in which the British Army has been involved since the end of the Second World War: the Falklands (Malvinas) campaign of 1982, and the Gulf War (Operation DESERT STORM) of 1990.

The Falklands campaign was the result of an unheralded attack on the islands by Argentine forces; the fact that it was unheralded reveals another failure of British diplomatic and covert sources of strategic Intelligence. A hastily assembled task force was sent 7,000 miles to the South Atlantic to retake the islands, and did so in a singularly successful and well-executed operation, thanks to excellent tactical Intelligence provided by the SAS and air photo-reconnaissance and by US satellite and SIGINT information. The Gulf War involvement was as part of an American/French/British force tasked to expel Iraq's forces from Kuwait; again, it was a brief and successful operation, in which satellite, air reconnaissance imagery and communications intercepts and SAS operations played a significant part.

The varied nature of the various post-war campaigns in which the field Army had been involved can thus be seen to have placed a heavy burden on those responsible for producing the tactical Intelligence on which the campaigns relied. The terrain varied from jungle to desert, from relatively flat and bare to mountainous and vegetation-covered, in climates varying from extremely hot and humid through hot and dry to cold and wet, while the languages in use in the countries concerned were ones in which few British soldiers had been trained. Nevertheless, the Intelligence organisation proved equal to the task, and in no case did tactical Intelligence or lack of security prove to have been a weakness.

In this summary of the tactical Intelligence requirements of the peacetime British Army during the Cold War, three failures of strategic Intelligence were mentioned – failure to predict accurately the Soviet detonation of its first nuclear device in 1949, Nasser's nationalisation of the Suez Canal and the Argentinian attack on the Falkland Islands. There were many more, including the USSR's exploding of its first thermo-nuclear device in 1953, its successful launch of

Sputnik, the first space satellite, in 1957, the erection of the Iron Curtain, the Berlin blockade, the erection of the Berlin Wall in 1961, the launching into space of the first manned spacecraft with cosmonaut Yuri Gagarin aboard in the same year, and the first multi-manned spacecraft, carrying a crew of three men, in 1964. At the same time, almost the only news of other Soviet weapon development came from photographs of items included in the annual May Day Parades in Moscow, taken by the British and Allied Service attachés there.

With the resources of the USA being deployed, however, this position was soon to change, thanks firstly to high-level air photo-reconnaissance and the UKUSA pact on the sharing of Intelligence. Flights over the USSR at very high altitudes above the range of the Soviet anti-aircraft defences by the Lockheed U-2 research aircraft were started by the Central Intelligence Agency, the US equivalent of MI 6, in 1956, and continued on a regular basis until 1960, when the Soviets managed to bring one down. Apart from the specifically military Intelligence that these twenty-odd flights produced, they enabled accurate maps of the Soviet Union to be made for the first time since Stalin had banned them in the 1930s.

The position was further improved by a succession of defectors to the West, both from Soviet military Intelligence (the GRU) and the Soviet secret Intelligence service (the KGB), encouraged by Gouzenko's successful escape from Soviet clutches. Three of these stand out: Colonel Oleg Penkovsky of the GRU, Major Vladimir Popov, also of the GRU, and Major Anatoliy Golytsin (alias Klimov) of the KGB. All were 'walk-ins', in that they volunteered their services. There will always be the suspicion in the minds of those receiving defectors that they might be 'plants'; even if they come bearing documents to add conviction to their story, these could well be forgeries, while without any documentary or photographic supporting evidence, doubt must be even greater. This is why a defector has to undergo a very detailed and lengthy interrogation process, often lasting several months, and sometimes even years, in which every answer is cross-checked with every other, as well as with facts that are already known. After interrogation, which will have taken place in a safe and remote location, defectors are generally resettled in the country of their choice, with a new identity and cover story, sometimes having had plastic surgery to alter their appearance, and some form of employment; some have even ended up as Intelligence consultants.

Popov volunteered his services in a letter dropped into the car of a US diplomat in Vienna in 1952, Golytsin by ringing the doorbell of the CIA station chief in Helsinki one evening in December 1961, and Penkovsky by persistently importuning Western diplomats at diplomatic functions in Moscow in 1961 with offers of his knowledge of Soviet plans. Penkovsky was persuaded to remain 'in place', and over the next two years, until his arrest for treason in 1962, supplied SIS with photographs of thousands of secret Soviet military and political documents through his Moscow contact, British businessman Greville Wynne. Wynne was arrested in Budapest in November 1962 and sent to Moscow, where he was tried with Penkovsky and, one year later, exchanged for the Soviet spy Konon Molody (alias Gordon Lonsdale); Penkovsky was sentenced to death and is believed to have been shot five days later, although another version has it that he was flung naked and screaming into the flames of the Moscow crematorium, watched by his GRU colleagues. Popov was also persuaded by his US handlers to remain 'in place', which he managed to do for six years. In that time he had passed bales of top secret Soviet documents to his CIA case officer, caused chaos in the GRU, caused the transfer of the chief of the KGB and saved the USA at least half a billion dollars in military research. He was arrested in 1958 by the Soviet authorities, found guilty of espionage on behalf of the USA, and executed the following year.

Golytsin did not remain in place, but defected with a vast knowledge of KGB agents and intentions, as a result of which leads were obtained by Western Intelligence to more than a hundred Soviet agents and sources within NATO, as well as information about the KGB's organisation and personnel. Golytsin, however, was a very difficult person, with a withdrawn and suspicious character; he was paranoid about Soviet disinformation and the ubiquity of Soviet agents in the USA and UK, and trusted very few people. Much of his early information could be cross-checked, and proved accurate, but he also managed to sow suspicion among the British and US Intelligence organisations with his allegations that both were penetrated at high levels by the KGB, which, despite very thorough investigation, could be neither proved nor disproved. There were therefore some in both organisations who thought that Golytsin was a KGB 'plant', tasked to spread disinformation and self-doubt in the Western Intelligence services.

The bringing down of Captain Gary Powers' U-2 aircraft over the USSR in May 1960 brought to an end, at least temporarily, this source of Intelligence on the Soviet Union. However, it was essential in the prevailing climate of the Cold War, with the difficulty of recruiting and communicating with agents in place behind the Iron Curtain, that knowledge of Soviet nuclear and missile development, testing and deployment should be available to British and US government planners. The advent of a more relaxed international climate, with the resulting arms limitation or reduction agreements such as SALT and START, did nothing to ease the requirement for overflights, as such agreements require some means of verification.

The success of the U-2 overflights had whetted the appetite of the Intelligence users for more of the same. Plans to augment, and ultimately to replace the aircraft overflights with satellite reconnaissance were given a boost in 1957 when the Soviets successfully launched their first satellite, Sputnik I. This event, showing that the USSR had not only caught up with but overtaken the USA, sent shivers through the West and thus ensured the availability of the funds necessary for the US National Aeronautics and Space Administration (NASA), the CIA and the US Air Force to close the perceived missile gap. When Powers' U-2 was brought down, it led to further pressure for the early introduction of replacement reconnaissance sources of similar or improved capability, and vast sums were expended by the US Government on the development of the necessary rockets, satellites and sensors, together with launch sites and launchers, control links and capsule recovery methods. As a result, the first launch of a Corona satellite (known to the public as the Discoverer weather/scientific satellite) took place in February 1959, and within a year of the last U-2 overflight of the USSR even the most remote parts of the Soviet Union had become accessible to US satellite photo-reconnaissance. The UKUSA agreement was bearing very valuable fruit indeed for the UK, which could not possibly have afforded either the money or the resources necessary for such a vast programme.

Between 1970 and 1984 the USA is believed to have launched some fifty-five reconnaissance satellites; the newer, larger satellites carry imaging sensors in both the visible, infra-red and ultra-violet spectra, as well as passive sensors to detect electronic and other emissions. The imaging sensors have an extraordinarily high resolution, enabling most detailed pictures to be transmitted back to base. By these means, many of the UK and US strategic Intelligence questions were answered, and the Soviet nuclear weapons testing sites, missile launching sites, anti-aircraft defences, ICBM silo complexes, tank and other arms factories were all pinpointed on accurate maps, enabling US and British nuclear missiles to be targeted accurately.

In October 1962 a nuclear world war was only narrowly averted after US U-2 and satellite reconnaissance over Cuba alerted the USA to the importation into Cuba of Soviet bomber aircraft and intermediate-range missiles capable of carrying nuclear weapons. Aerial reconnaissance thus became for the first time a provider of strategic Intelligence of prime importance; it has remained so ever since. Thanks to Intelligence-gathering satellites, the 'open skies' policy originally proposed by President Eisenhower became a reality, and the Soviet Union, which in 1955 violently opposed the idea, formally sanctioned the principle of aerial inspection with the signing of the Anti-Ballistic Missile Treaty of 1972. Satellite and high-altitude air photography again proved its worth later, in the Falklands campaign and the Gulf War.

Satellites are also used for the acquisition of signal Intelligence (SIGINT), a field in which great strides have been made since the Second World War with the advances in electronics and the development of the computer. The interception of government and military communications can be a very valuable source of strategic Intelligence; in the UK, responsibility for the gathering of such Intelligence lies with the Government Communications Headquarters (GCHQ) at Cheltenham, and in the USA with the National Security Agency (NSA) at Fort Meade in Maryland. Apart from satellites, both agencies employ listening posts around the world, as well as electronic surveillance aircraft and ships. The 'take' from all these sources is truly enormous, and the staffs employed by both agencies to collate and evaluate the Intelligence produced are correspondingly large. These methods of Intelligence-gathering are dealt with in more detail in Chapter 4, but it is enough to say here that their contribution to the strategic Intelligence picture, concerning not only the Soviet Union and its erstwhile satellite countries, but also China, Iraq, North Korea and other potential enemies, has been and continues to be very great.

The UKUSA pact that has proved so beneficial to both the UK and the USA was, however, severely tested after the defections of Burgess, MacLean, Philby and Blake, as well as the discoveries of the treachery of Fuchs, Blunt and Prime; for some time afterwards the US Intelligence agencies were very chary of passing sensitive Intelligence to their British counterparts, and equally distrustful of British Intelligence products. The balance was restored by the unmasking of a succession of moles and traitors within both the CIA and NSA, as well as by the capture by North Korea of a US eavesdropping ship, the USS *Pueblo*, with all its equipment intact. The first shock was provided in June 1960 by the defection to the USSR of two former naval cryptographers in the employ of the NSA, William Martin and Bernon Mitchell. They not only disclosed a great deal of highly classified information concerning the NSA, its methods and listening stations, but also compromised the relationship between the NSA and GCHQ. Subsequent investigation into their backgrounds revealed that neither of them should ever have been security cleared for access to classified information.

Even worse was the case of Sergeant Jack Dunlap, who had joined the NSA as a courier in 1958 and committed suicide in July 1963; he had been passing to the KGB copies of virtually all the classified documents he was carrying between the NSA's various buildings, and was only uncovered when his new-found wealth was finally investigated. On the same day that Dunlap died, the Soviet newspaper

Izvestia published a letter from another former NSA employee, Victor Hamilton (a.k.a. Hindali), revealing details of his work at Fort Meade. The capture of the USS *Pueblo* followed these disasters in January 1968, and precipitated the disbandment of the NSA's secret fleet of 'Ferret' listening ships.

That GCHQ was not immune to penetration was revealed shortly afterwards, with the arrest in September 1968 of a senior RAF technician, Douglas Britten, who had been employed on SIGINT work at RAF Digby; he had been spotted trying to contact his Soviet controller at the Soviet Consulate in London. Further cases of disloyalty within both the NSA and GCHQ continued to come to light as US and British security vetting procedures and counter-Intelligence skills improved. The US SIGINT surveillance satellite programme was revealed to the USSR by civilian employees of TRW and the CIA, Christopher Boyce and William Kampiles respectively, in 1977–78, but the traitor who caused the most damage to the Allied SIGINT effort up to this time was undoubtedly Geoffrey Prime, a Russian linguist who had joined GCHQ in 1968, having volunteered his services to the Soviets during his time at the RAF SIGINT station at Gatow in Berlin, and had since then been conscientiously passing everything relating to the Allied SIGINT effort on which he could lay his hands to his Soviet controllers. He resigned from GCHQ in 1978, but would have remained undiscovered had he not been arrested for his sexual assaults on young schoolgirls in 1982. The scale of his betrayal was difficult to assess, but the severity of his sentence, thirty-five years' imprisonment, gives some indication of the seriousness with which it was viewed.

Further cases of treachery continued to arise over the next decade, to such an extent that one wonders if there were any areas of the British and US Intelligence organisations of which the Soviet Intelligence agencies were not fully informed. A father-and-son team, John and Michael Walker, was arrested in the USA in 1985, accused and convicted of selling naval Intelligence secrets to the Soviet Union; the father, John, had spent most of his career in the US Navy as a communications specialist, handling classified cipher equipment, and for some seventeen years had been passing information to his Soviet controllers which included many of the operating manuals and cipher keys for the equipment installed in the USS *Pueblo*. The Walker case was followed in February 1994 by that of Aldrich Ames, the head of the CIA's Soviet counter-Intelligence section, who walked into the Soviet Embassy in Washington in 1985 with a plastic bag stuffed with papers which was later described as 'the biggest stack of secret documents ever smuggled out of the CIA'. These documents identified 13 CIA agents, of whom 9 were executed and 3 imprisoned. He continued to supply the Soviets and later the Russian Federation with information of the highest quality and security classification for nine years, as a result of which the CIA was forced to suspend operations world-wide to assess damage in the wake of this case. The damage done to British assets could still not be ascertained at the time of the issuing of the 1996 report of the British Intelligence and Security Committee. At Ames's trial it was revealed by the FBI that he had been paid a staggering $2.7 million by the Soviets and later the Russians for his services, more than twice the amount ever previously paid by the miserly Soviets to any other spy or spy network.

The motives and methods of the traitors named above will be considered in more detail in Chapter 4, but one factor common to all these cases is the lack of sufficient investigation into the backgrounds and suitability for recruitment of the people involved, coupled with a lack of regular follow-up checks into their lifestyle and standard of living. Efficient vetting would have uncovered all of them before much damage had been done, but this was lacking in both the UK and USA. Vetting procedures and standards have now been tightened on both sides of the Atlantic, but it has taken nearly fifty years for the lessons to be learned. It must not be thought that defection and treachery have been or are confined to the Western democracies, however; much good Intelligence has continued to result from the many defections from the KGB and GRU to both the UK and USA since 1945.

The whole picture of military Intelligence began to change dramatically with the demolition of the Berlin Wall in November 1989; the dissolution of the Soviet external empire in Eastern Europe soon followed. It had started in the USSR with the humiliating failure of its campaign in Afghanistan, and was fuelled by the collapse in oil prices; apart from armaments, oil was the Soviet Union's major export, on which it depended to pay for the imports from the West which were essential for the entire Eastern Bloc's economic survival. The miserably low Soviet standard of living was deteriorating at an increasing rate through the 1980s, and the Soviet social and economic system could not save itself. Mikhail Gorbachev, who had become General Secretary of the Soviet Communist Party in 1985, could not admit this publicly, but he did discuss (and allowed others to discuss) particular failures under his policy of *Glasnost* ('openness'). *Glasnost* spread rapidly in the Soviet Union, although it was repressed in most of Eastern Europe, whose regimes saw clearly that such an admission of failure would destroy them; spread it did, however, and in September 1989 the Poles were the first to elect a non-Communist government. Hungary, East Germany and Czechoslovakia soon followed, the revolution spreading from country to country by television and emulation. The world marvelled at the speed of the transformation, that it had happened peacefully, and above all, that the Soviet Union had permitted its external empire to collapse so rapidly. The Soviet Union itself started to dissolve in the 1990s, with several republics, notably Chechnya, declaring their independence. The USSR was formally dissolved on Christmas Day 1991, and the Cold War between the superpowers came to an end.

The ending of that war did not signal an end to the requirement for military and other categories of Intelligence, however. Russia is still a nuclear power, with a forbiddingly large nuclear weapons arsenal, the warheads of which are undoubtedly still aimed at Western targets, and a large and very active Intelligence organisation. Gorbachev may have abolished the KGB in October 1991, but its successor, the SVR (the Russian Foreign Intelligence Service), still includes many of the employees of the former organisation and runs many of the same agents. The GRU continues to operate on behalf of the armed services and seems to have even greater powers and responsibilities than before. Instability in the former Soviet Union means it must remain the most important single target for British military Intelligence, although the collapse of Communism in Eastern Europe has freed MI 5 resources from surveillance of Soviet Bloc embassies in London, and has allowed MI 6 to run down its stations in former Eastern European capitals and GCHQ to divert linguists specialising in the region to other tasks. The Defence Intelligence Staff (DIS) in the Ministry of Defence has shrunk a little during recent years due to staff shortages and cuts in the Civil Service element under the 'Options for Change' review instigated by the Conservative Government. The economic Intelligence directorate has been disbanded, and the DIS now concentrates its overstretched resources on trying to collect and analyse Intelligence on the armed forces in trouble spots such as Iraq and Bosnia, as well as the former Soviet Union and the People's Republic of China.

With the ending of the Cold War has come the predictable response of those who know little of the real world that our Intelligence organisations should be closed down to save money and that there should instead prevail an era of complete openness in government and diplomacy. This naive cry comes from many of the same people who saw no danger from the Soviets and who called, and continue to call, for a Freedom of Information Act on the lines of that introduced by the US Government. The British Government has responded to these cries with a certain amount of *Glasnost* by publicly announcing the locations of the HQs of both MI 5 (Thames House, Millbank) and MI 6 (an as yet unnamed monstrosity of a new building on the south bank of the Thames at Vauxhall Cross), as well as the names of the directors of both organisations.

The Labour Government published a White Paper on the subject of a Freedom of Information Act in December 1997. Under these proposals, although tens of thousands of bodies in central and local government, including the armed forces, would be open, security and Intelligence services and GCHQ would be excluded. Those who call for the opening of our Intelligence services' files to the public gaze, or even for the dissolution of our Intelligence agencies, are misguided, to say the least; the collection of Intelligence on the armed forces of potential enemies is an essential ingredient of preparedness for, and deterrence of, war. As the former Chairman of the KGB, General Vladimir Kryuchkov, said in 1990, 'Spying yields information that enables international problems to be solved by political, not military means.' To lay such services aside is equivalent to tying one hand behind one's back and accepting a needless handicap. The result of inadequate Intelligence was seen in the poor preparation of British armed forces and their equipment at the beginning of the Second World War, a situation which it would be criminally negligent to allow to occur again. Not knowing the full facts about the enemy to be faced calls for more rather than less Intelligence, and for more rather than less willingness to act according to the best analysis of that Intelligence.

The fact that Intelligence-gathering against the UK by Russia has continued since the Cold War ended has been confirmed by Parliament's Intelligence and Security Committee, who reported in May 1996 that as many as a dozen Russian agents of the SVR were believed to be operating in the UK. In the same month the Russian Federal Security Service claimed to have uncovered a British spy ring, and ordered nine British diplomats to leave the country. It thus appears that normal service has been resumed, and will presumably continue in the post-Cold War climate.

CHAPTER 4

Sources of Military Intelligence

It is often held, with what basis in truth it is impossible to say, that espionage is the oldest profession. In reality – like the oldest – it is more of a trade than a profession, practised very largely by people who do so for mercenary reasons, while others are forced into it by blackmail, and some do it for the thrill it gives them.

What can be said with certainty is that the use of people as sources of Intelligence, whether willing or unwilling, witting or unwitting, is as old as the human race itself. In fact, before the invention of the pictograph and writing, and before the advent of portable writing surfaces, human beings were the *only* source of Intelligence available concerning possibly hostile neighbours and rivals and their intentions. As befits the oldest Intelligence source, therefore, human Intelligence (HUMINT) is given pride of place in this discussion of the sources of military Intelligence, not least because it was also, until comparatively recently, the most prolific.

HUMINT can originate in many different ways: in wartime, tactical Intelligence can be provided by infantry or vehicle-mounted patrols into enemy territory or by prisoners of war under interrogation. Specialist units such as the Special Air Service Regiment (SAS) or the Royal Navy's Special Boat Squadron (SBS) especially can provide high-grade HUMINT from stay-behind or deep-cover sections or covert beach reconnaissance, as well as from the infiltration of snatch squads to take VIP prisoners.

In times of both peace and war, a high proportion of HUMINT will originate from covert sources, and this can be of both strategic and tactical value. However, the type of people who will voluntarily take up the trade of espionage are unlikely to turn out to be the most reliable, and this character defect has throughout the centuries marred the dependability of uncorroborated human agents as sources of Intelligence. Their motives for spying may be many and various, and they may well not be volunteers. Greed is a common motive, as it is in many walks of life, and so are bitterness, spite and a desire for revenge. Many agents are motivated by ideology, some by fanaticism, others by patriotism. Many more are compelled to take up espionage under the threat of blackmail to do with some episode in their past life which they would prefer not to be exposed to the gaze of the public, their spouse, their boss, their government or their police force.

Of these motives, only patriotism or idealism are likely to produce reliable agents. All the others are suspect for one reason or another. Greed, for instance, indicates that people will work for the highest bidder for their services. Bitterness, spite, a desire for revenge and fanaticism may well lead to biased or imaginative reporting. Few enter upon a life of espionage for the thrill of a James Bond-style life of adventure, and any who do so are as likely as not to find other sources of stimulation, which may either turn out to be more thrilling than espionage or lead to either discovery or blackmail, with the resulting danger of their being 'turned' against their employers.

The invention of the telephone in the late nineteenth century increased the potential of COMINT as a source of Intelligence, and during the First World War the tapping of the adversary's field telephone systems in the trenches by both sides added considerably to their knowledge of the enemy's order of battle.

With the invention of photography, also in the nineteenth century, a second string was added to the human Intelligence sources' bow. Now they would be able to substantiate their more unbelievable reports with photographic supporting evidence. The camera could not lie – at least not as easily as the human source – so that a new, and more acceptably reliable source, later to be known as 'imagery Intelligence' (IMINT), was eagerly seized upon by the military Intelligence community and put to great use. As cameras became smaller, lighter and more portable, and photographic emulsions became faster and capable of higher resolution, so they were increasingly supplied to agents, military attachés and other HUMINT sources to photograph foreign military equipment, documents, insignia, personalities, defences and other objects of military Intelligence interest. With modern high-resolution photographic emulsions it was soon found that, by photographing documents through a microscope, reproducible negatives of the size of a typescript dot or full stop could be produced; by substituting this reduced photograph, or micro-dot, for a normal full stop in an otherwise innocuous letter, documents or an agent's report could be transmitted without exciting the suspicions of censors or counter-Intelligence personnel. The invention of infra-red-sensitive emulsions also enables adequate flash photographs to be taken in full darkness without the subject being aware – a boon to counter-Intelligence surveillance operations. The photograph has proved its worth as an Intelligence source many times over, and now ranks as one of the most reliable sources available.

With so many obstacles in the way of passing Intelligence reports and human agents through enemy lines in war and through foreign passport and customs controls in peacetime, Intelligence agencies had for long looked longingly at the air as a means of by-passing them. Messages had in the past been attached to the legs of carrier pigeons and to arrows, but both these methods had disadvantages: they placed severe limitations on the size and weight of message which could be transmitted, and in addition, the range of the arrow was very limited and the pigeon very vulnerable to being shot down, if only for the pot. It was not until the siege of Paris by the Germans in 1870 that the hot air balloon was used for taking military messages over enemy lines, as well as for artillery spotting. The chief limitations of the balloon were its dependence on wind speed and direction, its vulnerability to ground fire and the unpredictable and sometimes violent motion of the basket swinging under the balloon, which limited the ability of the crew to observe, particularly through a telescope, as well as inducing motion sickness.

With the advent of the petrol engine and heavier-than-air flying machines, however, a new source of Intelligence known as air photo-reconnaissance came into being in the First World War. Not only was the aeroplane fitted with a camera able to take up-to-date and hitherto unavailable pictures of enemy activity and positions, it was also able to carry agents and their reports over the enemy lines in reasonable safety. This extension of IMINT, giving as it did an unusual bird's-eye view, needed expert interpretation for its full value to be realised. However, once the necessary interpreters had been trained, photo-reconnaissance (PR) became an extremely valuable source of military Intelligence, particularly in the Second World War. A good example was the coverage obtained of the German V-Weapon sites in France, and their testing and development establishment at Peenemünde, from which sufficient information was obtained for reasonably accurate predictions of the nature and performance of these weapons to be made by British military Intelligence.

The relative ease with which both telegraph and telephone could be tapped meant that a more secure means of communication was highly desirable. The introduction of wireless telegraphy in 1901 and wireless telephony in 1906 had seemed at first to be reasonably secure. Wireless telegraphy in particular had the additional advantage of giving this security over a considerable distance, especially if messages were securely encrypted. But what one person can make another can break, and it was not long before both sides during the First World War were detecting, listening to and decoding the wireless messages of the other side, thus bringing a new dimension to SIGINT. Certainly, the British had very considerable success in both World Wars with the recording and decryption of both the German armed forces' and diplomatic signals traffic. In the Second World War this success came close to being a war-winner.

Not only are radio signals easy to intercept, the interception is done by passive means, so there is no indication to either the sender or the receiver of the signal that interception is being carried out. This is a crucial difference between wire transmission and wireless transmission, as a 'tap' on a wire can be detected by one means or another. Another difference is that a wireless transmitter can be located from its transmissions by means of passive direction-finding equipment, again without either sender or receiver being aware that this has been done. In war, this can lead to the location of enemy headquarters or units; in both peace and war, to the location of hostile spies reporting clandestinely to their controllers. Finally, radio transmissions can be jammed by more powerful transmitters designed for the purpose, and radio equipment would very likely be disabled by nuclear explosions in time of war.

Radio was thus not the panacea that it had originally been thought to be, although despite its disadvantages, its advance into the military and Intelligence inventory was rapid. The risks of interception and location were reduced by introducing automatic encryption of speech and written messages, and high-speed transmission ensuring minimum time on the air; messages were recorded, speeded up and transmitted as a brief pulse of radio energy, being recorded and slowed down to normal speed on playback at the receiving end. The latest counter-measure to interception and jamming is frequency-hopping radio, in which time spent transmitting on any one frequency is reduced by hopping from one frequency to another in a sequence and at a rate previously agreed. Both automatic encryption and frequency-hopping have been made possible only by recent advances in electronics, particularly solid state and digital technology, which have enabled these very advanced techniques to be incorporated in radio sets which are minute by Second World War standards, as well as being cheaper. However, despite these aids to radio security, SIGINT is still a prolific source of Intelligence, more particularly at the strategic level; at the tactical level, the time required to overcome these security devices tends to reduce the value of SIGINT in the field.

For tactical Intelligence in the field, however, one development of radio has proved a very useful source, particularly for battlefield surveillance and the location of enemy mortars and artillery – radar, an acronym for RAdio Detection And Ranging, first used during the Second World War (and then called 'radio-location') for the detection and location of hostile aircraft. Radar provides one facet of another source of Intelligence which has, with the rapid advances in electronics technology in recent years, assumed an ever-increasing importance in the armoury of sources available to military Intelligence; not unnaturally, this source is known as electronic Intelligence (ELINT). Battlefield surveillance is a principal means of obtaining tactical information about the enemy in war, and surveillance radar provides one of the most important means of detecting physical activity: it can detect movement of vehicles and personnel at ranges up to 10 kilometres, by night and by day, in all weathers, while specialised versions can detect a gun or mortar shell in flight and, by working back down the trajectory, pinpoint the location of the weapon which fired it. As with radio, however, radar had the disadvantage of relying on the emission of electro-magnetic radiation, and these signals can be detected and traced back to their source by missiles mounting a warhead which homes in on such radiation.

Since radar can also be jammed, additional means of battlefield surveillance are necessary. One of these is optical, the other relies on presenting an optical image of the thermal differences of the battlefield scene; both rely heavily on electronics to amplify the minute electrical signals involved. Both are passive instruments, so emit no radiation on which enemy detectors or missile warheads can home. The first is the image intensifier, which, as its name implies, amplifies the available light many tens of thousands of times so that the image presented to the eye is visible as if in daylight; the second is the thermal imager, which is very much more sensitive, operates in the far infra-red band of the spectrum, and presents to the eye a positive or negative picture based on the temperature differences between the various parts of the scene.

The thermal imager can operate in pitch darkness and can see through smoke, mist and light foliage; the image intensifier needs a low level of available light, and is defeated by fog, smoke and foliage. A very effective use of thermal imaging is from the air, from both piloted aircraft and pilotless drones (remotely piloted vehicles – RPVs) for tactical Intelligence, or from aircraft or satellites at strategic level. Relying as it does on temperature differences to produce its images, thermal imaging (or 'linescan') can differentiate, for example, between active and disused factories, dummy and real aircraft and full or empty fuel storage tanks, as well as seeing through camouflage. Its pictures can either be transmitted by radio, in which case they are received in 'real time' but are vulnerable to jamming or interception, dropped by parachute over the processing base if urgent, or processed when the aircraft lands. Both of these latter methods impose a delay between the information being acquired and the analysts receiving it. Thermal imaging has greatly increased the usefulness and quality of IMINT as a source of military Intelligence.

The post-Second World War period has seen a meteoric acceleration in the development of electronics, with applications in most aspects of business and domestic life. Applications in the military field are also many and varied, and have led to a whole new category of military Intelligence known as ELINT, which has already been mentioned briefly in connection with battlefield surveillance radar, but covers very much more than this. ELINT embraces the whole field of electronic eavesdropping upon electro-magnetic emissions, for example from space satellites, nuclear explosions, radars and lasers of all types, missile control links, active homing and fusing systems for missile warheads, computer links and data storage systems, to name but a few. Much of this information – such as, for example, the frequencies used by foreign radar systems – is required in order that electronic counter-measures (ECMs) can be designed and developed. Similarly, other countries' ECMs have to be studied to enable electronic counter-counter-measures (ECCMs) to be developed, so that our own electronic equipment can function as required and without disruption by hostile ECMs. ECCMs are also based upon information provided by ELINT.

The gathering of ELINT is a very sophisticated and highly classified process, but sufficient information has been published over the past twenty years to enable at least some idea of the methods used by the former USSR and the USA to be gained. To provide the mobility required for the electronic detectors and the associated power, recording and computing equipment together with the personnel necessary to operate them, both countries have employed spy or 'ferret' ships. The former Soviet Union used vessels disguised as fishing trawlers, concealed among their large fishing fleets and fish-processing ships but distinguishable from them by the multiplicity of antennae with which they were equipped. The USA used elderly freighters for the same purpose, until the USS *Pueblo* was intercepted by North Korean ships off the Korean coast in January 1968 (see Chapter 3). This vessel was on its first mission, with the task of reporting on North Korean radar installations, radio transmissions and naval activity, and under strict orders to proceed no closer to the Korean coast than 13 miles. Although outside the 13 mile limit when intercepted, the freighter was nevertheless fired on and forced into the port of Wonsan. The crew was apparently unable to carry out its standing orders to destroy all classified equipment and documents aboard, despite having the means at hand to carry out this destruction rapidly. As a result, the vessel and most of its secrets fell into hostile hands, and other means had to be found to obtain the ELINT now compromised. The other US 'Ferrets' were mothballed and their functions taken over by satellites such as the SAMOS (Satellite And Missile Observation System), LASP (Low-Altitude Surveillance Platform), Discoverer and Big Bird series, aircraft such as the US EC-121, spy submarines and land-based listening stations.

Mention of spy satellites brings us to the immense improvements in IMINT which have been brought about by the developments in imaging techniques, electronic control, photographic film emulsions and lens materials resulting from the space programme. With vast areas of the former USSR denied to foreigners, rigid censorship imposed on the press and other Soviet publications and no means of knowing what the Soviets were doing or where, although it knew that the USSR was re-arming at an alarming and threatening rate, the USA was compelled to consider methods by which these forbidden areas could be penetrated and useful Intelligence concerning them gained.

Apart from SIGINT, COMINT and ELINT, pictures were needed of what was unknown terrain, giving details of roads, railways, rivers, canals, airfields, towns and cities, military training areas, factories, power stations, weapons testing sites, oil storage areas and many other things of military significance. It was therefore decided that a special aircraft was needed, able to fly faster, higher and with a longer endurance than any equivalent Soviet aircraft or anti-aircraft missile. The first such aircraft, the U-2, specially designed by Lockheed for the task, started operations in 1956, nine months after the prototype first flew. A special squadron with the cover name of 2nd Weather Observation Squadron was formed under the control of the CIA to fly the aircraft from bases in Turkey, Pakistan, Taiwan, Germany, Norway and England. From these bases the U-2s overflew not only the USSR but also all the other Warsaw Pact countries, the People's Republic of China and the Middle East. With the improved aerial photography cameras and film specially developed for the aircraft, they took remarkably detailed photographs in which each frame covered some 500 square miles of hitherto denied territory. The first flights were over the Middle East in May 1956, and were used to photograph the Anglo-French-Israeli preparations for the Suez operation that year; the first flight over the Soviet Union, from Turkey to Norway by way of Moscow and Leningrad, took place later that year.

The Soviet authorities had been aware of the flights over their territory from their inception because their radar was able to track them. They complained about the overflights through diplomatic channels at intervals over the next four years, but were unable to prevent them by other means. Once aware, the Soviets launched an urgent programme to develop a missile capable of intercepting and bringing down a U-2, and finally succeeded in June 1960 when an aircraft piloted by Captain Gary Powers crashed in the Soviet Union, alleged by the Soviets to have been brought down by a missile, but believed by others to have crashed due to sabotage at its base prior to take-off. It was only about the twentieth U-2 flight over the USSR, most of which had taken place between 1958 and 1960, but these had sufficed to cover the whole of the country. The Powers crash ended the U-2 programme over the USSR, but it was stated later by Alan Dulles, then Director of the CIA, to have been the most successful Intelligence operation ever carried out by the CIA or any other Intelligence organisation. The US Air Force stated that the information provided by the U-2 programme had forced it to alter completely its targeting of sites in the Soviet Union. Only 22 aircraft were built, of which 5 were acquired by the British and operated by them from bases in Cyprus and Turkey.

The end of the U-2 programme did not end the overflights of the Warsaw Pact countries by US reconnaissance, however. The time when the Soviets would be able to shoot down the U-2 had been foreseen by the CIA, and successors were being developed. The first of these was the SR-71 ('Blackbird'), and this was followed by the even faster A-11, both being designed and built by Lockheed. But Soviet missile development had been more rapid than had been anticipated by the CIA, and the scope for spy aircraft reduced accordingly. Luckily, by the time Powers had been brought down, the first of the Corona reconnaissance satellites (known to the public as the Discoverer weather and scientific satellites) had been launched successfully, and the series was fully operational by January 1961. Within a year of the last U-2 flight, space technology in the USA had advanced to such an extent that even the most remote parts of the Soviet Union had become accessible to photo-reconnaissance by satellite. In any event, the SR-71 took nearly ten years to deploy from the inception of the project in 1956, so in 1960 it was nowhere near ready to replace the U-2. It was a very much more sophisticated aircraft than the U-2, capable of sustained flight at an altitude in excess of 85,000 ft, at speeds greater than mach 3 (2,200 m.p.h.) and with a range of 3,000 miles. Its first flight took place in April 1962.

At the same time as the Corona system was being developed, another satellite system, known as SAMOS, was under development by the US Air Force. The first SAMOS satellite was successfully placed in orbit in January 1961. As a result of the Corona and SAMOS operations, a flood of photographic material started to become available to the CIA in 1961. The analysis involved required new techniques of interpretation, and took several months to complete for the first thousand photographs sent back by the first SAMOS satellite alone. The detail was such that in a photograph of a football game taken from a hundred miles up, all the players were clearly distinguishable even if the ball itself was not. Photographs could be taken not only in black-and-white and colour, but also with high-speed infra-red and ultra-violet films. The infra-red spectrum was particularly valuable for its mist and cloud penetration, as cloud or smoke over the target area could nullify a mission if it were dependent on normal visible-spectrum films or sensors. The rapid advances in IMINT as a result of the U-2 and satellite programmes, and the enormous increase in the quantity of IMINT material for analysis and dissemination, created a new requirement for photo-interpreters, and led in the USA to the creation of a National Photographic Interpretation Center under the Director of the CIA.

As a result partly of its own operations with U-2s and partly of the special relationship between British and US Intelligence organisations which had existed since early in the Second World War, a similarly large increase in the quantity of IMINT available took place in British military Intelligence, with a resulting increase in its importance as a source of Intelligence compared to other sources. Despite worries about the security of British Intelligence, resulting in particular from the Philby case, the CIA were anxious to share their information with the British, whose analysis and emphasis on quality over quantity they valued highly.

The reconnaissance satellite, despite the quality of its IMINT product, does have some limitations. It is in a predictable orbit, so that those being reconnoitred can tell in advance the area over which it will pass at any given time, it is over an individual target for a very limited time during each orbit, it has a very limited lifespan, and despite its ability to penetrate cloud up to a point, it is dependent for its success upon encountering suitable weather over the target, so unlike a reconnaissance aircraft or drone, it cannot be commanded to photograph a target at short notice. Its regular orbit obviously permits the target to be camouflaged before it can be photographed (Soviet camouflage techniques improved considerably in the 1970s and were able to provide some protection against US spy satellites).

The sheer quantity of information beginning to be provided by IMINT was being matched or exceeded by that from SIGINT, and the combined requirement for analysis and collation of information from both these sources was beyond the capacity of any conceivably sized human staff to complete within any useful time-scale without some form of artificial assistance. The answer lay in the electronics revolution, which was itself largely responsible for the very greatly increased flow of information for processing. The computers that had been developed by GC & CS at Bletchley during the war to carry out the decryption of the German Enigma-encoded signals had led to others of reduced size and power requirements but with greatly increased computing power, and the computer industry which had sprung up after the war as a result was called in to help solve the analysis problem.

Since the Second World War, computers have come to occupy an increasingly important position in all types of military Intelligence. From their early start in the decryption of SIGINT, their uses have expanded into the collection, collation, analysis and dissemination of both strategic and tactical military Intelligence from satellites, drones, manned aircraft, sensors, as well as the control of satellites, the navigation of reconnaissance aircraft and drones, and the control of the various sensors on board these reconnaissance vehicles. Computer imagery is used to build up three-dimensional views of weapons, buildings and installations from two-dimensional vertical or oblique aerial photographs, and computers are also used to enhance such photographs where the contrast or definition of the originals is inadequate. Computers are increasingly used both to encrypt and decrypt voice and facsimile transmissions over radio and landline at both tactical and strategic levels; they are also used extensively in ECMs and ECCMs for analysing and countering hostile radar and other electro-magnetic radiations.

Technology, and in particular the computer, was seen initially as a means of economising and cutting Intelligence staff levels, but the USA, for example, is currently spending more on computer hardware and software than on the entire defence budget: personnel are required to write the software, program the computers, maintain them and keep them on line, direct the analysis and collate and take action on the mass of paper generated by technical methods of Intelligence collection and analysis. Parkinson's Law still prevails, and programmes tend to expand to fill the available computing capacity, requiring ever more staff to evaluate the results. Computers have not fulfilled their early promise of reducing the number of personnel required – indeed, not only have staff numbers not decreased, but the skill levels required, and thereby the cost in salaries, have increased – but they have undoubtedly improved the efficiency and speed of response of the Intelligence organisation. Computers are also vulnerable to mechanical damage to hardware and software, to large changes in temperature and humidity, to power surges or failure, to static electricity, to electro-magnetic pulses from nuclear explosions, to breakdowns and to eavesdropping.

Despite these disadvantages, however, modern technical methods of collecting Intelligence, and of evaluating the results, could not function without the amazing recent advances in electronics which have led to the present generation of computers, with their remarkable increases in both computing power and computing speed coupled with their reduced power requirements and size. There is every reason to believe that computing speed will be increased by at least a further order of magnitude with the introduction of optical computing. Optical computers will use tiny flashes of laser light instead of pulses of electrons, which travel more slowly than light.

The two superpowers, the USA and the former Soviet Union, have had a virtual monopoly of satellite-produced SIGINT and IMINT for the past twenty years or so, and this has given them an Intelligence lead over other countries which will take several years to reduce. Despite their contributions to Western SIGINT, the British have been very much the junior partner in the special Anglo-American Intelligence relationship since the Second World War. Having no space-vehicle launching facilities of their own, the British are, and will remain, very much dependent upon the United States for all Intelligence collected by satellites. This is why so much of this chapter on British military Intelligence sources has been devoted to US spy aircraft and satellite development. The UK, as a country of the second rank, has no other source of IMINT on the former Soviet Union and any other potentially hostile country than the US space programme, but luckily, the UKUSA pact of 1947 is in place to ensure that it will continue to receive IMINT from the USA for the foreseeable future.

However, one of the consequences of the revolution in aerial reconnaissance and IMINT, as well as the enormous explosion in SIGINT from satellite and ground stations, is the glut of information coming in from all sources, which must surely exceed the analytical capacity of both British and US Intelligence organisations; despite the much larger staffs and the more sophisticated tools available to them. The eternal problem remains how to distinguish the wood from the trees, or the significant from the insignificant.

Another component of the information explosion is overt or open sources, such as foreign radio, television and the press. While they have not increased on anything like the same scale as SIGINT, IMINT and ELINT, much more information from such sources is now available, particularly in specialised magazines dealing with defence matters, weapons and all types of engineering. These sources are too often neglected in favour of information from more sophisticated or more highly classified sources, as the British JIC was found by the Franks Committee to have done prior to the Falklands conflict. Used sensibly, and collated with more highly classified information, where available, information from these open sources can answer very satisfactorily a very large proportion of the questions concerning military matters posed by the military Intelligence agencies. It is a matter of having the net spread widely enough to catch the right radio transcripts, newspapers, magazines, TV programmes and books, and of having a suitable collation system so that they may be found easily when required. The initial selection of press extracts, magazines and television programmes can be carried out very effectively by the military attachés on the staffs of the British Embassies in the countries concerned; the attachés forward them to the Ministry of Defence Intelligence Staff in London, where the information can be collated with that from other sources.

Mention of military attaché brings us to another source of HUMINT which has been widely used in military Intelligence organisations in Europe, although not in the British Army, since the beginning of the nineteenth century. Prior to that time, observing and reporting on a foreign country's capability and readiness for war and on its armed forces had been carried out by ambassadors or other diplomats, but as military weapons and organisations grew more complex as the nineteenth century progressed, governments began either to appoint military officers as ambassadors or to provide civilian ambassadors with military officers as attachés and expert advisers.

Despite the presence in London of a small corps of foreign military attachés, it was not until 1854 and the pressures of the Crimean War that Britain moved from its previous cold aloofness and took a first tentative step towards appointing its own attachés; in that year, liaison officers known as Commissars of the Queen were appointed to the headquarters of Britain's allies in Paris, Turin, Constantinople and the French HQ in the Crimea. After the war, only the officers in Paris and Turin were retained, becoming known as military attachés in 1860. By the late 1860s Britain had military attachés in five European capitals, and thereby greatly enhanced its ability to collect strategic military Intelligence. unfortunately, however, their reports were forwarded to the Foreign Office in London, where, due to the lack of anybody qualified to analyse raw military Intelligence, they remained undigested. It was not until the acceptance by Cardwell, then Secretary of State for War, of the recommendations of the Northbrook Committee in January 1871 that it was laid down that all military attaché reports would in future be sent to the Topographical and Statistical Department in the War Office for collation and analysis.

Today there is at least one Service attaché or adviser in the capitals of sixty foreign and Commonwealth countries, and in many of these there are separate naval, military and air attachés, some with assistant attachés as well for specialist matters. In the smaller countries, one officer will represent the interests of all three services and will be known as the Defence Attaché; in countries where two or more service attachés are in post, the senior will also be designated as Defence Attaché. British service attachés were formerly managed and directed by the directors of Intelligence of the service which they represented, and more recently by the Chief of Defence Intelligence (CDI). Since 1996, however, the responsibility for the attaché corps has been transferred to the Deputy Chief of Defence Staff for Commitments, where they are overseen by the Assistant Chief of Defence Staff for Policy (ACDS(Pol)), although they continue to serve the CDI.

The military attaché is in some ways an anachronism in these days of instantaneous communication by radio, television, e-mail, fax and telephone, as is the modern ambassador and embassy staff. The military attaché's brief is to monitor the media and military publications, attend army parades and manoeuvres, to visit training establishments and line units, to watch for and report on new military equipment, and generally to monitor the armed forces of the country to which they are posted. By international convention, military attachés should in no circumstances become involved in, or undertake any covert Intelligence work, but should act only as a channel for relaying to their Ministry of Defence information openly available to the public or provided by the host country, but this convention has frequently been breached by attachés of the former Soviet Union, its Warsaw Pact allies and by some Third World countries.

British military attachés operate to a frequently updated brief provided by the Defence Intelligence Staff in London, on whose behalf they pose questions to the Army foreign liaison staff of the host country and to whom they relay their replies, if and when received. A trained and experienced military attaché is an invaluable source of specialist information, and this information will often form the skeleton upon which can be hung the flesh of information from other and more exotic sources in the collation process. Military attachés also act as military advisers to the ambassadors under whom they serve, as well as accompanying or representing the ambassador on military ceremonial occasions.

Another valuable source of HUMINT is military defectors, of whom there have been a large number, particularly from the former Soviet Union and Warsaw Pact countries, since the Second World War. Motives for a soldier's defection are many and varied, ranging from the ideological through the greedy, the amatory, the disgruntled and the frightened to the plainly criminal. An example of ideological motivation was provided by one of the first to defect after the Second World War, Lieutenant Igor Gouzenko, a cipher clerk to the Military Attaché in the Soviet Embassy in Ottawa whose adventures were recounted in Chapter 3. Since his arrival in Canada in 1943 he had been very impressed by the freedom of the individual and the electoral process there, as well as by the quality and quantity of the goods available in the shops for purchase by anybody. The receipt from Moscow in August 1945 of orders posting him back to Moscow made him realise that he did not wish to leave this democratic heaven, so, taking with him some of the more highly classified and valuable documents to which he had access, he defected to the Canadian authorities with his family early the following month. There were very many more high-grade defections from the former USSR and its Warsaw Pact allies between the Gouzenko case and the ending of the Cold War, most of whom were genuine, and most of whom brought valuable information with them.

There is, however, another type of defector of a rather lower order who has provided a large volume of tactical military, and some economic Intelligence between the ending of the Second World War and the building of the Berlin Wall and the Iron Curtain in 1961. These were generally either privates and NCOs from the Group of Soviet Forces in Germany (GSFG), tempted by the higher standard of living in the West, or civilians such as doctors, teachers and technicians disillusioned with the repressive régime and the lack of opportunity in East Germany. It was to prevent the drain of educated personnel from East to West Germany, rather than, as was claimed, to prevent Berlin being used by the West as a base for sabotage and espionage against East Germany, that the Berlin Wall was built by the Government of the German Democratic Republic (DDR). The open frontier between East and West Berlin had been used as an escape route to the West from the oppressive régime of the East by some two million East Germans out of a population of eighteen million between 1949 and the building of the wall some twelve years later.

This is not to say that espionage by Western Intelligence agents had not taken place, nor to deny that the frontier between East and West Germany, and between East and West Berlin had been crossed many times by such agents or their couriers, but the Intelligence gained from them was, on the whole, of low quality. The same applied to the flow of defectors and other line-crossers, but the East Germans, as well as the Soviet forces in Germany, were obsessed by security to the point of paranoia, and there is no doubt that the building of both the barrier along the frontier between the two Germanys and the Berlin Wall reduced the former flood to a trickle, and then to almost nothing. In any case, the Intelligence provided by these sources had been tactical rather than strategic, and modern methods of surveillance by satellite had replaced an unreliable source with one of greater integrity.

Documents can be very important sources of military Intelligence. Documentary Intelligence has, like IMINT, COMINT and SIGINT, expanded very greatly in quantity and quality since the Second World War because of the great improvements in methods of copying and printing which have been introduced in this period. Since the invention of writing, documents have always been an important source of Intelligence, if only because they greatly reduce, or even eliminate, the human memory as a source of error. Queen Elizabeth I's Secretary of State, Sir Francis Walsingham, set great store by documentary Intelligence, as did Marlborough, Thurloe, who performed the same function for Oliver Cromwell, and most Intelligence officers since those times. These days, the flood of documentary Intelligence available on most military subjects, while not as great as the SIGINT and IMINT input, is nevertheless large enough to make its analysis a full-time occupation for a large number of people.

The range of documents of interest to the military Intelligence organisation is too great to be listed here in any detail: the quantities available vary in inverse proportion to their security classification, unclassified books, magazines and newspapers being easily the most numerous. There has been an upsurge of interest in military subjects on the part of the general public during the long period of relative peace since the end of the Second World War, and a consequent flood of books and periodicals covering these subjects. Many of these are authoritative, their information being provided by knowledgeable and enthusiastic sources, many of whom are former military personnel. Coverage of topographic, economic, communications and technical weapons and equipment subjects is especially good, and today's military Intelligence officer will tend to have a large, specialised library and periodical input as well as collation files upon which to rely in making analyses. Other useful sources of openly available information include lists of promotions, regimental magazines, patent applications, government statistics and other publications such as White Papers, technical handbooks, company brochures, scientific papers and proceedings of engineering institutes.

Classified documents will naturally be of greater interest, particularly if they are up to date, but these are naturally more difficult to obtain and consequently in shorter supply. Orders of battle, operational plans, mentions of new weapons and their performance, operators' handbooks for new equipment, code and cipher books, military standard operating procedures and identity documents fall into this category, along with many others too numerous to mention.

The problem with classified documents is the difficulty of either removing them from the building where they are housed or copying them, and the more highly classified the document the greater the difficulty. Furthermore, as the person wishing to remove or copy the document will be either an agent or an intending defector, there is the further problem, after having successfully removed or copied it, of getting it out of the country without being discovered in the process. The most common solution has been to photograph the document, leaving the carrier with only a small film to conceal and smuggle out; however, the making of copies by this means while under pressure is difficult, and many a mouth-watering prospect has proved in the past to be out of focus in a crucial part, or a vital portion has been missing because of hasty composition in the viewfinder, or the whole document has been blurred due to camera movement at the time of exposure. It is also less easy to tell from a photograph of a document whether or not it has been altered before being copied, and suspicion of forgery must always be in the mind of the recipient.

The Soviet defector Oleg Penkovsky, who was run for some eighteen months as an 'agent in place' by SIS, managed both to remove many classified Soviet documents dealing with their guided missile programme and to pass them to his SIS cut-out in Moscow before his discovery and arrest in October 1962, but there are still those on both sides of the Atlantic who hold that Penkovsky was a KGB 'plant', that his documentary information was deliberately doctored and therefore suspect, and that he was not shot after his trial, as claimed by Moscow, but is still alive under another name. For obvious reasons, classified documents from hostile countries can be obtained in peacetime only by covert means; in wartime, on the other hand, the majority of enemy classified documents will be obtained from the capture of headquarters, vehicles or personnel.

The Intelligence organisations of friendly foreign countries can be, and often are, useful sources of military Intelligence. Many crucial pieces of Intelligence have come from such sources, either unsolicited or in exchange for some other item of information. The Intelligence gained by MI 6 and GC & CS from the Polish and French Intelligence services concerning the German Enigma cipher machines before and at the beginning of the Second World War is a case in point; while the Anglo-US agreements on the sharing of Intelligence have proved a very fruitful source for British military Intelligence, as we have seen. The Americans are so far ahead of the British in technical and scientific methods of Intelligence-collection from satellites that British military Intelligence would have been virtually blind with regard to military activity and weapon developments within the former Soviet Union during the Cold War without the flow of information from the United States.

The sharing of information obtained from defectors to the United States and other Western countries has also led to the unmasking of agents working in the United Kingdom for foreign Intelligence services; John Vassall, for example, a clerk in the Admiralty who had been blackmailed into spying for the USSR as a result of a homosexual episode while serving in the British Naval Attaché's office in Moscow in 1955, was unmasked by two KGB defectors, Anatoli Golytsin and Yuri Nosenko, to the USA in 1961/62. The Portland naval spy ring of Harry Houghton and Ethel Gee, run by 'Gordon Lonsdale' (actually a Soviet KGB officer and 'illegal' named Konon Molody) and the 'Krogers' (otherwise known as Morris and Lona Cohen) was given away by a defector to the USA from the Polish Intelligence service named Mikhail Golenievski in 1960. All were tried at the Old Bailey in 1961 and found guilty of espionage; Molody was later exchanged for Greville Wynne, the British businessman tried in Moscow with Oleg Penkovsky; the Cohens, who had escaped the US round-up of Soviet agents in the late 1940s, were exchanged for Gerald Brooke, a British lecturer imprisoned in the Soviet Union for allegedly distributing subversive literature.

Intelligence has also been gained by the British from operations mounted jointly by SIS and the CIA, such as GOLD, the Berlin tunnel operation conceived in 1953 to attack the Soviet military communications landlines in East Germany. The plan involved the clandestine digging of a 500 yard-long tunnel from the West Berlin suburb of Altglienicke into East Berlin, to intercept the landlines from the Soviet military headquarters at Karlshorst to Berlin. As the tunnel would pass under the very feet of Soviet troops, precautions against noise had to be taken. With a diameter of 6 ft 6 in, the tunnel required the clandestine removal and concealment of more than three thousand tons of spoil. No ventilation shafts were possible along its length, so air had to be pumped into the tunnel mouth and then pumped out again. Because of the heat that would be generated by the electronic equipment and transformers, air conditioning was necessary; above all, pinpoint accuracy in aligning the tunnel was essential in order to end up at a 2 in diameter target only 18 in below a main road.

Digging started in August 1954, and was completed successfully in February 1955; 600 reel-to-reel tape recorders were installed to record the 'take', and they were using 800 reels of tape a day when the operation got under way. Aircraft loaded with tapes were flown for analysis out of Berlin to London and Washington weekly; care had to be taken by CIA in purchasing of such large quantities of recording tape in order not to distort the balance of the tape supply market in the United States. The task of translating and analysing the enormous quantity of intercepted information was monumental; in the USA alone, fifty CIA linguists worked two weeks on and one day off to keep up with the input. Almost exactly eleven months after the first message had been taped, however, the tunnel was accidentally discovered by Soviet engineers checking a faulty landline after exceptionally heavy rain, and was revealed to the Berlin press corps by the acting commandant of the Soviet garrison in Berlin; this propaganda move recoiled on the Soviet authorities, however, the general verdict of the press being in favour of the ingenuity and engineering skill shown in the tunnel's conception and construction.

The analysis of the backlog of tapes was not completed by the CIA for two-and-a-half years after the discovery of the tunnel; in the eleven months of its working life it had provided much order of battle information on the Soviet forces in East Germany, as well as information on the state of the East German economy and the fact that there was a spy in the SIS Berlin station, although his identity, George Blake, was not known until several years later.

A similar operation, this time originated by SIS but shared with and enlarged by the CIA, was Operation SILVER. The British had realised that it would be possible to monitor Soviet communications in post-war Vienna by tapping into landlines near a private house in the Vienna suburb of Schwechat. SIS bought the house, tunnelled 70 ft under a nearby road to the cables, and successfully listened to the Soviet traffic from 1949 until the Allies vacated Austria on 15 May 1955 in accordance with the Austrian State Treaty. To cover the comings and goings at the house, SIS opened a shop there selling Harris tweed; unfortunately, it became so successful and Harris tweed so popular that the SIS personnel found it difficult to devote time to the eavesdropping! The entry of the CIA into the operation greatly increased the scope of SILVER and the 'take' from it.

Information useful in military Intelligence can and often does come from the other two services and from other government departments; particularly at the strategic level, military Intelligence can derive useful pointers to future foreign military action from political and economic reports from foreign countries, based in some cases upon reports from British businesspeople returning from overseas visits, and in others upon reports from political and commercial staffs at British embassies and consulates abroad.

Casual one-off sources also play their part in the input to military Intelligence. A typical example from the Second World War is the 'Oslo Document' mentioned in Chapter 2, which was unfortunately not given the credence it deserved until its accuracy was gradually proved as the war progressed. In October 1939 the British Naval Attaché in Oslo had been offered anonymously certain secret German technical and scientific information, subject to his interest in receiving this information being affirmed by an alteration in the normal introduction to the BBC's German news. The requested alteration was made by the BBC at the request of 'C', as a result of which a package was delivered to the Naval Attaché early in November; the package was found to contain an electronic proximity fuse of advanced type and several typed pages of data covering various aircraft, rocket and other weapon developments previously unknown to British Intelligence. The package was forwarded to SIS headquarters in Broadway, and thence to Dr R.V. Jones, later the Assistant Director of Intelligence (Science) at the Air Ministry, who came to the conclusion that the information was genuine. Unfortunately, he could find nobody to agree with him; the feeling of those to whom he communicated his findings was that no one person could have had knowledge of all the projects mentioned in the document, and that the information was therefore probably a 'plant'. Jones, having at the time no experience in Intelligence, bowed to the 'superior' judgement of the doubters and, alone among the recipients, kept his copy of the document which, as the war progressed, was confirmed in every particular.

Finally, there is a source which does not fit into any of the categories so far mentioned – the eavesdropping microphone. The technique of electronic eavesdropping has become one of increasing sophistication since the end of the Second World War as part of the increasingly rapid development of electronics, and much Intelligence is produced by this means. Intelligence from this type of source tends to be of special value in counter-espionage, and the technique is therefore much used in this field by organisations such as the British Security Service (MI 5) and the US Federal Bureau of Investigation (FBI), but it is also of occasional value to other branches of military Intelligence.

The product of the eavesdropping microphone is generally recorded on tape and later transcribed for distribution. Although not specifically for military Intelligence, the microphone placed by the KGB in the Great Seal of the United States which hung in the ambassador's office in the US Embassy in Moscow, and which was discovered there in 1960, is an example of an eavesdropping device planted in the hope of gathering Intelligence other than for counter-espionage; a microphone concealed in such a place and remaining undetected could be expected, over the years, to pick up a variety of high-level Intelligence of all types, and it must have been a great disappointment to the KGB when the introduction by the CIA of new sweeping techniques led to its discovery. After its detection, the Great Seal was used to great effect in the United Nations by the US ambassador, Henry Cabot Lodge, as an example of the Soviet Union's perfidy in international relations.

The protection of all sources of military Intelligence is vital, and this is where security plays its vital part in the collection and dissemination process. 'Security' in this sense is the collective term used to describe all those measures taken to discover, assess and defeat the threat from hostile Intelligence services and subversive organisations. It has two distinct but related aspects: offensive and defensive. Offensive aspects include the acquisition of security Intelligence, while defensive security is the implementation of defensive measures to ensure the security of British forces.

In the words of Lord Radcliffe in his 1962 report on security procedures in the public service: 'the biggest single risk to security at the present time is probably a general lack of conviction that any substantial threat exists'. This is undoubtedly still true, but the espionage threat to the United Kingdom from hostile Intelligence services, both within the UK and overseas, is nevertheless as great as, or greater than ever. There is now also a significant threat from domestic and international subversive and terrorist organisations. The need for intelligent application of effective security measures is thus greater than ever. Within the Army, security is a command responsibility involving commanders and staffs, but while overall responsibility for security advice rests with military Intelligence, security is the business of everyone, and not only that of security staffs and unit security officers.

Within the United Kingdom and in areas of British influence overseas, the overall responsibility for security lies with the Security Service (MI 5); within the Army it lies with the Director of Security (Army) in the Ministry of Defence, who has representatives in the headquarters of commands both in the United Kingdom and overseas. The common objective of both is to frustrate the threat to the security of the UK and its armed services from espionage, subversion, sabotage and terrorism.

Espionage is the covert means by which hostile Intelligence services or subversive organisations attempt to acquire information affecting British national security to which they are not entitled. It is one of the disadvantages of a democracy that much valuable information is freely available which, in countries with more repressive governments, would be inaccessible; hostile Intelligence services can therefore concentrate their collection efforts on fewer, more highly classified targets, thus increasing both their chances of success and the difficulties of the British security organisations in frustrating their efforts. Suborning of personnel with access to classified information is one of the means used by hostile Intelligence services to obtain it, and here they make use of character weaknesses and the threat of exposure, ideology and sympathetic political beliefs, rapacity and the grudge of the embittered person as means of recruitment. The Positive Vetting system (see Chapter 3), if properly and regularly applied, will do much to prevent or reveal coercion of this sort.

Subversion is the adoption of illegal or unconventional methods in order to cause the overthrow of the legitimate government to the advantage of a subversive organisation. There are many techniques of subversion which can be employed by such organisations, among which may be included:

1. The use of 'front' organisations as cover for their real activities
2. The recruiting of influential people to operate, either consciously or unconsciously, on their behalf
3. Creation of a climate of mistrust and disillusion, leading to the discrediting of individuals and the government
4. The spreading of false, or distorted true information, to destroy confidence in leaders
5. Infiltration of education, local government, trade unions and other organisations, to use them for their own ends
6. Propaganda.

Modern methods of mass communication such as the press, the Internet, television and radio bring a very large audience within reach of subversive organisations with very little delay; satellite television enlarges this audience still further.

Provision of good security Intelligence is a prime function of the Security Service; within the Army, ultimate responsibility rests with the Director of Security (Army) in the MoD, whose organisation is represented down to unit level at home and overseas. Intelligence Corps security units, however, act in an advisory capacity only; they have no powers of arrest, and, should they discover a breach of security, they can only bring it to the attention of the commander of the unit or formation involved, or to the Special Investigation Branch (SIB) of the Corps of Royal Military Police. The SIB is the executive branch where arrest and interrogation of suspects is required, and its relationship to the Intelligence Corps security staff closely parallels that between the police Special Branch and the Security Service in the United Kingdom.

Which of all the sources of military Intelligence that have been mentioned are the most important, the most numerous, the most reliable? It is impossible to give an answer that is universally applicable, as the relative values and quantities vary so much from country to country and from year to year. One thing is certain: the vast majority of the information required by military Intelligence is available in the public domain, and most contemporary military Intelligence work is based upon openly available material. Of the other sources mentioned, IMINT and SIGINT are enormously productive, if limited in their coverage; ELINT is highly specialised, but invaluable in its specialised field, whereas HUMINT tends to be generalised and represents only a very small proportion of the total military Intelligence input. Agents or spies, in particular, occupy only a very modest place in the hierarchy of military Intelligence sources, although their role in counter-espionage work may be of crucial importance. All too often, the real function of Intelligence has been overshadowed by revelations concerning the achievements of this spy or that code-breaker, or by the hunt for hostile agents or 'moles' within the organisation itself.

CHAPTER 5

Covert Intelligence and Counter-Espionage

Generally speaking, it is true to say that some 80 per cent of the information required by military Intelligence organisations is openly available in one form or another. However, as with a jigsaw puzzle, it is always the missing part which is the most important. This means that considerable thought, time, money, ingenuity and resources have to be devoted to acquiring the remaining 20 per cent by covert means of one sort or another if the full picture is to be obtained.

Despite representing only a small proportion of the total Intelligence picture, it is the people and the methods used in the covert acquisition of Intelligence – rather than the humdrum and painstaking analysis of freely available information that occupy most of an Intelligence officer's time – that have always captured the public's interest and authors' imaginations. This undoubtedly accounts for the abundance of books on the subject, ranging from the speculative through the biographical to the highly imaginative and downright untrue, which have continued to appear ever since the spy scares that were so prevalent during the period immediately preceding the First World War.

The collection of Intelligence by covert means neither comes easily to countries with a democratic form of government, nor is it much admired in them. Secrecy is, on the whole, deplored in such countries, and the need for it in some areas of government is not widely understood – hence the Freedom of Information Act in the USA and the pressure by certain pressure groups and politicians for the introduction of a similar measure in the United Kingdom. In the former Soviet Union, on the other hand, and also in present-day Russia to a lesser extent, the secretive and suspicious Russian regime imposed rigid censorship on published information, keeping it to a minimum. The task of the Intelligence organisations of the former USSR and Warsaw Pact countries in gathering information about the NATO countries, for example, was therefore made much easier than that of NATO Intelligence organisations trying to do the same behind what was the Iron Curtain. Nevertheless, this easy access to information has done nothing to lessen the covert Intelligence efforts of Russia and other potentially hostile countries in the Western democracies; to such an extent that one wonders if it is possible for them to process and correctly interpret the mass of information which they so avidly and secretly gather and hoard.

Information concerning the organisations involved in the collection of covert Intelligence is rightly highly classified because of their covert function, and tends to be very out of date by the time it is published. In the United Kingdom, the two organisations involved in obtaining Intelligence by covert means are:

1. The *Secret Intelligence Service* (otherwise known as SIS, MI 6 or, colloquially outside the service, 'The Friends'), with its headquarters at Vauxhall Cross in London and headed by the Chief of the Secret Service, known as CSS outside the Service and as 'C' or 'The Chief' within it, is responsible for the acquisition of secret Intelligence overseas, and operates under the umbrella of the Foreign Office.
2. The *Government Communications Headquarters* (GCHQ), formerly known as the Government Code and Cipher School (GC & CS), with its headquarters in Cheltenham, Gloucestershire, and also under the control of the CSS, is responsible for the acquisition of secret communications Intelligence on foreign countries and the decryption of intercepts.

The organisation of SIS is a closely guarded secret, the latest available published organisation chart being that quoted by Nigel West (Rupert Allason, the former Conservative MP) in the Appendix to his 1983 book *MI 6*, enlarged upon by Kim Philby in *My Silent War*, published in 1969. This will undoubtedly bear very little relation to the current structure, although the basic division of the service into departments covering the three categories of Requirements, Production and Administration is likely to have been retained.

The formation of the service under its first Chief, Captain Mansfield Smith-Cumming RN, and the early years of its existence have been described in previous chapters. Smith-Cumming was succeeded as CSS in 1924 by Rear-Admiral Hugh ('Quex') Sinclair RN, a former Director of Naval Intelligence, who in turn was followed in 1939 by Major Stewart Menzies DSO, a former officer in the Life Guards; his tour lasted until 1952, when he was succeeded by his deputy, Major-General John Sinclair, a former Director of Military Intelligence. The post has since been occupied by:

Dick White	1956–68
John Rennie	1968–73
Maurice Oldfield	1973–78
Dickie Franks	1978–81
Colin Figgures	1981–85
Christopher Curwen	1985–90
Colin McColl	1991–93
David Spedding	1994–

For many years, the headquarters of SIS was located in Broadway Buildings at No. 54 Broadway, opposite St James's Park Underground station, a building described by Philby as 'a dingy building, a warren of wooden partitions and frosted-glass windows. It had eight floors served by an ancient lift.' It moved in the 1960s to Century House, an anonymous, modern, twenty-floor tower on Westminster Bridge Road near Lambeth North station, south of the Thames, which was inconvenient and actively disliked by the staff, and has recently moved again to its new, recently built and strangely blatant HQ at Vauxhall Cross.

The organisation of GCHQ, like that of SIS, is a closely guarded secret, and even the existence and function of this agency has only been publicly acknowledged since the publication in 1974 of Fred Winterbotham's book *The Ultra Secret*. Having its origins in the First World War, in the course of which a highly sophisticated British signal interception and decryption organisation had developed, GCHQ's predecessor, the Government Code and Cipher School was formed in November 1919 by combining the Navy's NID 25 (Room 40) and the Army's MI 1(b) cryptographic sections under the leadership of Alexander ('Alastair') G. Denniston, a naval cryptographer and former foreign-language master at the Royal Naval College, Osborne, Isle of Wight, and under the control of the Director of Naval Intelligence.

GC & CS was initially accommodated at Watergate House, Adelphi, near the Savoy Hotel, but moved in 1922 to new offices in Queen's Gate, South Kensington, when the Foreign Office took over responsibility for the organisation from the Admiralty. The following year, CSS was additionally appointed Director of GC & CS. At this time the GC & CS staff totalled ninety-one. In June 1926, GC & CS moved from Queen's Gate to Broadway Buildings, where it occupied the third and fourth floors, sharing the building with SIS. Between this date and 1936 its prime target was the Soviet Union, with Japan running it a close second, but with the rise to power of the Nazis in Germany in 1936 and the Spanish Civil War its priorities were changed to cover German and Spanish communications. In 1938, with the prospect of war looming larger and the likelihood of London proving an immediate target for enemy air attack, CSS arranged for alternative HQs for both SIS and GC & CS to be purchased; that selected for GC & CS was Bletchley Park, a large estate on the outskirts of the Buckinghamshire town, and the organisation moved to its new HQ in August 1939.

The exploits of GC & CS (or the Government Communications Bureau, as its new wartime cover name denoted it) in breaking many of the German Enigma codes in the Second World War have been covered in Chapter 2. It became known as GCHQ, and moved to Eastcote for a short time after the war, before finally moving to Cheltenham, where it remains. Its first Director, Alexander ('Alastair') Denniston, remained in charge of the organisation for twenty-four years, retiring in 1944 and being replaced by his long-time deputy, Edward Travis, who served until 1952. Among later directors were:

Eric Jones	1952–60
Clive Loehnis	1960–65
Leonard (Joe) Hooper	1965–72
Arthur (Bill) Bonsall	1972–77
Brian Tovey	1977–83
Peter Marychurch	1983–?
John Adye	1992–

The covert collection of counter-espionage Intelligence within the United Kingdom is the responsibility of the Security Service (MI 5). Formed in 1909 as part of the War Office Secret Service Bureau, its first head was Captain Vernon Kell of the South Staffordshire Regiment. He was a remarkable man, who was to run what became MO 5, and later MI 5, for more than thirty years, being promoted in the job until by 1939 he had reached the rank of Major-General and had been knighted. He retired, together with his deputy, Eric Holt-Wilson, in 1940, to be replaced by David Petrie, with Brigadier A.W.A. Harker as his deputy. Thereafter, Directors-General and their deputies were as follows:

Directors-General	
Percy Sillitoe	1946–53
Dick White	1953–56
Roger Hollis	1956–65
Martin Furnival-Jones	1965–72
Michael Hanley	1972–79
Howard Smith	1979–81
John Jones	1981–85

Antony Duff	1985–87
Patrick Walker	1987–92
Mrs Stella Rimington	1992–96
Stephen Lander	1996–
Deputy Directors-General	
Guy Liddell	1940–47
Roger Hollis	1952–56
Graham Mitchell	1956–63
Martin Furnival-Jones	1963–65
Anthony Simkins	1965–71
Michael Hanley	1971–72
Ronald Symonds	1972–76
John Jones	1976–81
Patrick Walker	1981–87
Mrs Stella Rimington	1990–92
Stephen Lander	1992–96
Hon. Eliza Manningham-Buller	1997–

The Director-General is now responsible to the Home Secretary, and the service comes under the aegis of the Home Office. The Security Service has no executive powers, however, and is dependent upon the Police Special Branch for the arrest and prosecution of suspects. Initially operating from the War Office in Whitehall and answerable to the Secretary of State for War, the organisation moved to 124–126 Cromwell Road, and thence in 1937 to two floors in Thames House, Millbank, while retaining an office (Room 055) on the ground floor of what is now the Old War Office Building as a contact office for other government departments, interviewees, etc. Rapid expansion in 1939 prompted a move of the administrative departments to Wormwood Scrubs, which proved a most inconvenient place from which to work; a further move to Blenheim Palace in Oxfordshire therefore took place, the headquarters of the organisation occupying offices in St James's Street, London. Smaller offices were also maintained in Piccadilly, Regent Street and Dolphin Square. In 1945, MI 5 moved its HQ and main departments to Leconfield House in Curzon Street, and its garages in Barnard Road, where they remained until the 1970s. The organisation returned to Thames House, Millbank, in 1995; prior to this move, the service had occupied nine buildings in central London, with branches scattered illogically around the city.

Contrary to the fears of some, covert Intelligence collection as practised in the Western democracies, and particularly in the United Kingdom, is neither evil nor immoral. The organisations involved are neither undemocratic nor attempts at secret government, although the undoubted need for secrecy in certain parts of the Intelligence collection and evaluation process may account for the disrepute in which the Intelligence function is held by some. It must surely be obvious that in the present state of the world, no country which aspires to the protection of its inhabitants and interests dares to be without an Intelligence organisation, and equally obvious that there must be areas of such an organisation which are of greater sensitivity than others and which it is not in the national interest to expose to the public gaze, and hence to a potential enemy. The same is true of most commercial businesses, where corporate pricing policy, market research results, competition analysis and product research and development, for example, are kept highly confidential, even from shareholders. The type of person who attempts to ferret out secret Intelligence information or who demands the right to see it under a Freedom of Information Act is either naive, unintelligent or has an ulterior motive.

The collection of covert Intelligence by whatever means demands a large and expensive organisation, and the value of the 'product', depending on the means used to obtain it, very often fails to justify the expenditure. Setting up the administration to gather and disseminate the Intelligence is also a lengthy process, involving the tightest security precautions at every stage and throughout the organisation. If it employs human agents, considerable care and time is necessary in their recruitment and training if they are ultimately to prove suitable.

Useful though they may be in war, clandestine sources are very much more useful to military Intelligence in times of peace. In war, so much tactical Intelligence is available from PoWs, photo-reconnaissance and captured documents that covert Intelligence, even at strategic level, is of only limited value to the Army. In addition, communication with covert human sources in war can be both difficult and unreliable, while other more technical sources can take a long time to process, often making the information out of date by the time that the interpretation and dissemination have been completed.

The four main covert means of Intelligence collection, HUMINT, SIGINT, ELINT and satellite reconnaissance, have already been mentioned in an earlier chapter. All have their uses and are complementary to each other, but their relative importance will depend on circumstances, so we will treat them as being of equal importance and discuss them in the order in which they are mentioned above.

To take HUMINT first; as we have seen, the spy is a member of the second oldest trade or profession, and in such a long history, the world's Intelligence and counter-Intelligence services have accumulated the hard way much experience in talent-spotting, recruiting and running secret agents securely. Most Intelligence services use similar methods, the generic term for which is 'trade-craft' (the use of this term might be seen as acknowledgement by those involved that espionage is a trade rather than a profession).

In countries such as the former Soviet Union and modern Russia there are several organisations with responsibility for the gathering of clandestine Intelligence; the two most notorious Soviet agencies were the KGB (Committee for State Security), responsible for both Intelligence and counter-Intelligence in the Soviet Union and overseas, and the GRU (Chief Intelligence Directorate of the General Staff), responsible for collection of military Intelligence overseas. Since the collapse of the USSR, the titles and functions of these organisations have changed, as described in the Appendix.

In the United Kingdom the Secret Intelligence Service (SIS, or MI 6) is responsible for all covert HUMINT overseas, and the Security Service (MI 5) is responsible for covert counter-espionage and security in the UK and British territories overseas. SIGINT in the UK is the responsibility of Government Communications Headquarters (GCHQ). In the USA, the Central Intelligence Agency (CIA) approximates to the British SIS, the Federal Bureau of Investigation (FBI) to MI 5 and the National Security Agency (NSA) to the British GCHQ.

Nobody knows how many people in the world are engaged in the collection and dissemination of covert Intelligence, but in 1989 the CIA alone was believed to employ some 18,000 staff, and the former Soviet KGB and the GRU together some 25,000. Of the latter, at least 5,000 were serving in the field in some 90 countries. No exact figures are publicly available for the British SIS or GCHQ, but estimates by analysts put the total staff of MI 6 at about 2,000, while GCHQ is estimated to have a staff of approximately 5,000. A reply to a Parliamentary Question in December 1997 quoted MI 5's personnel as totalling 1,860, only slightly below the estimates of 'around 2,000' previously given by Intelligence experts. These figures indicate the size of organisation required nowadays to run a covert Intelligence collection and dissemination operation worldwide. The CIA (known to its members as 'The Company') may be taken as typical, and is well described in Philip Agee's exhaustive study of the agency, *Inside the Company*, which is the most detailed description of a real-life covert Intelligence organisation to have been published in recent times. The CIA is headed by a director, under whom are four deputy directorates:

1. The Deputy Director Intelligence (DDI) is responsible for setting Intelligence requirements and the collation, analysis and dissemination of Intelligence. Sub-branches are organised by subject.
2. The Deputy Director Operations (DDO) is responsible for production of

clandestine Intelligence (also known as Clandestine Services – CS). Sub-branches are organised by geographical area.

3. The Deputy Director Science & Technology (DDS&T) is responsible for setting requirements, the evaluation and dissemination of Intelligence on scientific and technical subjects, and also for development of new technical methods of Intelligence collection.
4. The Deputy Director Administration (DDA) is responsible for organisation and management, personnel, training, security, finance, information services, communications and logistics.

The main areas of responsibility in the headquarters can thus be summarised as Administration, Requirements (and Dissemination), Production and Science & Technology. These correspond basically with the British SIS organisation as described by Kim Philby in his book *My Silent War*, and probably also with the organisation of the clandestine Intelligence-collection agencies of most major countries, which are covered in greater detail in the Appendix.

Overseas, the CIA's collection effort is organised into a series of 'stations' or 'bases', manned by US nationals. These are based generally on US diplomatic missions in each country, and if US forces are stationed in the country, probably also upon military bases there. The station is the CIA office in the capital of the country in which it is located, and operates under a station chief who probably has diplomatic cover in the political section of the embassy or consulate. The majority of the Station Chief's subordinate staff will also operate under diplomatic cover from the embassy or consulate, possibly in the economic or consular sections. Bases are subordinate offices to the station, and may be located in other cities or elsewhere. If the station is on a US military installation, only the chief and a bare minimum of his subordinates will have diplomatic cover, the majority being properly assigned civilian employees of the Department of Defense. Subordinate staff at stations and bases consist of case officers, technical specialists, secretarial staff, drivers and others necessary to the conduct of successful clandestine operations. Communication between stations and bases, and between stations and headquarters at Langley, Virginia, is generally by radio, cable and the diplomatic bag.

Having briefly covered the type of organisation necessary to programme, coordinate and support the clandestine collection of Intelligence by human agents, let us now look at the agents themselves. Much care and forethought is required in the selection, recruitment, training and running of secret agents, or spies, and this is the job of the case officer. The case officer will be a national of the country whose Intelligence service is running the agent, and a career officer in that service. He is the last link in the chain between the agent and the government on whose behalf the agent is working. The case officer can be responsible for running several agents, each of whom may run several sub-agents or sub-sources. For reasons of security, however, no agents can be recruited before they have been thoroughly checked out, and approval for recruitment given by the headquarters of the case officer's organisation.

Case officers are continually on the look-out for potential new agents, both for the mounting of new operations and for the improvement of existing ones. The ideal case officer will have the ability to remain completely detached while manipulating agents, although at the same time being able to develop personal rapport with them. Within the station, the case officer will have access to the technical and other support necessary in certain types of operation: locksmiths, surveillance teams, photographic equipment and experts, secret writing facilities, eavesdropping and communication equipment and expertise, micro-dot readers and safe-breakers are just a few of the facilities which, if not all available within the station, can be called upon from the headquarters of the organisation when specialist support is required.

The process of selecting potential agents is known as 'talent-spotting': suitable candidates are cultivated and tested, and their potential assessed by the case officer in consultation with headquarters. The majority of secret agents will be nationals of the country in which they are carrying out their espionage. If, after all the available data has been duly evaluated and weighed, the potential agent is cleared, and approval for recruitment is given by headquarters, the process of recruitment starts. This can take many forms, depending upon the type of operation for which the agent is required and the relationship which will have developed between the agent and the case officer during the cultivation and testing phase. Generally speaking, however, it is a delicate process which has to be approached very carefully, taking the agent's personality and character into consideration.

Agents are sometimes told for whom they will be working, in which case they are said to be 'conscious' or 'witting'; often, however, agents may provide information knowingly, but without being formally told its destination, in which case they are said to be 'semi-conscious'. An agent who passes information without knowing its destination is said to be 'unconscious' or 'unwitting'; an example of this type of agent could be a Communist Party member in a Third World country recruited under a threat appearing to come from the local security service. In nearly all cases involving conscious agents, the case officer establishes a direct personal relationship with the agent, developing a rapport while at the same time giving firm guidance and maintaining full control. As most operations involve money and most conscious agents are in the pay of the service running them, control can often be maintained by delicate handling of financial matters.

The ideal agent works at the highest level in the target country, actually creating the events or developing the weapons upon which they report and which the Intelligence service running the agent is trying to forecast. Excellent examples of the talent-spotting, recruitment and running by the pre-war Soviet Intelligence service of such agents are provided by the so-called 'Cambridge Five', a network of five bright Cambridge undergraduates with potential, comprising Harold ('Kim') Philby, Anthony Blunt, Donald Maclean, Guy Burgess and John Cairncross. Talent-spotting was carried out by a Cambridge don and another undergraduate, James Klugmann (later Secretary of the British Communist Party), and suitable talent, recruited by Soviet 'illegals' Arnold Deutsch and Theodor Maly, was then run by Soviet case officers operating under diplomatic cover from the Rezidentura in the Soviet Embassy in London.

Philby was talent-spotted for the KGB while at Cambridge as an undergraduate in 1933, and recruited by them a little later. He joined MI 6 at the behest of the KGB in 1940, and rose rapidly through the organisation to become, by 1949, the senior MI 6 representative in Washington, responsible for liaison between that organisation , the FBI and the CIA. He had even been earmarked by Major-General Sir Stewart Menzies, the then CSS or 'C', as his probable successor, until he had to dismiss Philby in 1955 for his association with Guy Burgess, another Soviet agent recruited at Cambridge while an undergraduate in the 1930s, who had been serving the KGB in the British Foreign Office until he fled to Moscow in 1951. During most of that time Philby had been in a position to 'blow' to the KGB all British SIS agent-running operations against the Soviet Union and its Warsaw Pact allies, as well as, for part of the time at least, some of those initiated by the CIA. For his services to the USSR Philby was decorated with the Soviet Order of the Red Banner in 1965; he had been one of the most phenomenally successful 'agents in place' ever, and his value to the USSR must have been beyond price.

John Cairncross, an undergraduate at Trinity reading French and German, was another recruit destined to occupy high-level positions of trust in MI 6, the Foreign Office, the Treasury and as private secretary to Lord Hankey, the Minister without Portfolio in Churchill's wartime government, and over many years he provided priceless information on the organisation and personalities of the SIS, MI 5 and the War Office, as well as detailed information about the British development of the atomic bomb.

Anthony Blunt, another of the Cambridge Five, was employed in MI 5, where he was able, over a period of several years, to pass to his Soviet masters vital information concerning British security operations against Soviet agents as well as other counter-espionage and organisational Intelligence. After leaving MI 5 at the end of the Second World War, but not before passing over to his Soviet masters a comprehensive list of MI 5 agents and sources, Blunt went on to become, first, the Surveyor of the King's Pictures, then the Director of the Courtauld Institute, and finally the Keeper of the Queen's Pictures, for which he was knighted in 1956. His knighthood was rightly withdrawn, together with his honorary Fellowship of Trinity College, before his death in 1983.

The final member of this treacherous quintet was Donald Maclean, who reached a responsible position in the Foreign Office, but who defected to Moscow with Guy Burgess after being warned of their impending discovery.

The facts that the Cambridge Five were recruited as early as the 1930s by the KGB, and that most of them reached positions of trust and great responsibility in the British establishment while remaining loyal to their Soviet masters, show the far-sightedness of the KGB and the shrewdness of its talent-spotters and recruiters at a time when SIS was shunning the universities as a recruiting ground and the CIA was non-existent. The fact that they were all successful in being taken on by such organisations as MI 5, MI 6, the Foreign Office and the Treasury without question despite their known Communist leanings while at university shows the appalling laxity of the British security vetting procedures up to and including the Second World War, the lack of continuing periodic checks during their employment by the British establishment, as well as the efficacy of the trade-craft taught them by their Soviet case officers. The failure on the part of MI 5 to uncover any of these traitors is significant when one remembers the speed and comprehensiveness with which it rounded up the German espionage organisation in the United Kingdom during the Second World War, particularly when it is also remembered that the USSR and its missions in the UK, as well as the CPGB, had been the subjects of such intensive counter-espionage work by MI 5 between the wars. The existence of a highly placed and possibly unidentified Soviet 'mole' in MI 5 during and after the war probably explains these and other failures on the part of the Security Service against Soviet espionage and agents in the UK.

In the absence of top-level agents, who because of their position in the government of their country are least likely to reveal their country's secrets to a foreign Intelligence service, an agent with access to writings or plans emanating from the top level can be almost as useful. People at this level may betray their leaders' confidence for a variety of motives, some of which have already been mentioned. One such was Günther Guillaume, an East German antagonistic to the West whose doctor father had been instrumental in tending Willy Brandt's wounds and saving him from capture during the Second World War. Guillaume was in the employ of the East German Intelligence service, the Hauptverwaltung Aufklärung, and was encouraged by them to seek employment with Brandt, who had by then become Federal Chancellor of West Germany. Brandt took him on and employed him as a valued aide and confidante. His discovery and exposure as an East German spy by a defector led to Brandt's resignation as Federal Chancellor in 1974 and to the arrest and conviction of Guillaume and his wife. The East German Intelligence service made much use of this type of agent before the unification of East and West Germany, particularly favouring the use of attractive male case officers to subvert middle-aged spinster secretaries of ministers and high-level civil servants in federal government offices, often with considerable and long-term success.

A third and lower grade of prospective agent is someone who has access to a target area. They may be trained to open secure filing cabinets, copy classified documents or place listening devices in conference rooms or offices where conversations on classified subjects take place. Lastly, there are agents who can assist in operations without themselves having access to the source of information: for example, by renting houses or other accommodation, buying vehicles or other equipment, acting as a courier or operating a radio.

The types of agent mentioned above might be termed 'primary sources', but 'secondary' operations are often necessary to target these sources. Secondary operations can involve using surveillance teams to follow people in the streets, setting up of observation posts (OPs) to watch comings and goings to and from target buildings, photography in its various forms, telephone tapping and 'bugging' buildings and vehicles, opening mail and gaining access to airline and ship passenger lists and cargo manifests. Such operations may well yield high-grade Intelligence in their own right, but they are more often used to identify the really important target for possible recruitment. They are very useful for acquiring knowledge of a target's personality, which may be helpful in assessing their probable reaction to a recruitment approach, as well as how best to make the approach to ensure the greatest chance of success.

To keep agent-running and support operations secure and free from discovery or penetration involves the use of 'cover' and 'trade-craft': cover is the story woven around a secret operation to give it an apparently legitimate purpose, while trade-craft comprises all the tricks and tools of the trade to keep a covert operation secret. Cover involves the use of cover names and pseudonyms by the case officer and their colleagues and the provision of cover employment for them, for example as an employee of a government department or as a legitimate businessperson. The maintenance of a high standard of trade-craft in any operation is essential: human lives are often at stake, and agents will continue to work more happily for an organisation that maintains their security, and hence their morale, than for one in which security is poor. The agents themselves will almost certainly require considerable training in the necessary techniques, as well as in the use of technical and communications equipment. These techniques will include how to select places for clandestine meetings, counter-surveillance techniques prior to and after clandestine meetings, concealment devices, safety and danger signals, how to counter audio penetration of meeting sites, use of the telephone, use of disguise, use of 'cut-outs' or go-betweens to reduce the frequency of meetings between agent and case officer, and methods of communication, to name but a few.

Communication with agents is perhaps the most difficult and yet the most crucial element of trade-craft. While a personal meeting between agent and case officer is both the easiest and the most efficient method of communicating, it is also the most insecure and dangerous, and can therefore be used only sparingly. Such meetings can be arranged in hotels, public buildings such as museums, other tourist attractions, houses or flats ('safe houses') obtained for the purpose, vehicles, public parks or isolated woods, railway or underground stations, or other places where eavesdropping or surveillance is difficult. Wherever they take place, they require the most elaborate security precautions and cover. Normal communications are better arranged through third parties ('cut-outs') or hiding places where messages can be left ('dead drops' or 'dead letter-boxes' in SIS and CIA jargon, *dubok* in the Soviet services), such as hollow trees, loose bricks in walls or special portable containers designed to look like discarded rubbish or stones. The latter were particularly favoured by the former KGB as it is easier to find places where they can be used unobtrusively. An agent will normally be given several alternative dead-letter drops, which will be used in an agreed sequence but not in rotation. They will have been told how to signal in some way, such as a chalk mark on a wall or lamp-post, when they have loaded the drop, as well as being given a system whereby they can indicate danger, safety, a request for a meeting or for its postponement, and other things when necessary. Another method of passing an agent's report is the 'brush contact', which can be used, for instance, in public lavatories or pedestrian subways where motion is uninterrupted and surveillance more difficult. In totalitarian countries with highly effective counter-espionage organisations, such as the former USSR, different methods of agent communication are necessary: encoded transmissions in normal radio programmes are often used to give agents their tasks, while their reports are often sent through the international civilian mail to a 'post-box' in a non-Communist country, using secret writing techniques to hide the real message in an apparently innocuous letter.

Agents will almost always require continuous training in the writing of reports, as well as in all the other aspects of cover, trade-craft and communications already mentioned. They must learn to separate fact from rumour or opinion, to specify clearly the source for each piece of information, to make sure that dates, names, numbers and places are accurately recorded, and that the specified format for reports is always followed. Particularly in military matters, where formation signs, vehicle numbers and other markings on uniforms and equipment can be of crucial importance, they must be taught to draw or describe such things accurately. With equipment of all types, but particularly with radar and other antennae, gun calibres, munitions and vehicles, some indication of dimensions must be given. Agent or secret source reports are normally disseminated to the evaluators with a separate cover sheet giving the source's degree of 'consciousness', their access to the type of information given in the report, and their previous reliability, together with their pseudonym. Also issued with the report will be a sheet, for return to the issuing agency, on which the recipient can grade the report for value and probable accuracy, as well as a detailed criticism of the report for the guidance of the case officer, including requirements for further information from the agent.

If agents are discovered or 'blown', they may be 'turned' against the service by which they are employed by the counter-espionage service of the country against which they have been spying, and this is always a danger to be carefully considered and guarded against when using human agents. Such an agent is known in the trade as a 'double agent' or 'double', and the use of this type of agent against their employers is known as 'playing them back'. A classic example of this type of operation was the 'turning' by the British of nearly all the German agents sent to the UK during the Second World War: Operation DOUBLE-CROSS, run by MI 5 and the Twenty Committee, succeeded in deceiving the Germans into believing that they had a large and successful network of agents in the UK, as a result of which they were ready to believe the deceptions fed to them via these turned agents concerning the Allied invasion of north-west Europe in June 1944.

Another successful use of a double agent was in Australia in the early 1960s, when a Soviet secret agent, Lieutenant-Colonel Boris Animisovich Skoridov, was unmasked by this means. Skoridov, under his operational name of Ivan Skripov, was posted to Canberra in July 1959, as the first Soviet diplomat to take post there after the resumption of diplomatic relations between the USSR and Australia; these had been broken off five years previously because of Soviet espionage in Australia. Skripov was officially the First Secretary at the Soviet embassy, but his real task was to set up a new espionage network to replace the one smashed five years earlier by the Australian security service. His mission failed, firstly because

1. Charles Wilson, Director of the T & S Department of the War Office in 1871 and, as a Lieutenant-General, responsible for reorganising military Intelligence after the débâcle of the Crimean War. (National Army Museum)

2. Colonel (later Lieutenant-General Sir) Henry Brackenbury, the first Director of Military Intelligence at the War Office in 1885. (National Army Museum)

3. Major-General Sir John Ardagh, who became DMI in 1896, in Staff full-dress uniform. A brilliant DMI, he was cleared of blame in 1903 for the lack of Intelligence prior to the Boer War. (National Army Museum)

4. Major-General Sir Vernon Kell, the head of the Security Service MI 5 from 1909 until 1940. (Author's collection)

5. *No. 20 St James's Square, London, formerly Adair House and home to the War Office Intelligence Branch from 1874 until it was moved to Queen Anne's Gate in 1884. (Author's photograph)*

6. *Nos 16 & 18 Queen Anne's Gate, London, which were home to the War Office Intelligence Branch from 1884 to 1901, when it moved to Winchester House in St James's Square. (Author's photograph)*

7. The War Office (now known as the Old War Office Building) in Whitehall, to which the Directorate of Military Operations moved in 1906. It remained the home of much of the Directorate of Military Intelligence until the 1960s. (Author's photograph)

8. The underground office of MI 10(a) in Montague House Annexe, Whitehall, in 1945. This building was demolished to make way for the new MoD Main Building. (Author's photograph)

9. The Ministry of Defence Main Building in Whitehall, which houses much of the Defence Intelligence Staff; some specialist branches, however, work from various other buildings in the area. (Author's photograph)

10. No. 54 Broadway, London (Broadway Buildings), the pre-1939 and war-time HQ of both the Secret Intelligence Service and GC & CS, as it is now after rebuilding. (Author's photograph)

11. The new headquarters of the Secret Intelligence Service at Vauxhall Cross, London. (Author's photograph)

12. Thames House, Millbank, the present headquarters of the Security Service. (Author's photograph)

13. The 'Enigma' cypher machine, showing the typewriter-type keyboard at the top and the plugboard on the front. Behind the keyboard are the rows of lamps which lit up to indicate the letters being transmitted, and behind them are the three rotors. (Royal Signals Museum Collection)

14. The 'Enigma' machine with the top cover removed, showing the lampholders and the three rotors, each of which carried the letters of the alphabet. (Royal Signals Museum Collection)

15. The American TR-1 high altitude reconnaissance aircraft. Under its alternative designation of 'U-2', this was the type of aircraft in which Captain Gary Powers, USAF, was brought down over the Soviet Union in May 1960. (USAF)

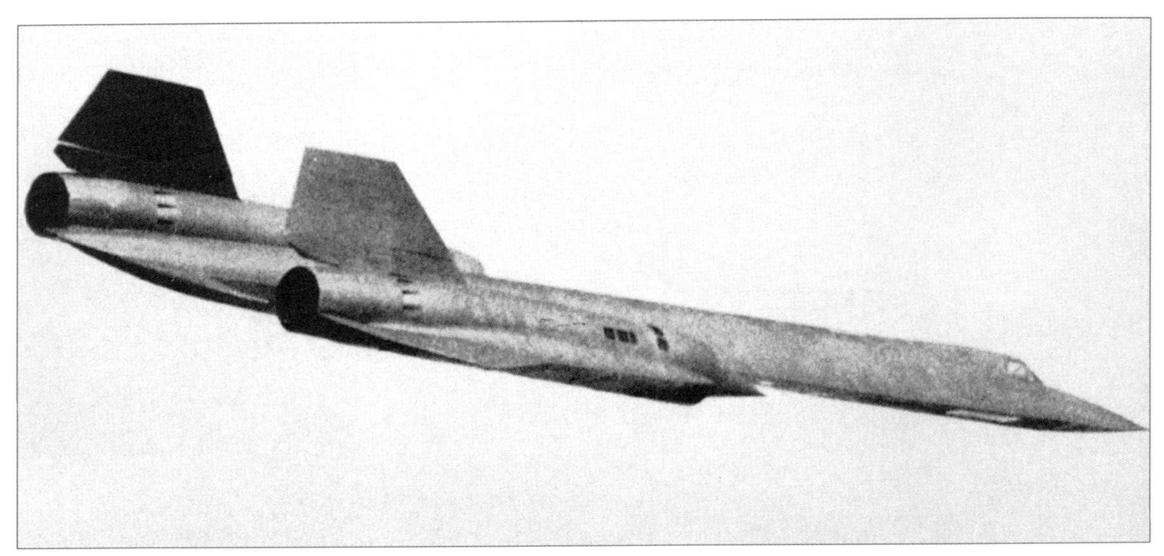

16. The Lockheed SR-71 high altitude reconnaissance aircraft flying over RAF Mildenhall in an air display. The SR-71 replaced the TR-1/U-2 for high-level, high-speed reconnaissance missions. (Barry Jones)

17. The ZB-298 battlefield surveillance radar enables troops to detect movement out to a range of 10,000 m by both day and night. As it can see through smoke and in complete darkness it complements the image intensifier; the latter is a passive instrument, emitting no detectable radiation, but the radar is active and therefore vulnerable to detection. (Marconi Avionics Ltd)

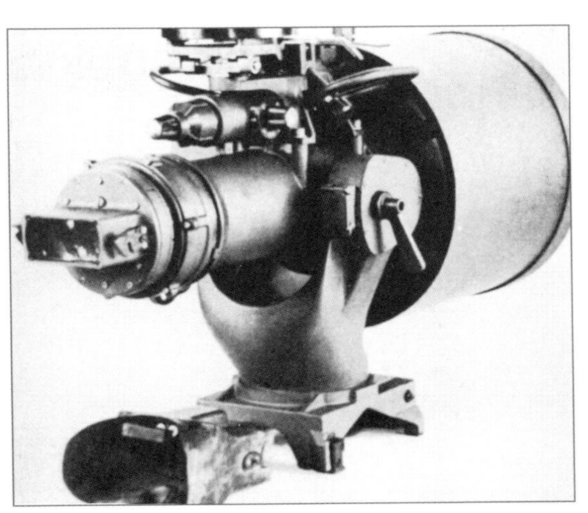

18. The night observation device (NOD) is the largest of a range of passive image intensifiers in service with the British Army for observation by starlight. (Pilkington PE Ltd)

19. The Cymbeline mortar and gun-locating radar is the third of the modern systems for battlefield surveillance in service with the British Army. Passive far infra-red thermal imagers form the fourth. (EMI Electronics Ltd)

20. Infra-red linescan image of the Imperial War Museum at Duxford, Cambs., by day, from an altitude of 1,000 ft. (W. Vinten Ltd)

21. Infra-red linescan image, taken by night, of the IWM at Duxford, also at 1,000 ft altitude. Compare this with Plate 20. (W. Vinten Ltd)

22. Computer-enhanced image, from a US reconnaissance satellite, of the Russian Nikolaiev 444 shipyard, showing a 75,000 tonne nuclear-powered aircraft carrier under construction there. (Associated Press)

23. An oblique satellite image, computer-enhanced, of the Russian aircraft carrier shown in the vertical view in Plate 22, under construction in 1984 at the Nikolaiev 444 shipyard on the Black Sea. (Associated Press)

24. The first public appearance of the Soviet heavy tank Iosef Stalin 3 in the Berlin Victory Parade in 1945. The unique and sophisticated armour layout, its low silhouette and its combination of a high velocity 122mm (4.8in) gun with thick and well-sloped armour shook Western tank designers and users. (Tank Museum 2448/D5)

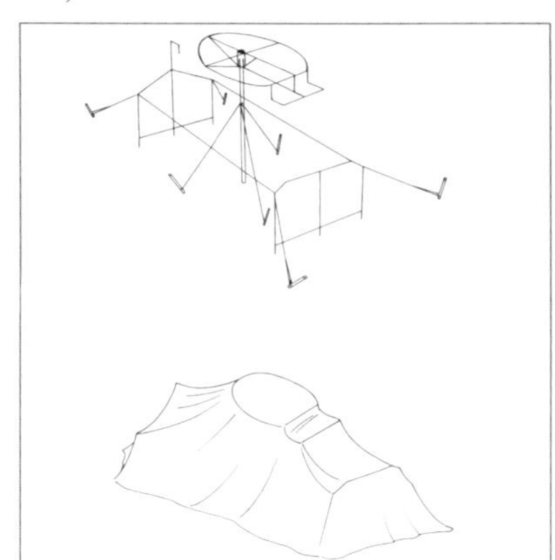

25. An early dummy tank scheme produced by 'A' Force in the Western Desert. It consisted of a simple framework over which was draped a camouflage net or tarpaulin.

26. A later wooden dummy tank built by 'A' Force, mounted on a truck chassis to make it more mobile and quicker to install. (Imperial War Museum)

27. A tank-track simulator, consisting of a length of tank-track wrapped around the wheels of a two-wheeled trailer, towed by a mobile dummy tank. (Imperial War Museum)

28. A 'Sunshield' mounted on a cruiser tank to disguise it as a truck. (Imperial War Museum)

29. The ultimate in dummy tank design – an inflatable, fully detailed model Sherman tank with traversing turret and all markings. (Dunlop Ltd Archive Project)

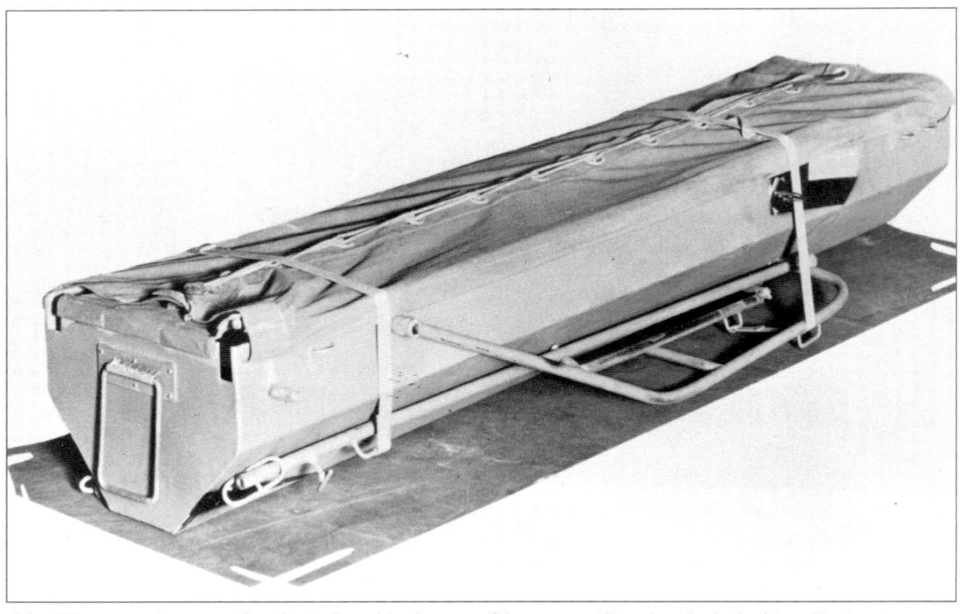

30. The carrying case for the inflatable dummy Sherman. (Dunlop Ltd Archive Project)

the Australian security service, alerted by the earlier Soviet espionage efforts, was particularly vigilant, and secondly because, unknown to him, a woman agent to whom he entrusted a particularly important task was a member of the Australian service. This woman was played back to Skripov as a double agent by the Australians until, in 1963, enough evidence had been gathered against him for him to be declared *persona non grata* by the Australian Government and expelled.

Recruitment of 'agents in place' in closed societies such as the former Soviet Union is extremely difficult, and greater success is achieved in recruiting nationals of such countries when they are outside their own countries in diplomatic missions, international organisations, press agencies, airlines or visiting on business. The pressures experienced by former Soviet personnel overseas due to the rigidly conformist routine imposed upon them, for largely internal security reasons, tended to generate a natural dissatisfaction when contrasted with the greater freedom of thought, movement and communication which they saw all round them in the West. The aim of the Western Intelligence services was therefore to spot those already some way down the road to defection and to help them along the rest of the way, persuading them to remain 'in place' as long as possible. Recruitment possibilities were, and still are limited, as only certain designated persons in Soviet and Russian missions and offices abroad can have personal relationships with foreigners; permission for such relationships is normally limited to Intelligence officers and those diplomats and administrative personnel whose need to deal with foreigners is legitimate. Nevertheless, much success has been achieved by Western Intelligence agencies in obtaining Intelligence in this way.

As mentioned above, attempts are always made to persuade the potential defector to remain at work, in order to remove or copy files and other documents or to install audio eavesdropping equipment. Elaborate arrangements for safe houses to keep the agents hidden before relocation to their destination country and for their eventual evacuation have to be made and reviewed well before the actual defection, and account must be taken of the reaction to be expected from their embassy or office, and responses to it. The reaction of the Soviet embassy in Ottawa to the Gouzenko defection mentioned in Chapter 4 was fairly typical.

Another type of agent much favoured by the former Soviet Union was the 'illegal', who tended to be a Soviet national, provided with the identity of a national of the target country who had died abroad and whose age, height and weight resembled that of the 'illegal'. 'Illegals' are often the offspring of mixed parentage, with fluent knowledge of the target country's language, and may spend years in training and perfecting their cover story (or 'legend', as the Russians call it), into which much work and research will have gone. Their cover is often so deep that their real identity can only be revealed after yet another cover identity has been peeled away, like the skin of an onion. In addition, they will usually travel to the country in which they are to operate under a third, temporary, cover. After safe arrival in the country against which they will be operating, and having fully established their cover there, 'illegals' are used as head agents, in communication with their case officers either in the embassy or agency HQ, recruiting their sub-agents as required from suitably placed nationals of the country of their adoption.

To enable the adoption by 'illegals' of alternative but genuine identities, the Soviets required a large number of genuine foreign passports ('shoes' in their jargon), and their quest for these from the effects of dead members of the International Brigade and others who fought in the Spanish Civil War is another example of their Intelligence foresight. They also used the identities of Westerners who have visited Russia and other former Warsaw Pact countries and who have died there, thus acquiring not only a passport but also a birth certificate.

An 'illegal' cannot hope to operate or travel under a fictitious identity in a modern bureaucratic society. Even in a country such as the UK, where identity cards are not issued to everybody, individuals accumulate a mass of official and unofficial documentation, starting with birth registration, as they progress through life, and no fictitious identity could stand up to investigation once it was checked against the records. The Russians overcome this difficulty by taking a genuine identity and weaving a 'legend' around it, mixing fact with fiction.

The interlinked cases of Rudolf Abel and Konon Molody, in the USA and UK respectively, serve to illustrate the extreme care taken by Soviet Intelligence, both in building up the cover of their 'illegals' and in training them. Abel carried a US passport identifying him as Andrew Kayotis. The real Andrew Kayotis had been born in Lithuania and had become naturalised in the USA. In 1947, Kayotis was granted a visa to visit relatives in Lithuania, but he subsequently died in hospital there. Abel used this identity to travel from France to Canada, and thence across the border into the United States, in the autumn of 1948. After his arrival there, he abandoned the identity of Kayotis and assumed that of a certain Emil R. Golfus, a US citizen who had died shortly after his birth in New York in 1902. Under this identity, as an artist and photographer, Abel organised, and ran for ten years until his arrest in 1957, a network of Soviet agents in the USA. After his arrest he never admitted that he was a spy, only that he was an illegal immigrant. Imprisoned for espionage, he was exchanged four years later for the captured US U-2 pilot Gary Powers. According to Soviet sources, his real name was Aleksandr Ivanovich Belov, born in the USSR in 1903, but even this may have been another of his many aliases, as the name Rudolf Abel had been used in France in the 1920s by several Soviet agents, and 'Abel' is a combination of the initial letter of his first name and the first three letters of his surname. After his death in the USSR in 1971, his gravestone in Moscow revealed his name as William Fisher, born in England!

Two of Abel's associates in the New York spy ring managed to evade arrest; they were Morris and Lona Cohen, who escaped to Canada. They then went via Singapore, and possibly Moscow, to New Zealand, picking up en route birth certificates and a wedding certificate in the names of a New Zealand couple, Peter and Helen Kroger, who had died some years earlier. In December 1954, with New Zealand passports, they arrived in the UK, where they set themselves up as support agents for another Soviet 'illegal', Gordon Lonsdale. Peter Kroger opened an antiquarian bookshop in London, and the couple settled into a bungalow in Ruislip which became the main base for what became known as the 'Portland spy ring'. It was also, possibly by design, near to the GCHQ headquarters, then located at Eastcote, and also to the US Army base, the signal traffic from which could be expected to mask the occasional transmission to Moscow from the Krogers' clandestine radio transmitter.

Gordon Lonsdale was the cover name used by Konon Trofomovich Molody, another Soviet 'illegal', born in the USSR the son of a prominent writer and taken to the USA at the age of ten by an aunt who passed him off as her own son. After education at a private school in Berkeley, California, his aunt gave him the option of applying for US citizenship or returning to the USSR. He chose the latter, and returned to Moscow in 1938. During the Second World War he was recruited into the GRU, to whom his knowledge of English and his American accent made him an attractive proposition, and he is believed to have spent eight years training for his assignment and learning his cover. The real Gordon Lonsdale had been born in Canada of a Canadian father and a Finnish mother who separated in 1932; he went to Finland with his mother, and that was the last heard of him in the West.

Molody arrived in Canada in 1954 under an unknown identity and surfaced as Lonsdale in Vancouver. After starting work as a salesman and collecting various documents, such as a driving licence, to support his new identity, he went to Toronto, where he obtained a passport in the name of Gordon Arnold Lonsdale. On this passport he crossed into the USA and travelled to the UK in 1955, having contacted Rudolf Abel in New York en route. In London he enrolled as a student of Chinese at the School of Oriental Studies, and entered the vending and amusement machine business as a cover for his Intelligence work. When the Portland spy ring was rolled up by MI 5 in January 1961, Molody was sentenced to twenty-five years' imprisonment; however, he too served only a small part of his sentence before being exchanged for another Western agent held by the USSR, British businessman Greville Wynne. In his writings after his return to Moscow, Molody continued to insist that he really was Gordon Lonsdale, but this fiction was well and truly destroyed by the doctor who had circumcised the real Gordon Lonsdale as a baby; Molody was not circumcised, and this had been the fatal flaw in Molody's carefully constructed 'legend'.

If the Soviet task of planting 'illegals' in the bureaucracies of the West is difficult, requiring much forethought and many years of preparation, how much more difficult must it be for Western Intelligence agencies to do this in the very much more closed societies and more rigid bureaucracies of the former Soviet Union and its allies? Western Intelligence organisations nearly always prefer to employ 'illegals' who are natives of the country being penetrated, and to recruit these behind the Iron Curtain was a virtual impossibility. In this case it is preferable to rely upon the technological advantage which the UK and the USA currently enjoy over the former Warsaw Pact countries.

The days when spies such as Abel and Molody were of crucial importance to Intelligence collection are coming to an end – if they have not already done so – and in their place are the technical collection systems involving satellites, electronic detectors and computers. The highest priority of military Intelligence collection in the nuclear age is the size, location, range, targeting and yield of the opposing side's nuclear arsenal, and the chances of human agents being able to gain access to this level of information, to communicate it to their masters and, above all, to keep it up to date are minimal. There is, however, a reluctance by many in the secret Intelligence services of the world to admit this. Traditionalists and even romantics at heart, they remain convinced that however costly agents may be to train, run and support, a human spy on the ground is worth more than a satellite in space. The truth lies somewhere between these extremes: covert Intelligence from human agents still has its uses, particularly in regional conflicts where the level of technology is relatively low, such as in Afghanistan, Central America and the Near East, but between nuclear alliances such as NATO and the former Warsaw Pact, high-technology methods produce better and more reliable results.

It is often said that one picture is worth a thousand words, and this has been an overwhelming advantage of the air photo over the human agent since the first hand camera was carried aloft in an aircraft in the First World War. After the initial difficulties of interpretation had been overcome by special training of interpreters, air photos gained a high reputation for accuracy, speed of response and reliability in the plotting of enemy positions, gun emplacements, forming-up areas, stores and dumps, defensive works, roads and other communications such as railways and waterways. Air photos could give the big picture, whereas agents could give only a part of it, and that as it was when they had last observed it, days or even weeks previously. Since the outbreak of the Second World war, the development of this form of Intelligence collection has been very rapid, due to the introduction of jet-propelled aircraft with greatly increased speeds and operating altitudes, and developments in computerised and inertial navigation aids and imaging techniques in both the visible and other spectra made possible by the discovery of new lens, detector and film emulsion materials. In peacetime, however, countries do not take kindly to the unauthorised overflying of their territory by foreign aircraft, and with the post-war developments in anti-aircraft radar, there are now few countries in the world incapable of at least detecting, if not engaging, such overflights.

The US Government had foreseen this situation, especially with regard to its overflights of the former Soviet Union and its Warsaw Pact allies with the U-2 and SR-71 aircraft. However, it was essential in the prevailing climate of the Cold War, with its consequent difficulty both of recruiting and communicating with 'agents in place' in these countries, that knowledge of Soviet nuclear and missile development, testing and deployment should be available to US Government planners. In addition, prior to the U-2 overflights very little was known of the geography, communications, industrial capacity and factory locations of the USSR. The advent of a more relaxed international climate, with the resulting arms limitation or reduction agreements such as SALT and START, did nothing to ease the requirement, as such agreements require verification, and the reconnaissance satellite is one of the few means available of acquiring this verification that is accepted internationally.

Developments in satellite reconnaissance have been described in Chapter 4. Since a satellite can be detected and its orbit predicted with great accuracy, it can scarcely be said to be covert in its overflight of foreign territory; what is covert is its task. The most usual tasks of reconnaissance satellites are to gather IMINT and ELINT, and the sensors involved in the collection of these types of Intelligence have hitherto been 'passive' in operation: they emit no radiation themselves, but detect electronic or thermal radiation from the equipment, particularly radar, and the countryside over which the satellite is orbiting. It is thus not possible for hostile equipment to detect the type of reconnaissance being carried out by the satellite, or even whether or not the satellite is in fact engaged in reconnaissance of a military nature. Passive sensors, however, whether operating in the visible or the far infra-red spectrum, are severely affected by adverse weather in the target area; cloud cover is not penetrable by these means, and other methods of imaging, using radar or some other 'active' system, have to be employed in these circumstances. Such a system has already been tested on the US space shuttle and will probably by now be operational on US reconnaissance satellites; while guaranteeing results regardless of the weather conditions over the target area, the active nature of the imaging system alerts the country over which the satellite is passing to the fact that reconnaissance is being carried out by the satellite. The mission therefore becomes overt rather than covert.

However, a reconnaissance satellite, even with passive Intelligence-collecting sensors, is of little use unless it can transmit the information it has gathered back to its base, and for Intelligence to be timely, this must be done as soon as possible after it has been collected; it is in this phase of the operation that the satellite ceases to be passive or covert and its Intelligence 'take' becomes vulnerable to interception.

Various methods of transmitting the information from satellites have been tried; the first Corona/Discoverer satellites relied upon recoverable photographic capsules, ejected from the satellite by a trigger mechanism and parachuted to earth, but these were vulnerable to bad weather as well as to failure of the parachute to open, while defects in the ground radar sometimes made it impossible to find capsules that had successfully re-entered the earth's atmosphere. Defects in the ejection mechanism added to the difficulties with this type of system, of which 15 out of the first 16 satellites launched failed to operate correctly, and the Corona system did not achieve dependability until January 1961. A similar but improved method of parachuting the capsules to earth was employed in the next series of US military reconnaissance satellites, the SAMOS (Satellite And Missile Observation System). With this series, the capsule was ejected at prearranged times and parachuted into a preselected area of the Pacific Ocean, in which US warships were standing by to pick it up. Unfortunately, there were usually several Soviet trawlers in the area, and occasionally they managed to get to the capsule first; for this reason, the method of pick-up was changed and specially adapted aircraft were employed to catch the capsules in the air. Nowadays, the information from satellites is encoded and transmitted to base by radio; it is vulnerable to interception, but this method does at least have the advantage that the information is received back at base in real time. The decryption of the transmitted information is a very difficult and lengthy task, however.

The Soviets employ similar if technically less sophisticated sensors on their military reconnaissance satellites; these are numbered in the Cosmos series, well over 2,000 of which have been launched so far, and which vary widely in both size and function. They are launched from the missile bases at Kapustin Yar, Tyuratam and Pelsetsk, and they also generally use a capsule ejection system to send their information back to earth, in this case over former Soviet territory. Apparently, Russian satellites continue to employ small nuclear reactors to power their sensor and communication systems. As was found when Cosmos 954 broke up on re-entry and fell to earth on Canadian territory, this type of power generator can pose a radiation hazard, and it was abandoned by the USA some years ago in favour of the lighter, less dangerous and technically more advanced systems currently in use.

While little is known about Russian reconnaissance satellites, it is a relatively easy matter to identify those engaged on military reconnaissance missions by their low-altitude polar orbits and their relatively short flight life. On this basis, it appears that the Russians have launched an average of some thirty missions of this type annually throughout the period of their operations in space, equivalent to about one-third of all Russian space launches in this period. In addition, the cosmonauts manning the Salyut and Mir space stations are believed to have carried out photography for military Intelligence purposes. The USA, on the other hand, is believed to have launched some fifty-five reconnaissance satellites in the period from 1970 to 1984, according to the publication *Aviation Week and Space Technology*, all launched on Titan rockets and most carrying simple, high-resolution cameras. Their newer, larger KH-11 satellites can transmit their reconnaissance images digitally by radio to base, a method that increases the active life of the satellite by removing the limitations imposed by carrying only limited supplies of photographic film, as well as both simplifying and speeding up the image-collection process.

Apart from their imaging sensors, reconnaissance satellites carry passive sensors to detect electronic emissions from the territory over which they are passing; they thus play their part in the covert collection of both ELINT and SIGINT. Satellites in geo-stationary orbit above fixed points on Earth can also be used for secure communication with human agents in hostile territory. The former Soviets positioned one of their Cosmos satellites over Iran for this purpose prior to the Islamic revolution there, obtaining reports of troop movements and defensive installations along the Iranian frontier with the former USSR from agents by radio until the Iranian counter-espionage service caught one of them in the act of transmitting. Geo-synchronous orbiting satellites in the Rhyolite series have been positioned by the USA over former Soviet and Chinese missile ranges to intercept the telemetry involved in Soviet and Chinese missile launches. The Rhyolite series replaced the earlier, classified Ferret electro-magnetic reconnaissance satellites of the US Air Force.

Signals Intelligence has proved a valuable and increasingly prolific source of covert Intelligence since the First World War. In wartime, the interception and decryption of signals between the opposing High Command and its subordinate commands in the field gives a very much more up-to-date and accurate picture of the enemy's strategic situation and proposed actions than any number of human agent reports, however well-placed the agents involved may be. In peacetime, in the absence of prisoner of war reports and captured documents, SIGINT can be even more valuable, particularly when combined with reconnaissance satellite imagery Intelligence. SIGINT is collected passively, and provided the security of the resulting information and its source is well guarded, the potential enemy has no idea that its communications have been penetrated. However, the delay between the interception of a message and its decryption and dissemination to those interested can limit the usefulness of this source of Intelligence in wartime to the strategic rather than the tactical; in addition to the delay involved in identifying and breaking the enemy codes, the sheer quantity of information produced demands a large expenditure of staff time and computer-power, as well as posing a problem of priorities in both decryption and dissemination.

The official history of British Intelligence in the Second World War has, somewhat belatedly, revealed the part played by GC & CS and SIGINT in that war, with the result that the biographies and memoirs of several Allied commanders, as well as the official campaign histories, have had to be reassessed. As a result of this, the pendulum has swung too far the other way, and the impact of SIGINT during the war across the whole spectrum of military Intelligence has been exaggerated. For instance, with regard to technical Intelligence on the weapons and equipment of the German Army, the effect of SIGINT was virtually nil; the vast majority of technical Intelligence came from prisoners of war, captured documents and the examination of captured equipment, SIGINT contributing no more than confirmation of the name of a new weapon reported by prisoners of war, and warning of its issue to units.

In the important area of new weapons developments, such as nuclear, biological and chemical (NBC) weapons, there was no indication from SIGINT, or indeed from any other source, that the Germans had developed, tested and stockpiled not one but three different nerve gases by the end of the war. Similarly with the V-weapons; virtually all the information on which the British appreciation of German wartime missile development was based came from captured documents, air photo-reconnaissance, prisoner of war interrogations and examination of rockets and components which had gone off course and crashed in Sweden. It is also fair to say that the majority of tactical military Intelligence during the Second

World War came from the same types of source, with some additional information from tactical 'Y' intercepts. The SIGINT emanating from GC & CS was too late, too vague and at too high a level. Where SIGINT came into its own was at the strategic and political level, where processing delays of weeks or even months had less effect. Such delays at the tactical level would have been quite unacceptable and would have turned Intelligence into history.

In peacetime, however, in the absence of prisoner interrogation and with a paucity of documentary Intelligence, SIGINT comes into its own, particularly when attempting to gather Intelligence on a secretive and closed country such as Russia or the People's Republic of China, and particularly when combined with imagery Intelligence from reconnaissance satellites. Such is the flood of accurate and timely Intelligence from these two sources that the temptation must be to rely entirely on these technical sources rather than to take the risks involved with human sources. However, if belt and braces are reckoned to be a safe combination, how much better to have the string of HUMINT in addition to the belt of SIGINT and the braces of IMINT to prevent us being caught with our trousers, or defences, down.

The advent of wireless brought into existence a new field of Intelligence, the comprehensive study and analysis of communications systems which later became known as signals Intelligence or SIGINT. This study involved:

1. Intercepting wireless messages – a process which in the British Army came to be called 'Y'
2. Breaking down the codes and ciphers in which they had been transmitted – a process known as cryptanalysis
3. Locating their place of origin – a process known as direction-finding (DF)
4. Establishing the characteristics of the communications networks involved – a process later known as traffic analysis (TA), so that their behaviour, procedures and techniques could yield further information
5. The interpretation of the resulting information by specialists.

The terminology was standardised in October 1943, the generic term SIGINT covering all the above processes and any Intelligence produced by them. The term 'Y' Service covered both interception of signals and operation of DF, although in the USA this was known as 'radio Intelligence service' (RI). The term 'traffic analysis' covered the study of communications networks, signals procedure, call-signs and low-grade codes; 'low-grade' in this sense refers to the degree of security provided by the code, not the importance of the traffic using it.

In the UK and USA, both the existence and the purpose of organisations specialising in the interception, decryption and dissemination of military and diplomatic communications of friendly and enemy countries alike was a very well kept secret for many years after the end of the Second World War. The secrecy was essential to the continued functioning of this highly successful passive and covert method of collecting Intelligence, but if only one ill-judged report or remark was acquired or heard by the target country, the flow of information would be cut off instantly and, in that cipher, permanently. Such ill-judged disclosures were made in 1920 by the British Government when it published a series of intercepted messages between the Soviet Government and the Soviet trade delegation in the UK in an attempt to expose Soviet encouragement of subversion in British industry and the suborning of the British Labour movement. Not satisfied with the results obtained from the first such disclosure, which the Soviets virtually ignored, further extracts from intercepted Soviet telegrams were leaked to the British press in September 1920 – again, incredibly, without noticeable Soviet reaction. It was not until January 1921 that the Soviet codes were finally changed for another reason, and not until four months later that the GC & CS were again able to decrypt at least some of the Soviet communications between Moscow and its trade mission in London.

Continued British dissatisfaction with the USSR, both for its support for the Communist Party of Great Britain and its subversion in India led to further disclosures of British intercepts of Soviet communications by the British Foreign Secretary, Lord Curzon, in an ultimatum to the Soviet Government in May 1923. Amazingly, this disclosure, although acknowledged by the Soviets as showing that the British were reading their official communications, again had little effect on the interception and decryption of those communications by GC & CS until late that year; then the Soviets introduced a new range of codes which for some months defeated the best efforts of GC & CS to decrypt.

As if their earlier efforts to compromise the best source of British Intelligence on the USSR had not been sufficient, in May 1927 the British Government made further disclosures of successfully decrypted Soviet communications in support of their charge of Soviet espionage in the UK and in justification of their decision to break off diplomatic relations with the Soviet Union. In the parliamentary debate on this decision, government ministers fell over themselves in an orgy of indiscretion: in addition to quoting verbatim from intercepted Soviet telegrams, the Foreign Secretary quoted from intercepted Comintern correspondence, while the Home Secretary divulged counter-espionage information concerning Soviet espionage networks and agents.

This third British indiscretion produced the result that should have followed from the first – the Soviets switched to the 'one-time-pad' for encoding their communications with their overseas representatives, and this system, which, if correctly used, is virtually unbreakable, proved to be so to the decrypters of GC & CS. The result was that from that date until the Second World War, the British Government was deprived of its most valuable and reliable covert source of information on the USSR and its Intelligence-gathering organisations. It is tempting to speculate whether, if the British had continued to have access to Soviet diplomatic traffic up to the war, Philby, Blunt, Burgess and many others could have survived as Soviet agents to inflict their damage on British and Allied foreign policy, Intelligence and counter-espionage agents and operations, nuclear weapons, and other technical and scientific research and development programmes.

If senior government ministers, politicians and their senior civil service advisers are unable to understand the vital importance to national security of preserving the integrity and secrecy of valuable covert Intelligence sources such as SIGINT, how much less is the average member of the press or public likely to do so? Calls from vested interests for freedom of information and the abolition of the Official Secrets Act appeal to the average citizen's sense of justice and fair play, and find ready and sympathetic listeners among the public. Without revealing too much, it is difficult to educate the public to understand the vital necessity of keeping certain things completely secret, and for a very long time. A priceless source of reliable information on a secretive and closed society such as the former Soviet Union must never again be compromised by politicians or government officials who do not understand the importance or scope of a covert source such as SIGINT. The irresponsible behaviour of the British Government of the 1920s in this regard was culpable in the extreme.

It is at first sight unfortunate that so much has already been revealed since the ending of the Second World War, although with Philby in the USSR from January 1963 until his death in May 1988 and the information on subsequent British and US developments in SIGINT passed to the Soviet Union by the Walkers, Prime and other British and US traitors, it must be assumed that both the British and US organisations, equipment and capabilities in the field of SIGINT have been known to the former Soviet Intelligence services. However, the books that have been written on Ultra and the GC & CS organisation since the Second World War have at least helped to educate the public, and possibly also the politicians, as to the existence, purpose and value of SIGINT, even if they reveal little about post-war progress in this field.

Signal Intelligence derives from the interception and decoding of coded foreign radio messages. The interception of radio signals is a relatively easy task; in fact, in the early days of wireless, with fine tuning not yet invented and the variable strength and direction of transmissions due to poor understanding of antenna design and atmospheric effects, it was sometimes difficult to prevent unwanted interception of strange signals interfering with the clear reception of the desired station. It was fortuitous interception of German signals on the Western Front during the First World War which led to the deliberate British interception efforts. The Army organisation responsible was MI 1(b) in the War Office, and it was this branch, together with the corresponding Admiralty organisation NID 25 (Room 40), formed the foundation upon which the post-war SIGINT establishment, GC & CS, was built in November 1919.

If interception of radio signals is easy, however, decryption of their enciphered contents is not. It is a very different and specialised matter, and in the early days of British SIGINT during the First World War both the Admiralty and War Office MI 1(e) found it necessary to form specialist teams of decryption experts. These too were absorbed into GC & CS on its formation. The battle between the encoders and the decrypters has been going on for centuries, and like that between attack and defence, will probably never end. What one person's ingenuity can invent, the ingenuity and persistence of another will disentangle in due course. The more complicated the code or cipher, the longer it will take to decipher, and the longer the decryption process takes, the less timely will be the Intelligence contained in the result – this is why, in wartime, SIGINT's value to a commander of a field formation in action may be limited.

The introduction of Enigma mechanical encoding machines into the German service in the late 1920s represented a major advance for the encoders in this battle. It was known in GC & CS, from experiments they had made with similar machines that, properly used, the ciphers generated by these machines were unbreakable by cryptanalysis, and the future for the British organisation therefore looked poor.

The Enigma machine resembled a primitive typewriter; above a conventional QWERTY keyboard it had a series of matching illuminable windows (the lampboard) lettered to correspond to the keyboard layout. Where the platen of a normal typewriter would be were three moving rotors, each carrying the twenty-six letters of the alphabet on its rim. The front face of the machine's case (the plugboard) also carried the letters of the alphabet, arranged in three rows, as on a typewriter keyboard, each letter having two plugholes for a two-pin plug. By varying the setting of the three rotors, the encipherment could be changed. Typing a letter on the keyboard caused another letter (which one depended on the setting of the rotors) to light up on the lampboard, and varying the rotor settings gave a choice of some 17,500 permutations. By the additional use of the plugboard, the number of permutations could be increased to 5×10^{92}, representing a cryptanalytical task quite beyond the unassisted human brains of GC & CS to solve. The machine did have disadvantages, however: it was slow in use, as the message had first to be typed letter by letter, and the corresponding letter illuminated on the lampboard had to be noted and written down in the text to be transmitted; also, any numbers had to be spelt out in full, as there were no numerals on the key-, lamp- and plugboards.

The story of how the pendulum swung back in favour of the decipherers, with the help of the Polish and French SIGINT organisations, was told in Chapter 2, although it must be emphasised that many German Enigma ciphers, correctly used, were never broken. It was largely as a result of the problems posed to GC & CS by the German introduction of electro-mechanical enciphering machines that the computer was born during the Second World War, but at first electro-mechanical devices known as 'bombes' and based on one or more modified Enigma machines were developed. These moved the machine's rotors through the very many permutations required to find a particular key, a process that could take up to two hours. Eventually, the GC & CS organisation employed some 100 bombes of increasingly sophisticated design and large size, spread over several sites and operated by some 2,000 WRNS personnel.

The bombes were electro-mechanical predecessors of the present-day electronic computer, and since the war, GCHQ (the successor to GC & CS) and the NSA (its US equivalent) have been in the forefront of computer development. The first computers had to rely on the thermionic valve, and were thus of very large size, with limited computing power and generating very large quantities of heat; in addition, the valves used had only a very limited life, and breakdowns – often at embarrassing times – were frequent. The first breakthrough in size reduction, increased capacity and reduced power consumption came with the introduction of the transistor; a further one came with the invention of the micro-chip and its micro-circuits, and data-processing speed will be further increased with the introduction of the optical computer.

However, such developments help the cryptographer as well as the cryptanalyst in the eternal battle between them. Codes and ciphers of ever-increasing sophistication and complexity can be both invented and broken by their use, and it is not too difficult to imagine the SIGINT organisations of the world's powers growing ever larger in size, but being gradually drowned in an ever-deepening sea of computer-inspired but largely unintelligible paper. In this connection, however, it is encouraging to believe that Russian and Chinese capability in computer design lags somewhat behind that of the UK and USA, a belief strengthened by the strenuous efforts made by these countries to overcome the West's bans on export to them of the latest Western technology and to gather, by espionage, details of the latest Western advances in electronics and computer technology.

To the military Intelligence complex, SIGINT can be a major Intelligence source of crucial importance in both peace and war. In war, its tactical usefulness can be limited by the time taken to decrypt and disseminate its contents, but this time-lag can be less of a drawback where strategic matters are concerned. Tactical usefulness can also be inhibited by considerations of security, limiting access to the information and preventing disclosure of its source to unindoctrinated personnel. However, it is possible to foresee an even greater importance for SIGINT in the future, as advances in electronics enable photographs, drawings, maps and documents to be transmitted over radio networks as well as by wire. The interception and interpretation of this type of information will greatly increase the value of SIGINT, especially to the technical and scientific branches of military Intelligence organisations.

The last, but not the least, of the four main sources of covert Intelligence mentioned earlier in this chapter is electronic Intelligence (ELINT). As could be deduced from the comparatively short history of electronics, ELINT and its extension, electronic warfare (EW), are comparatively recent arrivals on the Intelligence scene, having made their first tentative appearance during the Second World War with the development by both sides of radar and air navigation aids. With the extraordinary progress made in the development of electronics since that war, ELINT has kept pace as a part of EW, and now represents a very important and thriving source of military Intelligence, covering a wide spectrum of emitters of electro-magnetic radiation.

A radar set consists basically of a transmitter, a receiver, a highly directional antenna and a viewing screen. The transmitter emits pulses of electro-magnetic energy from its antenna which, if they encounter an object such as an aircraft in their path, are bounced back from it to the receiver; the time that elapses between the transmission of a pulse and the arrival of its reflection at the receiver is measured by the set, and knowing the speed at which electro-magnetic waves travel, can be converted into the distance to the object. The radar operator can thus read on the screen both range and bearing of a target. It was in this form, as an improved method of detecting and engaging enemy aircraft from the ground, that radar made its first successful appearance during the Second World War. Since that time, it has branched out into many forms, land-based, airborne and ship-borne. It can be used as a navigation aid for ships and aircraft, as a form of battlefield surveillance, as a fire control system for weapon systems on land, sea or in the air, for airborne mapping, for mortar and artillery location, for missile tracking and guidance, and for many other purposes.

In all these applications, radar has been highly successful, although, as with any new weapon, after the initial advantage gained by its early success, measures to counter it have not been far behind. Radar is an 'active' system, dependent for its working upon the emission and reflection of a stream of electro-magnetic pulses; it is not difficult for these pulses to be picked up by receivers other than that in the radar set, and it is on this inherent weakness that the measures employed to counter radar are based. These measures are known as electronic counter-measures (ECMs) and form another facet of EW for which ELINT is essential. Radar, while not itself an instrument of EW, is nevertheless its main target, and it is on hostile radars that electronic reconnaissance is carried out. ELINT arising out of electronic reconnaissance provides, among other things, much of the information on which the design of ECM and radar warning receivers can be based. It can also provide similar information regarding ECMs, from which suitable electronic counter-counter-measures (ECCMs) can be developed. ECMs are basically composed of deception and decoy techniques together with jamming, and can be deployed against communication networks as well as against radar and missile guidance systems. Of these techniques, jamming, being an active system, is the easiest to detect and to beat. In addition to information concerning the frequencies and operating characteristics of hostile radar systems, ELINT can provide the geographical locations of such systems; by putting this information together with technical and other Intelligence on hostile radar systems, the Intelligence organisation can build up the hostile order of battle.

To gather ELINT, listening and analysis systems are deployed in aircraft, ships, ground stations and space satellites as near as possible to probable sources of hostile radar emissions. The hostile radars are provoked into operation by the intrusion of either the listening vehicle itself or by another into the operational ambit of the target, and the resulting electronic emissions are recorded for analysis either then and there or back at base. It is for this purpose that Russian Bear and Badger aircraft constantly overfly the territories of NATO countries and Russian trawlers and shadowing aircraft dog the naval exercises carried out by the NATO navies on the high seas.

The USS *Pueblo* and U-2 incidents, in which the specially equipped US former merchant vessel was captured by the North Koreans off the Korean coast and the US electronic reconnaissance aircraft was brought down over the former USSR have already been mentioned, but there have been many other similar incidents of the shooting down by the former USSR of US and British aircraft engaged in electronic reconnaissance since 1950, in Europe, over the Baltic, off the Russian coast, and in the Far East. At least one was brought down in error, for which the former Soviet Government paid compensation to the US Government, but there is little doubt that others were involved in clandestine activities over and around the former Soviet Union, although the full facts are unlikely ever to be made public. Nigel West, in his book *GCHQ*, gives details of several such downings of US reconnaissance aircraft from 1950 to the present, as well as mentioning the electronic reconnaissance efforts of the British and Swedish ELINT organisations.

Not unnaturally, ELINT operations are highly sensitive and given the highest security classification by the governments concerned. Little is known about such operations outside the limited circle of those involved in them, and such little information as is publicly available has come mainly from the trials of the shot-down U-2 pilot, Gary Powers, the captured crew of the *Pueblo* and various US and British traitors spying for the former Soviet Union and found guilty of having handed over secrets relating to the US and British ELINT organisations, their equipment and operations.

The most damaging spy from the British point of view was Geoffrey Prime, a long-term senior employee of GCHQ in Cheltenham, who had been passing the secrets of this most secret of establishments to his controllers for ten years prior to his arrest in April 1982. He was caught not because of any counter-espionage effort or suspicion, but because, after his arrest for sexual offences against young girls, he told his wife of his espionage activities and she in turn told the police. After one of the most far-reaching and detailed counter-espionage investigations ever to have been carried out in the United Kingdom, Prime made a full confession in June; he had apparently been recruited by the Soviets in 1968 and, since that date, he had told them everything he knew about GCHQ organisation, personnel, locations and operating procedures. After being found guilty of espionage at his trial in November 1982 he was sentenced to thirty-five years' imprisonment, a mighty sentence, but one which could scarcely match the damage to national interest caused by his crime.

The NSA in its turn suffered, along with GCHQ, when two members of its organisation, William Martin and Bernon Mitchell, defected in 1960. Close, even intimate friends, they had both had considerable experience in the US Navy prior to joining the NSA in 1957. At a press conference in Moscow some time later, both made damaging allegations concerning GCHQ and the NSA, but it was the investigation into their defection that caused even greater repercussions – it revealed that they were homosexuals, who, as Communist Party sympathisers, should never have been allowed access to classified information. Worse, it brought to light twenty-six other NSA employees who were sexual deviates, two Directors (of Security and Personnel) who had been parties to forgery of employment records, and one Communist.

The worst leakage of NSA secrets, however, occurred from 1958 to 1963 through a chauffeur and courier, Sergeant Jack Dunlap. Dunlap had joined the NSA in 1958 as a chauffeur, but it was after he became a courier carrying classified documents between various NSA buildings that the damage was done. Apparently, he sold to the KGB copies of the documents with which he had been entrusted, to such good effect that he was able to run three cars, two boats and a mistress; it was this expensive lifestyle that led to his being investigated and his subsequent suicide in July 1963. It was never possible to discover just how much Dunlap had passed to the KGB, but as he was estimated to have been paid some $60,000 by them, it seems probable that he photographed virtually every document that passed through his hands and passed copies to them.

It is hard to overestimate the damage done to the NATO ELINT effort by spies such as Prime and Dunlap, defectors such as Martin and Mitchell, and the equipment and documents captured in the *Pueblo* and U-2 incidents. Several other lapses of security have occurred, for which personnel involved in the Intelligence collection effort have been tried and acquitted or transferred to less sensitive posts. Meanwhile, Russian efforts to penetrate the British and US ELINT and SIGINT organisations have continued unabated while both organisations have tightened up their vetting and security procedures in an attempt to counter them.

Despite *Glasnost*, *Perestroika* and the apparent growth of détente between East and West, national security requirements dictate that the cut and thrust of the Intelligence war will continue and increase in intensity for the foreseeable future. Certainly, the British Parliament's Intelligence and Security Committee, reporting in 1996, said that available information suggested that Russian espionage was being stepped up, particularly in the commercial and industrial fields. Both the SVR (Russia's foreign Intelligence service, its replacement for the Soviet KGB) and the GRU (the Russian military Intelligence service) have renewed their efforts to post Intelligence officers to London under diplomatic or media cover.

CHAPTER 6

British Military Deception, 1939–45

Deception lies at the heart of Intelligence, of all kinds and not only military. The agents with their cover stories, the case officers with their false names and cover stories, the heads of station with their cover jobs in the embassy or trade mission, the government ministers who deny the existence of an Intelligence organisation – all are practising deception, and in many cases their lives and the lives of others are dependent upon it being practised successfully.

In military operations, success is very often dependent upon surprise being obtained. Von Clausewitz wrote that surprise lies at the root of all military activity, and surprise comes from successful deception. Deception in military operations, briefly mentioned in Chapter 2, has been employed both strategically and tactically since time immemorial, and many notable examples of its successful application are to be found in the history books; two early ones which spring immediately to mind are the wooden horse used to bring about the fall of Troy and the pretended retreat of the Norman cavalry during the Battle of Hastings.

The land battle on the Western Front in the First World War gave little opportunity for either tactical or strategic surprise, although every opportunity to try to hide troop concentrations by means of camouflage or to mislead the enemy by concentrations of dummy tanks or guns was taken. In fact, the British Armies in the Battle of the Somme disdained surprise, so confident were they of their superiority in numbers and firepower, but such cases have been rare and are seldom successful. In that war, the best examples of deception leading to the achievement of surprise came from General Allenby's campaign in Palestine.

All surprise in war rests upon concealment, both of one's strength and of one's aim, and security is one of the basic principles of war. But few commanders will be content merely to conceal their strength and intentions. Intelligent commanders wishing to impose their will upon the enemy will try to deceive them as to both. Weak commanders will try to give an appearance of strength, while if attacking, they will try to weaken the enemy at the point chosen for attack by feinting at other parts of the front. They will try to get inside the enemy commander's mind, assess his appreciation of the situation, and then provide, by all available means, the information that will lead the enemy commander to make the dispositions that will best suit their own plan. The object of deception is to affect the actions of the enemy.

To be successful, therefore, deception demands not only good security, but also good Intelligence; the latter will give the commander an accurate picture of the enemy's strength and dispositions, and probably a good idea of the enemy commander's appreciation of the situation and plans for dealing with it, while the former will keep from the enemy a commander's true intentions and means of implementing them. At the lowest tactical level it is possible to anticipate enemy reactions with a fair degree of certainty, particularly if the enemy's military doctrines have been available for study and if the commander has gained experience of enemy tactics in previous encounters. The higher one goes up the tactical scale towards the strategic, however, the more the psychology of the individual enemy commander enters the equation; within a theatre of war at the more senior levels of command, considerations of personality, logistics and even of politics become increasingly dominant. For those directing the war at the highest level, it is normally so difficult to make a sufficiently accurate assessment of enemy capabilities and intentions that it is rarely possible to impose a deception plan plausible enough in all its aspects to affect the enemy's actions.

The Second World War produced many more deception plans, both successful and unsuccessful, than any previous war, perhaps due largely to the many more channels for deception that modern technology, particularly radio, had opened up, as well as the more mobile nature of the warfare involved compared to that on the Western Front in the First World War.

Tactical deception, at unit or formation level, is a comparatively simple operation involving few outside agencies or facilities; a few dummy tanks here, extra camouflage there, radio silence, artillery barrages on wrong targets can and often are employed to implant the wrong idea in the enemy commander's mind. Intelligence is probably limited to interrogation of a few prisoners, air photo-reconnaissance, patrols and possibly radio intercepts from 'Y' (tactical SIGINT), while security of the operation in the shortened time scale of tactical operations is easily maintained.

Strategic deception at theatre command level is more complicated, involving the Intelligence-collection agencies, especially SIGINT, the security services (including military field security), a specialist deception organisation and air photo-reconnaissance. However, strategic deception of an enemy's high command as distinct from its forces in the field is a very different matter, involving lengthy and complicated planning, the coordination of many disparate organisations, the availability of strategic Intelligence of the highest reliability and at the highest levels, and a very high level of security throughout the planning and execution stages. While the execution of the plans will be an operational matter and a military responsibility, the Intelligence and security services involved will be largely civilian, and the relationship between them and the military staffs can be delicate and often acrimonious.

Because of the scale of the problems presented by such strategic deception plans, they can be attempted only rarely, and are successful even less often. British (and, later, Allied) use of deception in the Second World War covered all these levels and reached a high degree of competence in planning and execution. It started in the United Kingdom after the evacuations from Dunkirk and Cherbourg, when the consequent weakness and disorganisation of British armed forces and the constant and very real threat of invasion made deception of the Germans regarding the strength of the defences of the British Isles essential. While the Axis powers in the Second World War successfully employed strategic deception – prime examples being the German invasion of the USSR in June 1941 and the Japanese attack on Pearl Harbor in December of that year – it was the successful British, and later the British and US, employment of tactical and strategic deception on the largest scale which provides the best illustrations of the art of deception in war.

United Kingdom, 1938–42

The British deception campaign began almost accidentally, when MI 5 and, later, GC & CS and MI 6 found that they had the means of misleading the enemy. Even before war had been declared, a German agent known by the British as 'Snow' and to the Germans as 'Johnny' reported to the British security authorities in September 1938 that he had been nominated by the Abwehr as their senior agent in the UK. This appeared to be confirmed when the Abwehr provided him with a radio set the following year. Just to be on the safe side, he was detained in Wandsworth prison when war broke out, where he was reunited with his radio set and commenced transmitting reports to Germany under the guidance of MI 5, which gradually provided him with a notional network of sub-agents. By the summer of 1940, MI 5 was running a network of some half-dozen agents which appeared to command the full confidence of the German Intelligence service.

MI 5 did not then realise that this network represented the sum total of the German Intelligence agents operating in the UK at this time; in addition, the Intelligence supplied to the enemy through this network of double agents was very much on an *ad hoc* basis, as MI 5 was not yet properly organised or equipped to maintain it. Because of the many tasks confronting the security authorities in the dark early years of the war, it was not until the summer of 1941 that B Branch of MI 5, under Captain Guy Liddell, was eventually able to concentrate its subordinate branch B1(a) fully on the running of its double agents.

Nevertheless, during the 'phoney war' from September 1939 to June 1940, the 'Snow' network was able to satisfy the Abwehr's requirements for Intelligence from the UK. After the fall of France, however, with the probability of an imminent German invasion, the Abwehr was suddenly required to provide a flood of information on the United Kingdom, and hurriedly recruited, trained and despatched to the UK, by air and sea, as many agents as it could find. However, as they were provided with forged identity and ration cards based on information provided by 'Snow', they were easily identified on arrival, and there was little difficulty in recruiting most of them as double agents.

During this same period, the British Isles were constantly being overflown by Luftwaffe reconnaissance aircraft, which, enjoying air superiority, could photograph more or less at will and as required. The aim of British deception measures at this time was therefore to exaggerate the strength of its defences, both fixed and mobile, and conceal the location of factories and airfields by means of the use of camouflage and dummies. Concrete anti-tank barriers and barbed wire entanglements were conspicuously erected along the south and east coasts of England, and many daytime and night dummy airfields were constructed. From June to October 1940 the dummy airfields were so successful in deceiving the Luftwaffe recce flights that they absorbed twice as many attacks as did the airfields they were protecting. Dummy factories and rail depots were built, giant smokescreen-generating plants were installed to conceal real factories, and deceptive fires known initially as 'Special Fires' and later as 'Starfish' were installed in 1940 near eighteen important industrial towns and several airfields – these were lit after the first wave of bombers had attacked a target, to draw subsequent waves away from the target and on to open country. Responsibility for the coordination of deception arrangements involving camouflage within the United Kingdom was given to a new department headed by Colonel Sir John Turner, a retired officer who was the Director of Works in the Air Ministry; not surprisingly, the department was known only as 'Colonel Turner's Department', to conceal its real purpose. Initially, Colonel Turner was only to advise the

Ministry of Home Security on deception schemes other than camouflage, but his remit was broadened in 1940 to cover all deception schemes

Deception in the United Kingdom in these early war years was thus divided between the dummies, decoys and camouflage provided by Colonel Turner's Department and the false information being fed to the Abwehr by the double agents of MI 5. With the possibility that the UK could at any moment become a theatre of war, the military authorities considered, not unreasonably, that the handling of double agents should be their responsibility, and certainly MI 5 was experiencing increasing difficulty in extracting convincing information from the military authorities to be passed on via the double agent network. The problem clearly extended beyond the competence of the military, naval and air authorities while at the same time being of great sensitivity.

After some discussion between the chiefs of the armed services and others involved, the 'W' Board, composed of the three Service Directors of Intelligence, Captain Guy Liddell of MI 5, the Director of SIS and the Chairman of the Home Defence Executive, came into being in January 1941 with the task of coordinating all aspects of deception within the United Kingdom. The 'W' Board had no terms of reference, and no limits were placed upon its responsibilities. Its main task was to give guidance on deceptive material to be passed to the Germans via the double agent network, and the Twenty Committee (running Operation DOUBLE-CROSS) was set up at the same time, with executive responsibility for the selection and approval of such material. Like the 'W' Board, the Twenty Committee had no terms of reference, but its task, broadly speaking, was to elicit, collate and obtain approval for the traffic passed via the double agents, and to act as a point of contact between the service Intelligence directorates, MI 5, SIS and the Home Defence Executive.

Despite the ministrations of the 'W' Board, however, MI 5's B1(a) branch continued to have difficulty in extracting approval from the service departments, and particularly from the War Office, for the traffic submitted to them. To MI 5 they seemed to be more concerned with emphasising the areas in which information could *not* be passed than those in which it could. But as Sir John Masterman wrote in his book *The Double-Cross System in the War of 1939–45*:

> The War Office . . . pointed out that we were still on the defensive, and that the great gains of deception could only be garnered when we passed to the offensive. In a defensive phase the chief merit was concealment; in an offensive phase the misinformation we could pass to the enemy.

The important thing, however, was to obtain enough information to make the traffic credible, and MI 5 was able to do this. Throughout 1941 the double agents continued to build up their credibility, although the War Office continued to doubt MI 5's claim that they now controlled 80 per cent of German espionage in the United Kingdom. Luckily, this claim was soon to be substantiated by SIGINT: the hand ciphers used by the Abwehr for communicating with their agents had been broken by GC & CS at Bletchley Park in December 1940, and their Enigma ciphers were broken a year later, enabling MI 5 not only to claim control of 80 per cent of German espionage networks in the United Kingdom, but also to confirm the Abwehr's acceptance of the reliability of these networks. It was confirmation of this acceptance that enabled the Allied deception schemes produced to cover Allied offensive operations later in the war in Europe to be so outstandingly successful. Not only were the British able to influence German thinking on British economic and military matters, but from the briefs which the German case officers supplied to their agents, MI 5 was able to learn where German information was weakest and what their priorities were for the acquisition of information.

This satisfactory situation was complicated early in 1942, when Bletchley started reading the Enigma traffic between the Abwehr station in Madrid and Berlin. This revealed that reports were being received and passed by the Madrid station, allegedly from a German agent in the UK, which were rich in ludicrously inaccurate detail – so inaccurate, in fact, that it was clear not only that the agent could not be resident in the UK, but also that he had in all probability never visited the British Isles. His identity remained a mystery until he contacted a representative of MI 6 in March. It transpired that he was a young Spaniard of good family who had become profoundly disillusioned with totalitarian régimes as a result of the Spanish Civil War and was passionately devoted to promoting a British victory. After recruitment by the Abwehr he had retired to Lisbon with a map of the United Kingdom, a *Guide Bleu* for England, a Portuguese study of the British fleet and an Anglo-French dictionary of military terms, from which slender resources coupled with a lively imagination he had compiled a series of some forty lengthy reports from his own 'observations' and those of a notional network of sub-agents.

MI 6 initially told MI 5 nothing of his existence, but after his recruitment as 'Garbo', the Twenty Committee was finally informed in March 1942. As a result, he was brought to England, where he came under MI 5's B1(a) Branch in April, but neither MI 5 nor the Service Intelligence representatives on the Twenty Committee were informed of the existence of the decrypts of the Abwehr traffic between Madrid and Berlin, and a highly anomalous situation resulted. In their ignorance of this traffic, they regarded 'Garbo' with understandable suspicion, based on their knowledge of his obviously invented reports, and it was not until MI 6 released the decrypts in June 1942 that 'Garbo' was enabled to be incorporated in the double agent orchestra playing to the Abwehr from the UK. Now the services had to be persuaded to make more positive use of the powerful weapon which the combination of the double agent networks and SIGINT had placed in their hands.

Quite how powerful a weapon this could be was outlined in a memorandum presented by the B1(a) representative to the 'W' Board in July 1942, extracts from which are reproduced below:

> It is reasonably certain that the only network of agents possessed by the Germans in this country is that which is now under the control of the Security Service.

Three supporting arguments were advanced: first, a watch on mail sent to known Abwehr cover addresses had revealed no uncontrolled agents; second, there was no evidence of payments being made to any uncontrolled agent through the usual channels in either Lisbon or Madrid; third, the Radio Security Service (RSS) had not detected any uncontrolled agents operating. The memorandum went on:

> It is inconceivable that there should exist in England any organisation or network of agents so carefully concealed, so different in its nature from anything of which we have knowledge, and so wholly divorced from the network which we control that it is able to operate without colliding at any point with the controls we have described above . . . It follows from this that if we, being in control of the network, choose to say one thing, and a single agent who is not controlled to say another, it is we who stand a better chance of being believed . . . we have been able to watch the Germans making arrangements for the [agents'] despatch, discussing arrangements arising from payments sent to them or letters received from them, and passing on from one Stelle to another their reports and comments on them . . . it follows that the General Staff in this country have, in MI 5 double agents, a powerful means of exercising influence over the German OKW.

The 'W' Board and the Twenty Committee had been created to supervise the supply of information and misinformation to the Abwehr via the double agent network, but neither body was responsible in any way for the formulation or implementation of deception policy. Although in the early, defensive, years of the war there was no British deception policy, overall responsibility for deception rested with the Joint Inter-Service Security Board, a body established in February 1940 under the auspices of the Chiefs of Staffs' Joint Intelligence Sub-Committee. With no clearly defined operational targets at this time, there could be no deception policy to back them up, but tentative steps in the direction of strategic deception had been taken in 1941, when Colonel Oliver Stanley MC had been appointed as Head of the Future Operational Planning Section of the Joint Planning Staff, a cover title for his real job as Controlling Officer in charge of strategic deception. A tentative plan for a notional attack on the Norwegian coast (Operation HARDBOILED) was approved by the Chiefs of Staff in December 1941. Although it gave the deception organisation some useful experience in the planning of strategic deception operations, it is not known whether or not it was successful in deceiving the Germans into reinforcing their Norwegian garrison.

In July 1942, during the visit to the UK of the US Joint Chiefs of Staff, the decision had been taken to launch an Allied invasion of French North Africa. The combination of the B1(a) memorandum with the fact that there was now a clearly defined positive operational plan for the services was the spur required to establish an overall deception policy and the means of coordinating and controlling it. In August, the London Controlling Section of the Chiefs of Staff Committee was formed, with Lieutenant-Colonel J.H. Bevan of the War Cabinet Office as its head. His appointment, and the creation of the organisation he headed, was inspired by General Sir Archibald Wavell's experience with a similar organisation which he had created in the Middle East during his tenure as C-in-C Middle East from 1939 to 1941.

THE MIDDLE EAST, 1939–42

After the evacuation of British troops from the Continent of Europe in 1940, the Middle East was the only theatre of war in which British forces were engaged. With the entry of Italy into the war in June 1940, the British Army in Egypt was faced with an enemy greatly superior in numbers, while based in countries whose populations were indifferent if not actively hostile, forming a society of a complexity difficult for foreign security organisations to understand, let alone control. There was therefore no possibility of imposing in territory occupied by the British the complete control over sources of information which was possible in the United Kingdom; in addition, any information supplied by double agents was liable to be contradicted by information from undetected enemy agents or the freelance purveyors of information who abounded in the soukhs of Cairo, Alexandria and Beirut. This region has been well described as an Intelligence officer's paradise and a security officer's hell.

Apart from the numerical superiority of the enemy and the difficulty of controlling sources of Intelligence and counter-Intelligence in the Middle East theatre, the terrain was highly unfavourable for tactical or strategic deception. The Western Desert is a fairly featureless landscape, in which it is difficult if not impossible to hide large forces or their movements; there is little natural cover, and movement of vehicles is immediately given away by the clouds of dust thrown up by their wheels or tracks. If deception was to be employed, therefore, it had to be of a specialised kind designed by specialists. A specialist organisation known as 'A' Force, under the command of a Lieutenant-Colonel Dudley Clarke, was therefore set up for the purpose in November 1940 by the C-in-C Middle East, General Sir Archibald Wavell, a highly imaginative officer who had learnt the art and value of deception in a similar environment in Palestine in the First World War at the feet of his idol, General Sir E.H.H. Allenby.

In addition to the military General Staff Intelligence and Field Security staffs, the British Intelligence organisation in the Middle East theatre comprised the Combined Bureau Middle East (CBME), a cryptanalytic centre and offshoot of GC & CS at Bletchley Park, Security Intelligence Middle East (SIME), which filled many of the functions filled by MI 5 in the UK and had close affinities with it, and the Middle East Intelligence Centre, which coordinated Intelligence both for GHQ Middle East and the JIC in London. 'A' Force was officially constituted in March 1941 as Advanced HQ, 'A' Force, Dudley Clarke working under conditions of great secrecy in a converted bathroom in the GHQ building, receiving his orders directly from General Wavell and dealing only with the Chief of Staff and the Directors of Operations and Intelligence at GHQ. He had two officers and only ten other ranks to assist him, the other ranks forming the basis of two notional units, known initially as 38 RTR and 39 RTR, which were responsible for the manufacture, erection and display of dummy tanks, artillery and trucks.

Initially, these dummies were of simple construction, consisting of collapsible wooden or metal frames forming the skeleton of the weapon or vehicle with canvas tacked to the frame to form the skin. As time went by and experience of sandstorms and other vagaries of the desert weather was gained, the construction of the dummies became more solid and more sophisticated, better able to stand up to the forces of nature. Tank outlines made of wood were mounted on lorry chassis to make them more mobile, while tank covers in the shape of trucks and known as 'sunshields' were built in large quantities to disguise concentrations of tanks as parks of soft-skinned vehicles. Later still, in Italy and NW Europe, tank and gun dummies were made out of inflatable rubber, and were very realistic indeed, even at close range. Aural deception was added to the visual deception devices in early 1942 by the use of recordings of tank movement, played over a public address loudspeaker system mounted on a truck or tracked vehicle. Dummy tank tracks in the sand were made by the ingenious adaptation of two-wheeled trailers with lengths of tank track wrapped around their wheels, towed by trucks.

'A' Force itself was a notional brigade of the 'Special Air Service', itself at that time a notional body based in Transjordan; the SAS later became '1st SAS Brigade' and 'A' Force became just that, with the role of the 'control and administration of units of GHQ Troops operating dummy weapons'. The notional 'Special Air Service' was formed as a result of the capture of an Italian officer's diary which disclosed the Italians' fears of the possibility of airborne landings in their rear; these fears were played on by the notional arrival of the '1st SAS Brigade' in January 1941, followed by others, and the deception was augmented by bogus radio traffic, displays of dummy gliders built by 'A' Force's craftsmen and by the judicious leaking of rumours. At the same time, the arrival of a notional '10th Armoured Division' was projected to enemy Intelligence. Although the success of these deceptions was unknown, experience in the dissemination of false information and the display of dummy equipment was being gained by the British which would stand them in good stead when it came to the large order of battle deceptions successfully practised in the run-up to, and the execution of the Allied landings in south-east Europe and France in 1943 and 1944.

'A' Force was also responsible for working with MI 9, the prisoner escape organisation, and for running its own agent and double agent networks. However, the latter were not a majority of the enemy's secret sources of Intelligence, and were therefore likely to be less influential on the enemy's appreciation of the situation than were those in the United Kingdom. It was not until December 1941 that 'A' Force was given the advantages enjoyed by the Twenty Committee in the UK of being made privy to the operations and developments of the Abwehr Intelligence networks, in this case controlled from Ankara and Istanbul, by GC & CS breaking the Abwehr Enigma cipher. 'A' Force could now identify and deal with agents controlled by the Abwehr, verify the credibility of its own double agents as well as seeing which of their planted messages gained credibility and which did not, and finally, in conjunction with the reading of the enemy's operational traffic, gain a reliable insight into the enemy's fears and expectations.

By March 1942 'A' Force was sub-divided into three sections: Control (with responsibility for plans, policy and administration), Operations (with responsibility for physical execution of plans and tactical decepton) and Intelligence (with responsibility for implementation of deception schemes through the channels controlled by the Intelligence and security bodies). These latter were now numerous, the recently promoted Colonel Clarke having built up an extensive network of sub-operators stationed in East and South Africa, Cyprus and the headquarters of the

Eighth Army in Egypt and Ninth Army in Syria. To enable the planting of deception information, the sub-operators had at their disposal correspondents in Ankara, Istanbul, Lourenço Marques, Malta and Asmara. In the summer of 1942, when Lieutenant-General Maitland Wilson organised Persia & Iraq Force (PAIForce), 'A' Force opened a linked HQ there, operating mainly from Persia.

The first major strategic deception plan which the enlarged and reorganised 'A' Force was called upon to execute was the cover plan for the invasion of Madagascar in April 1942, in which the notional objective of the invasion force was painted as the Dodecanese Islands. The deception was successful enough to ensure that the German garrisons of Rhodes and Leros were placed on full alert. The success of this ploy, playing on the real and known fears of the Germans regarding these islands, encouraged 'A' Force to repeat it the following June, when cover was required for a convoy which the Royal Navy was urgently trying to get through to the beleagured island of Malta. Rumours of an imminent attack were circulated in the Middle East, while all communications between the outside world and Iraq, Palestine, Syria and Egypt were cut for forty-eight hours. No explanation was given, but 'A' Force channels indicated that an attack on the Dodecanese was imminent. These measures caused a gratifying stir in enemy Intelligence circles, but he failed to act and Colonel Clarke therefore judged that the deception failed; no forces were diverted to the defence of the Eastern Mediterranean and the convoy suffered heavy losses. Similar failure attended the attempt by 'A' Force the following month to persuade the enemy that an attack on Crete was imminent, in order to prevent forces from the garrison of the island being rushed to reinforce Rommel's troops in Cyrenaica; the threat of attack was duly relayed by the Abwehr but was ignored, and the reinforcements were despatched despite all. But although it would be difficult to identify any significant occasion on which the strategy and dispositions of the Axis forces in the Middle East were affected by the imaginative efforts of 'A' Force between May 1941 and July of the following year it must be remembered that this was a period of trial and error, and only since December 1941 had the advantage of access to the Abwehr Enigma material been available to 'A' Force. Change began with the initiation of Operation CASCADE in March of 1942, the first comprehensive order of battle deception plan for the whole of the Middle East theatre of operations and one which formed the basis for all subsequent deception plans for the cover of the Allied invasions of western Europe, both from the Mediterranean and from the United Kingdom.

The groundwork was both intricate and complicated; a start had already been made by 'A' Force in 1941, with the invention of the SAS Brigade (which later came into being) and 10th Armoured Division to add to the actual forces in the

Western Desert and 7th Division to add to the Cyprus garrison, but CASCADE was a comprehensive plan for inflating the notional strength of British and Commonwealth forces throughout the Middle East. The notional units and formations had to be created in Army Orders and Army Council Instructions just as real ones, and they had to be shipped out from their home bases in the United Kingdom, New Zealand, India and South Africa; this meant close liaison with the army staffs in the countries concerned, as well as the creation of orders of battle within the formations, divisional signs and some visible evidence of their presence if they were likely to be seen by uncontrolled enemy agents. Within range of enemy intercept services they had to generate their own radio traffic, and their movements and administration had to be documented; and, once created, they had to stay in existence or some plausible reason for their elimination from the order of battle to be provided. In 1942, 'A' Force created a notional Corps HQ (25 Corps), seven notional infantry divisions (including two Indian and one New Zealand) and the notional 15th Armoured Division. The following year they added a bogus 12th Army, a bogus 14 Corps, eight more infantry divisions (including two Polish and one Greek), three armoured divisions and one airborne division; all of these formations and units had a real core in a training or L of C unit, and careful records were kept, both in Cairo and London, showing where they really were, where they notionally were, the enemy's probable knowledge of each one and, from SIGINT and captured documents, the conclusions the enemy had drawn. An analysis of documents captured during and after the Battle of Alamein, carried out by 'A' Force in November 1942, showed that the greater number of these bogus formations and units had been accepted by enemy Intelligence and incorporated in their estimates of the British order of battle; British strength in armoured units was over-estimated by 40 per cent and in infantry units by 45 per cent. What is more, these inflated figures remained in the German Intelligence estimates until the end of the war.

UNITED KINGDOM, 1942–43

We left the United kingdom deception organisation in August 1942 with the reconstitution of the London Controlling Section and the appointment of Colonel J.H. Bevan to head it. The reorganisation could not have been more timely, with the agreement of the British and US Combined Chiefs of Staff to a landing on the coast of French North Africa later that year, but a more gruelling test for the new-born organisation could scarcely have been devised. While the full details of the operation had still to be decided, it was clear that a landing on a probably hostile shore had to be mounted from two widely-separated bases, each thousands of miles from the objective; one (combined US and British) assault force was to sail from Britain, a distance of some 2,800 miles, and the other (entirely American) was to sail from the USA, 4,500 miles distant. The convoys carrying these assault forces would have to sail through sea areas in which German U-boats were both active and successful, while the arrangements for combining the land, sea and air elements of these Allied forces with very different operating procedures were formidably complicated, with massive communications involved. It would, as a result, be very difficult to maintain secrecy, but the preservation of secrecy was essential to the success of the operation; it was probably more for this reason than for any notable success shown by previous deception operations that deception was made an intrinsic part of the planning for Operation TORCH, as this operation came to be known.

London Controlling Section received its brief even before any operational planning had been started. Its task was twofold; first, although the western Allies had decided that an invasion of NW Europe was not possible that summer, everything possible had to be done to persuade the Germans that it was still a possibility so that no forces would be transferred either to the Mediterranean or the Eastern Front, and, second, a cover plan had to be prepared for TORCH itself, concealing the real objective of the assault forces by indicating a plausible alternative. Within a week, Colonel Bevan and his colleagues had prepared outline plans and presented them to the Chiefs of Staff on 5 August.

For the solution to the first task they proposed a feint at the Pas de Calais, and for the second, Norway as the alternative destination for the TORCH convoys, as the Germans were known to be especially sensitive where the Norwegian theatre was concerned. The proposed feint across the Channel was approved by the Chiefs of Staff on the 18 August, and was christened Operation OVERTHROW. It was to be implemented partly by means of visual displays and partly by judiciously planted rumours via the double agent networks controlled by MI 5. The visual displays were the least satisfactory, although a little could be done by assemblies of shipping, the construction of 'hards' for the loading of landing craft and the overflying of the French coast by reconnaissance aircraft. The double agents, on the other hand, were more effective, especially 'Garbo', who sent ominous accounts of troop movements in southern England.

By mid-September, London Controlling Section had already achieved its aim and kept von Rundstedt on the *qui vive* for another two months, so OVERTHROW must be judged a major success. Throughout the summer and autumn of 1942, up to the eve of the TORCH landings, German forces in north-west France remained on the alert in expectation of an imminent Allied attack. The Germans' lack of suspicion about the Allies' real intentions can be attributed to a great extent to London Controlling Section's cover plan.

The notional attack on Norway known as Operation SOLO I, which was designed to disguise the TORCH assault forces' real destinations, was only part of the deceptive web woven by the LCS around Operation TORCH. The Allied assault forces themselves were the victims of another deception, Operation SOLO II, designed to hide from them their real destinations, while the all too visible preparations at Gibraltar were covered by Operation TOWNSMAN, and Operation KENNECOTT was designed to deceive the enemy as to the real destinations of the convoys once they had put to sea. With regard to the Norway deception, the LCS found themselves pushing at an open door: Hitler's worries concerning the Norwegian defences were well known and continual, and he put the whole of Central and Southern Norway on full alert on 2 November, as well as having maintained a substantial part of the German fleet in northern Norway. Operation SOLO I was therefore as successful in achieving its aim as OVERTHROW had been.

The real difficulty, however, arose once the TORCH convoys had put to sea and once the unusual activity at Gibraltar indicated that something must be about to happen in the Mediterranean. A carefully planned timetable had been prepared by LCS, indicating the nature and the purpose of the several stories to be disseminated through various channels. During August, emphasis was to be placed on rumours and signals forecasting the forthcoming relief of Malta, for which supplies would naturally be stockpiled in Gibraltar. In early September the emphasis would switch to troop concentrations in Scotland, calls for Norwegian interpreters, guide books and currency, and the manufacture and purchase of snow chains and anti-freeze for vehicles. Later that month the assault forces were to be warned to prepare for a long sea voyage, vaccinated against tropical diseases, issued with mosquito nets and anti-malarial drugs, and lectured about tropical hygiene. Simultaneously, attention was to be concentrated upon troop movements in Kent and Sussex, the display of 'hards' for the loading of landing-craft along the Thames, Medway and the south coast together with the deployment of anti-aircraft guns for their defence, and the story circulated that the Dieppe raid had been a rehearsal for an attack on a large scale on the French coast. At the end of the month, a spate of diplomatic indiscretions would occur, pointing to increasing British interest in Scandinavia, the improvement of relations between the British Government and General de Gaulle, and the intention to relieve Malta's desperate situation. In October, mountain clothing was to be issued to selected units in Scotland, and reports were to be circulated of the evacuation of civilians from the south coast area, the preparation of large numbers of hospital beds and of army convoys practising driving on the right of the road; at the same time, other stories would be circulated about the demand for Italian interpreters, guide books and currency, the imminence of heavy air raids on Italian cities and the attachment of Roman Catholic priests to units because of their knowledge of Italy.

The feedback from SIGINT enabled the LCS to assess the success of their efforts as they went along. It seemed to indicate that they were almost too successful, with rumours proliferating throughout Continental Europe suggesting Allied landings anywhere along the Atlantic coast from Narvik to Dakar. The most accurate accounts came from the Vatican: Abwehr agents there reported in mid-September that the Americans would land at Dakar and the British at Algiers in October, an alarmingly accurate assessment that was, luckily, lost in the general noise of rumour. When the convoys were sighted on the 6 November, the German military attaché in Madrid reported Spanish opinion as favouring the relief of Malta as their aim, going on to land behind Rommel's Army in Libya; he expressly discounted the idea that they might be destined for either French North Africa or Italy. The TORCH deception cover plans can be considered a major success: two great armies had been transported thousands of miles across the ocean in conditions of near total secrecy to land at the very last place the enemy had expected, and not even the most sceptical of critics can deny Lieutenant-Colonel Bevan and his colleagues the credit for a remarkable achievement. It was the first success for British strategic deception, and was to be the precursor of many more. The parts played by the Twenty Committee's network of double agents and the feedback from SIGINT were, of course, crucial to its success.

THE MEDITERRANEAN, 1942–43

The reorganisation of 'A' Force and the network of agents throughout Africa and the Middle East built up by Colonel Clarke to pass false information to the enemy meant that by the summer of 1942 it was possible for 'A' Force to indulge in activities ranging from tactical deception in the battles of the Western Desert to participation in the strategic deception plans of the London Controlling Section for covering Operation TORCH. Its role in the latter was to help in the misleading of the enemy with regard to both the build-up in Gibraltar and the destination of the TORCH convoys.

At this time the Eighth Army was at bay in Egypt on the El Alamein line. At the end of July, Allied plans concerning the landings in French North Africa having been settled, the British Prime Minister, Winston Churchill, visited the

Middle East theatre on his way to Moscow. During this visit he replaced the commander-in-chief, General Sir Claude Auchinleck, with General Sir Harold Alexander, and the commander of the Eighth Army with Lieutenant-General Sir Bernard Montgomery. 'A' Force was called upon to produce and implement a cover plan to mislead the enemy Intelligence organisation about the PM's movements, and this plan was called Operation GRANDIOSE. Deciding that it would be impossible to conceal the visit of so many VIPs, 'A' Force chose instead to report its itinerary more or less accurately but two or three days late. By this means, the credibility of the channels used to disseminate the inaccurate information would not be compromised, but it would not be possible for the enemy to take effective action on it. Again it was impossible to tell whether or not the deception was successful, but the fact remained that the PM and his entourage were able to complete the visit without coming to harm.

Dudley Clarke's brief from Montgomery was simple: 'A' Force was to do everything possible to delay the Axis attack which SIGINT showed to be imminent. It was already attempting, with little evident success, to divert reinforcements intended for Rommel's forces to Crete by mounting a notional threat (Operation ROYAL) against the island; this consisted of displays of dummy landing craft in harbours in Cyprus, dummy gliders on Egyptian airfields, putting Greek troops in the Nile Delta on standby, spreading rumours, and bogus radio traffic. In addition, a dummy support line was constructed behind the British Alamein positions, manned by two of the notional divisions; this was supported visually by dummy minefields, trenches and tracks, and the story spread that this was to be the main British defence line. Although the inflated British order of battle was accepted by German Intelligence, however, these deceptive measures had no effect on Rommel's plan or its execution. By now the Allied air forces had achieved air parity, and even local air superiority, in North Africa, so the effectiveness of visual displays of dummies was reduced due to the restriction loss of air superiority placed upon the enemy's ability to carry out air reconnaissance. There was still a requirement for such displays, however, as enemy air reconnaissance could not yet be completely eliminated.

The reasons for the relative lack of success of 'A' Force's deception plans thus far became clear at the end of July 1942, when the German intercept HQ was overrun by the Australians. The documents captured revealed that there had been two major sources of leaks in the UK's security in the theatre, which had given Rommel such reliable insights into British intentions and movements over the preceding twelve months that it was not surprising that 'A' Force's efforts had met with so little success. The first leak was identified as coming from the US

Military Attaché in Cairo, Colonel Fellers, whose cipher used for communications with Washington had been broken by the Germans. Fellers had been given free access to all British military Intelligence at GHQ and had passed it to Washington in the broken cipher. This leak was plugged by Colonel Fellers changing to a new and unreadable cipher. The second leak came from lax signal security within Eighth Army and the Desert Air Force, whose traffic had been freely read by the German tactical SIGINT intercept stations since early 1941. This was cured by tightening and changing radio procedures within the two organisations, thus denying Rommel a vital source of Intelligence. In addition, several German agents in Cairo were 'blown' by the capture of the documents from the German intercept HQ and arrested, thus leaving a clearer field for the double agents such as 'Cheese' run by 'A' Force for the dissemination of false information.

With these advantages, therefore, 'A' Force was now able to play a full part in the preparations for the Battle of Alamein; these involved a strategic plan (Operation TREATMENT) and a tactical plan (Operation BERTRAM), by which the enemy was to be led to expect an attack in the south on 5 November, when the actual plan was for an attack in the north a fortnight earlier, on 23 October. It was obviously impossible to conceal the fact that an attack was pending, but the enemy could be misled as to its time, place and aim. Operation TREATMENT aimed to convince the enemy that the British did not intend to launch a major offensive in the Western Desert at all, worried that the German advance to the Caucasus threatened their rear; Montgomery's aim would notionally be limited to improving his tactical positions and to testing his force under battle conditions, while the major British offensive would notionally continue to be directed at Crete. To lead the enemy away from the last week in October as the probable time for the British attack, a notional conference in Tehran was arranged, to take place on the 26 October, and to be attended by the Commanders-in-Chief of Middle East, Persia & Iraq and India commands; complete preparations were made for their travel and accommodation, and the conference was cancelled only when the attack at El Alamein was well under way. The last week in October was scheduled as a leave period for the Eighth Army, and units were encouraged to arrange a round of social and sporting engagements. This time the deception appears to have been successful: not only was Rommel still on sick leave when the attack started, but Hitler only ordered him to return on 24 October, not having thought the situation serious until then.

For BERTRAM, the tactical deception plan, most of the implementation was visual, supported by bogus radio traffic. In the south, where the notional attack was to be simulated, an entire dummy logistical network of supply dumps, camps, pipelines and pumping stations was carefully simulated and not too carefully camouflaged, with construction work carried out at a pace which would suggest completion not before the end of November. In the north, where the actual attack would go in, the situation was more difficult: dumps had to be built up but very carefully concealed, so that stores and ammunition were brought up at night and then buried or camouflaged as camps or vehicle parks. The 10 Corps' armour and artillery was camouflaged too, by first creating soft-skinned vehicle parks in the concentration areas and then gradually replacing the soft-skinned vehicles with tanks and guns moved in at night and disguised as 'B' vehicles by the use of 'sunshields'. In the north some 1,000 'sunshields' were used, while in the south the bogus concentration employed 550 dummy tanks, 150 dummy guns and 2,000 dummy vehicles of all kinds.

There can be no doubt that these deceptions were successful in misleading the Germans. Tactical surprise was complete, and not until three days after it had opened did Rommel feel confident of the true thrust of the British attack, by which time the Allied forces were established well inside the Axis defences. It was unfortunate that Colonel Clarke was unable to witness the success at last of 'A' Force's deceptive ploys; by this time he was heavily involved in London with the LCS plans for covering the TORCH operations, but his deputies in the Western Desert continued to mount minor tactical deceptions as the Eighth Army advanced westward towards Tripoli, as well as using their double agents, and especially 'Cheese', to continue to suggest that Crete and Italy were threatened by imminent attack. These threats to Crete were taken seriously, especially by Hitler; throughout the winter of 1942–43 the Abwehr stations in Athens, Prague, Bucharest, Istanbul and Rome reported on news of Allied plans to retake Crete once the North African coast had been cleared, all these reports being read, decrypted and passed to 'A' Force and LCS by GC & CS, many obviously originating from sources other than those controlled by the Twenty Committee and 'A' Force. However, it was significant how many of the reports classified by the Abwehr as originating from 'very reliable' sources were in fact emanating from the sources under British control.

UNITED KINGDOM, 1943

Although Colonel Clarke was unable to witness the success of 'A' Force's deception plans for the Battle of Alamein as he was in London at the time, his visit to London had more important objectives, coinciding as it did with the presence there of Colonel Peter Fleming, his counterpart from India, and Lieutenant-Commander Cook and Major-General Strong of the US Joint Security Control organisation, the US equivalent of the LCS. Under the aegis of Colonel Bevan, they were able to finalise not only the cover and deception plans for TORCH, but also to work out an Allied organisation for planning and implementing future deception work. Up to this point, due to the pressure of events, the London Controlling Section had had to assume virtually sole responsibility for the TORCH deception, cooperating on a more or less ad hoc basis with the US Joint Security Control, but this type of arrangement would not be adequate for the sustained deception that would be required over a period of months and possibly years for the planned operations to come.

The plan for the Allied organisation was finalised in December, when Colonel Bevan visited the United States for the purpose; London Controlling Section was to be responsible for deception in Europe, North Africa, the Middle East and India, while the US Joint Security Control would assume responsibility for the Western hemisphere, covering Canada and the Pacific, including Australia and New Zealand and China (except for one or two channels run from India by Colonel Fleming). Liaison would be effected by an LCS representative attached to the British Joint Staffs Mission in Washington. The reorganisation of 'A' Force needed to enable it to cover these increased responsibilities is described later in this chapter.

It was fortuitous that the finalisation of the Allied deception organisation was completed in time for the Casablanca Conference, to which the Chiefs of Staff were summoned in January 1943, and at which the next phase of the war was planned. The decisions reached at this conference were to impose heavy new loads upon the deception staffs, loads which were to be further increased as the year progressed. It would be no exaggeration to say that by the summer of 1943, the entire responsibility for pinning down German forces in north-west Europe and preventing them sending reinforcements to either the Mediterranean or the Eastern Front lay with Colonel Bevan and his colleagues on the staff of Major-General Sir Frederick Morgan, the Chief of Staff to the Supreme Allied Commander (COSSAC), who had been appointed to plan the Allied invasion of northern France in 1944 with the organisation set up after the Casablanca Conference.

In the absence of any further guidance from the Chiefs of Staff, in December 1942 the LCS had put forward proposals for the continued flow of deception information through the double agents, which was vital if they were to continue to be credible to the enemy. The LCS proposed that they continue to maintain the notional threat to Norway through the winter of 1942–43, that the strength of Allied forces in the United Kingdom and their readiness for an assault on the Continent of Europe be exaggerated, and that the notional threat in the eastern Mediterranean to the Aegean and Greece should also be maintained. In February 1943 these proposals were accepted with little alteration by the Chiefs of Staff, who had agreed at Casablanca that the major operation that year should be the invasion of Sicily (Operation HUSKY), with additional limited amphibious offensive operations launched from the United Kingdom against the French coast according to the availability of forces. Then followed a long pause: HUSKY was to be a large operation, involving some 160,000 troops and 3,000 ships and landing craft, and no serious deception plans could be made until the details of the operation they were designed to cover had been worked out.

Towards the end of April, COSSAC finally received a directive from the Combined Chiefs of Staff instructing him to plan for a full-scale attack on the Continent of Europe as early as possible in 1944, and to prepare an elaborate camouflage and deception scheme designed to keep the enemy pinned down in the west and to keep alive its expectations of an attack in 1943. General Morgan gave responsibility for deception operations to a section of his HQ known as Ops B. In conjunction with the LCS, Ops B drew up details of these under the umbrella title Operation COCKADE, which comprised three distinct operations: STARKEY, WADHAM and TINDALL. STARKEY was to be a notional attack by fourteen British and Canadian divisions to establish a bridgehead on either side of Boulogne between 8 and 14 September. WADHAM was a notional follow-up by two corps, one from the UK and the other from the USA, to capture Brest; this operation would be called off for various reasons, and in its place TINDALL would substitute a notional attack against Norway, with five divisions seizing Stavanger and striking as far inland as Oslo.

However, before any of these operations could be set in train, the Germans had to be persuaded that there were enough forces available to carry them out. There were only 22 British and 4½ Canadian divisions in the UK in June 1943, while the bulk of the US troops so far there were administrative and logistic units, but the LCS had been quietly building up a notional and highly exaggerated order of battle for both the British (DUNDAS) and US (LARKHILL) forces, and feeding them to the Germans via the double agents of the Twenty Committee. The German OKW Intelligence branch, Fremde Heer (West) (Foreign Armies West), treated the agent reports as credible, and reported in November 1943 that the Allies had available for a landing in north-west Europe a total of 43 divisions comprising 26 infantry, 14 armoured and 3 airborne divisions, compared to the actual figure for British forces in September of that year of 1 airborne, 12 infantry and 4 armoured divisions.

Although the Germans had taken the order of battle bait, they conspicuously failed to accept the supporting visual displays of dummies, the bogus radio signals and the troop and shipping movements that accompanied the agents' reports. These had been noted by the OKW, but they continued to brief von Rundstedt, the

German Commander-in-Chief West, that the main objective for an Allied landing in Europe was in the Mediterranean, and would in all probability remain there. In fact, in August 1943 von Rundstedt's staff noted that the composition and quantity of agents' reports prompted the suspicion that the information was being deliberately planted. A week later they wrote of the somewhat too obvious preparations for attacking the Channel coast, which were conspicuously slow in completion. From SIGINT, the British learned of the lack of German reaction to the feints they had been making, which had culminated on 9 September in minesweeping operations by three flotillas of minesweepers from Dungeness towards Le Touquet and the sailing of a convoy of some thirty ships to within ten miles of the French coast. This apparent lack of reaction was naturally disappointing, but at the time they had no way of knowing that the Germans considered these measures to be a large-scale rehearsal for a genuine attack to be launched against their west coast defences at any time before the onset of the autumn gales.

Operation WADHAM fared little better, although Hitler's extreme sensitivity where Norway was concerned ensured that in spite of the demands of the Mediterranean theatre, the German garrison in Norway never fell below twelve divisions in strength. The deception was carried out by means of shipping movements and troop deployments reported by the double agents, by airfield displays of dummy aircraft and by a certain amount of radio traffic, starting in July 1943 and coming to a climax at the end of August. German headquarters in Oslo reported that agents' reports led them to expect a landing in the first two weeks of September, an opinion shared by Fremde Heer (West), but these views had no effect on von Rundstedt's HQ or the OKW; forces and shipping in southern England were sufficient for a major operation, and as late as the end of November von Rundstedt reported that even making allowance for possible deception, a major landing must be expected soon. But by now deception was beginning to merge into reality with the completion of the Allied landings in Italy and the consequent build-up of Allied forces and shipping in the United Kingdom.

THE MEDITERRANEAN, 1943–44

'A' Force had worked closely with the London Controlling Section in implementing the deception plans which had so successfully covered Operation TORCH, and during his visit to London in October 1942, Colonel Dudley Clarke had agreed with Colonel Bevan a framework for future cooperation which effectively merged the deception organisation in the Mediterranean theatre with the organisation centrally controlled from London. 'A' Force continued to function at both the tactical and strategic level in accordance with the principles which it had developed over the preceding two years, receiving only the broadest of directives from the LCS. This maintained the principle constantly reiterated by Bevan that officers engaged in deception operations had to be fully integrated with the operations staffs of the commanders in the field, whose plans they had to implement, and whose resources had to be used in implementing their own.

This now posed a problem in the Mediterranean theatre, as the Supreme Allied Commander for the theatre, General Dwight D. Eisenhower, had his headquarters in Algiers, whereas 'A' Force and the whole deception apparatus for the theatre was based in Cairo, and had been since 1940. It was from there that all his links to the eastern Mediterranean, the Middle East, Turkey, Greece, the Balkans and Italy were operated, and it was all the more essential, now that the centre of gravity of Allied operations in the Mediterranean had moved westward, that these contacts and the flow of information to and from them should be maintained. The maintenance of a credible threat in the eastern Mediterranean remained a continuing necessity and a highly successful part of Allied deception plans well into 1944.

A reorganisation of 'A' Force therefore took place to eliminate the problem. Its Main HQ was to remain in Cairo, to continue the control of its agents throughout the Middle East and North-east Africa, while a so-called 'Rear HQ' at Nairobi similarly controlled activities in East and South Africa. An Advance HQ, headed jointly by Lieutenant-Colonel M.H. Crichton from Cairo and Colonel E.C. Goldbranson of the US Army and with a substantial US element, was established at Algiers, working directly with General Eisenhower and controlling outstations in Malta and North Africa, while a new Tactical HQ under Lieutenant-Colonel D.I. Strangeways took responsibility for tactical deception in the field. The Tactical HQ worked directly under General Alexander when, in February 1943, he set up his 18 Army Group with its HQ at Constantine in Algeria, and later accompanied him to Italy, where it implemented tactical deception schemes up to the end of the war in Europe. After the TORCH landings 'A' Force's agent resources were considerably enhanced when General Darlan aligned himself with the Allies, and the French Intelligence service in North Africa (the Deuxième Bureau), placed its resources at General Eisenhower's disposal, including a large number of double agents allegedly working for the Abwehr.

However, although 'A' Force now controlled an impressive array of enemy agents in the Mediterranean theatre, unlike B1(a) in the United Kingdom it did not control them all, and a certain (and unknown) amount of true information continued to filter through to the Abwehr together with the falsehoods planted by the double agents. To control the information passed through these, a number of 'Thirty Committees', analogous to London's Twenty Committee, were established throughout the Mediterranean theatre and the Middle East. Eventually, there were twenty-one of these, stretching from Lisbon to Baghdad and from Nairobi to Florence, each consisting of an 'A' Force officer as chairman, an MI 6 officer as secretary and an MI 5 member. 'A' Force was responsible for the text of the messages to be passed, MI 6 provided staff, communications, ciphers and finance and ran those agents operating in territories not under Allied control, while MI 5, as in the UK, ran the agents in territories under the control of Allied forces. In Algiers, where the French played a significant part in running the double agents, a French representative was added to the triumvirate, and the body was known as the 'Forty Committee'.

The overall plan for deception in the Mediterranean for 1943 was known as Operation BARCLAY, and was worked out by 'A' Force to conform to the LCS outline approved by the Combined Chiefs of Staff and received by 'A' Force in February. Their plan was produced in March and approved by General Eisenhower in April. The objective was to secure the greatest possible surprise for Operation HUSKY (the invasion of Sicily) by posing credible threats elsewhere, and to reduce to a minimum air and naval attacks on the shipping being assembled for the assault on Sicily in the UK, North Africa and Egypt.

Much of the legend on which the deception was to be based was already to hand. It will be remembered that 'A' Force had been positing a notional threat to Crete (Operation WAREHOUSE) ever since the Battle of Alamein, with the aim of containing the Axis forces in the Balkans and Aegean and preventing both the despatch of reinforcements to Rommel in North Africa and the opening of a new front in Turkey and Persia. A further plan (Operation WITHSTAND) was added in January 1943, projecting the worries of the Allies concerning the danger of a German invasion of Turkey through Bulgaria, and positing a pre-emptive attack on Crete and the Dodecanese. This plan had the added objective of emphasising to the Turks the degree of Allied concern regarding a possible German attack on their country, thus making them more open to accepting the help being offered by Winston Churchill during his visit to Adana after the Casablanca Conference. In addition to the visual displays of amphibious forces mounted in Cyprus and other eastern Mediterranean ports and the reports submitted by the double agents, British armoured units, judiciously reinforced with dummies, manoeuvred ostentatiously in Syria within easy range of the Turkish frontier from January into May.

Through SIGINT it was possible to monitor the considerable success of the rumours spread from Cairo, but in February an indication that 'A' Force might have overdone it came when the OKW issued a general warning that the reports of Allied landing intentions showed that the Allies were practising deception on a large scale. Nevertheless, the OKW concluded that major Allied landing operations would take place in the following month, beginning with attacks on, in order of probability, Sicily, Crete, Sardinia and Corsica.

Sicily was the obvious next target for the Western Allies, and the task facing 'A' Force was therefore fraught with very great difficulties: until Sicily was in Allied hands, passage through the Mediterranean could never be regarded as safe, and it must have seemed unlikely to German Intelligence that the Allied forces being gathered in Tunis and Bizerta were intended for another more distant target. The difficulties were enhanced by the reluctance of the Allied air force commanders to diversify their attacks on the scale considered necessary by 'A' Force to add verisimilitude to the deception; with the limited resources available to them they did not feel able to provide the intensity of bombing of the cover targets of Corsica, Sardinia and France for which 'A' Force had asked. The concentrated air attack on Pantellaria and its subsequent capture in June pointed all too clearly to Sicily as the Allies' next objective, especially as during the following four weeks targets in Sicily were bombed twenty times, and in Sardinia only once.

Despite these difficulties, however, through air photo-reconnaissance, naval reconnaissance and beach raids 'A' Force managed to obtain details of all the notional targets. Actual amphibious training was carried out by Greek and British troops in Egypt and by French troops in Algeria, appeals were circulated for Greek interpreters and for fishermen with knowledge of the bays and inlets of southern France, Corsica and Sardinia, Greek drachmas in large quantities were purchased in Cairo and Alexandria, pound notes were overprinted 'France', 'Greece' and 'Bulgaria', and maps of the notional objectives as well as pamphlets about Greece and Axis forces in the Balkans were issued to troops training for the Sicily invasion.

Radio deception was also a high 'A' Force priority; as much as possible of the real traffic generated by the Allied command centres in Malta and Tunis was carried by landline, while an elaborate programme of bogus wireless traffic was generated at 'Twelfth Army HQ' in Cairo. Confusion concerning the date of the operations was also carefully sown, and a massive display of dummies was erected in the Western Desert (Operation WATERFALL) for the benefit of German air reconnaissance, representing the notional '8 Armoured Division' and deployed within reach of the Cyrenaican harbours of Tobruk and Bomba. Dummy glider squadrons were added in early June, and all these forces were brought to maximum readiness in the third week of that month, when they began to move to the harbours for notional embarkation.

In total, 700 men were engaged full-time on the project, and real workshops, fuel installations and an anti-aircraft brigade were deployed in the Tobruk area. Unfortunately, much of this effort was wasted due to the German loss of air superiority in the Mediterranean by this time, but as Colonel Clarke reflected afterwards, the risk always remained that a single photo-reconnaissance aircraft on one day alone could have vitiated the whole of the rest of the deception effort had the visual displays not been carried out.

In pursuance of the HUSKY cover plan, what was to become the best-known and most successful deception operation of the whole war, Operation MINCEMEAT, was carried out. This plan, a variation of the 'planted false plan' ploy that is as old as war itself, came to the public's attention after the war in Ewen Montagu's book *The Man Who Never Was*, of which a film was also made. The scheme was the brainchild of Montagu, then a Lieutenant-Commander RNVR, and his colleague in the LCS, Flight-Lieutenant Charles Cholmondley RAF, and was inspired by the washing ashore on the coast of Spain of an RAF crewman from a British aircraft which had crashed into the sea in September 1942; the body was carrying documents which the Spanish authorities made available to the Abwehr before returning them to the British. In this case the documents had been unimportant, but Cholmondley proposed that another corpse, dressed as an official British courier and carrying documents of an apparently highly confidential nature, be obtained and dropped from an aircraft at a point off the Spanish coast where currents would take it ashore to be discovered. Enquiries were made of the London coroner, Sir Bentley Purchase, and the pathologist, Sir Bernard Spilsbury, both of whom were encouraging, and a suitable corpse was obtained. Montagu and Cholmondley then reported to the Twenty Committee that the cadaver would be fit for use any time within the next three months.

Operation MINCEMEAT was then put in train, but the original proposals were changed so that the body would be sent by submarine rather than by aircraft, and floated ashore at Huelva on the Spanish coast, where the currents were favourable and where the Germans had a highly competent Vice-Consul. The body itself was notionally identified as a 'Major Martin' of the Royal Marines, serving on the staff of the Chief of Combined Operations, Vice-Admiral Lord Louis Mountbatten. The confidential documents it was carrying would be in a briefcase chained to the body, and would consist of a letter of introduction from Admiral Mountbatten to Admiral Sir Andrew Cunningham, a personal letter dated 23 April from the VCIGS, General Sir Archibald Nye, to General Alexander, and the proofs of a manual on combined operations sponsored by Mountbatten and with a foreword by Eisenhower. The letter from General Nye indicated that the Allies were planning an assault-landing, code-named HUSKY, in Greece, that the idea of using Sicily as a cover for this operation had been rejected in favour of its use as cover for another operation, and that General Maitland Wilson, the notional commander of the Greek landing, should use the Dodecanese as his cover target.

The submarine, HMS *Seraph*, sailed on 19 April, but 'Major Martin' carried in his pocket two theatre stubs for the evening of 22 April, to make it appear as if he could not have left London before that date, and so must have been travelling by air. He was duly floated ashore at Huelva together with a capsized rubber dinghy early on 30 April, and the body was discovered by fishermen later that morning. The corpse was impounded by the Spanish authorities, the documents it was carrying were copied, and the copies were passed to the Abwehr. The corpse and the original documents were then returned to the British authorities, but the copies were sent by the Abwehr to Berlin and their subsequent progress was traced, with interest, by the British by means of SIGINT.

Although the fake documents told the Germans nothing they did not already expect, they did cause them to give priority to the defence of Greece over the next two months. For once Fremde Heer (West) was convinced both of the importance and of the genuineness of their Abwehr source's information, as a result of which the OKW ordered all German commands and headquarters concerned with the preparation of defences in the Mediterranean theatre to co-operate in strengthening them in the threatened areas in the shortest possible time, in particular Greece. Hitler himself regarded Greece as the area most threatened, and the OKW continued to give priority to its defence. The Abwehr made preparations for the evacuation of its stations there, the planting of stay-behind agents and the sabotage of installations, all of which was revealed by SIGINT.

However, the success of these deception operations was not solely responsible for the fact that when the Allies invaded Sicily in Operation HUSKY on 10 July 1943 only two German divisions were available to assist the Italian 6th Army in repelling them. Hitler's well-founded belief was that the Italians were unwilling to remain in the war, and he naturally lacked the desire to commit German forces in an area where they might be lost in the aftermath of a general Italian surrender. For whatever reason, the invasion was a success and achieved a fair measure of surprise, for which the deception operations may fairly claim some responsibility. The assault on Sicily did not lead the OKW to reassess the Allies' strategic intentions, which they continued to believe involved a landing in Greece rather than in Italy as the next Allied move, but the false picture of the Allied order of battle so carefully built up by the deceptionists over the preceding months led the

Germans to overestimate the forces available to the Allies twofold, giving credibility to their fears as to the Allies' next move.

This next move had not been decided at the Washington Conference in May 1943, Churchill favouring proceeding on to the Italian mainland after the conquest of Sicily, and the Americans resisting any extension of the Allies' activities in the Mediterranean theatre. However, the collapse of the Italian Army a few days after the Allied invasion of the island persuaded the Americans to reconsider, and on 26 July General Eisenhower was ordered by the Combined Chiefs of Staff to mount an attack on Naples with available forces. This assault consisted of two operations: the first (BAYTOWN), by the British Eighth Army, was across the straits of Messina, with the object of freeing the Straits for Allied naval use and pinning down the Axis forces in Calabria; the second (AVALANCHE), by the US Fifth Army, was in the Bay of Salerno as a preliminary to seizing Naples. Operation BAYTOWN was launched on 3 September, and AVALANCHE six days later.

The deception plan covering AVALANCHE was known as Operation BOARDMAN, and gave 'A' Force the task of both weakening Axis forces in Italy (especially in the south and the centre of the country) and holding the maximum number of the enemy in the Balkans (especially on the Greek mainland). Because the German appreciation of Allied long-term intentions had always considered the Balkans to be their objective, and this appreciation was well known to British Intelligence, 'A' Force's task was made easier, and BARCLAY glided seamlessly into BOARDMAN. Operation BOARDMAN postulated a notional attack against Sardinia by the corps actually destined for Salerno, and one by a combined French and US force against Corsica. The possibilities of attacks on either the south of France or the Italian mainland between Leghorn and Genoa were also kept alive, as were notional attacks on the Peloponnese by the notional 'British Twelfth Army' and on Apulia in Italy's heel, to open the Straits of Otranto. This last merged into a tactical deception plan, Operation BOOTHBY, which called for the simulation by all the usual means of an attack on Crotone, on the ball of Italy's foot, from Sicily.

Rumours of these notional attacks mingled with many others circulating in the Mediterranean via the double agents in Tangiers, Madrid, the south of France, Egypt and other places. Whether or not 'A' Force's deception plans covering the Italy landings added much to the German Intelligence organisation's confusion is not known; certainly, the haste with which the landings on the Italian mainland were mounted did not give 'A' Force the same opportunities as had the long-prepared plans for the invasion of Sicily. If they did not achieve all they were intended to do, however, there is no doubt that they helped to maintain the long-held illusions of the Germans about Allied long-term objectives; even the Italian landings failed to convince them that General Eisenhower's eyes were not fixed upon the Balkan Peninsula. German situation reports in September and October showed much more concern about the threat to the Balkans than about the situation in Italy, and this was reinforced by the attacks on Cos, Leros and Samos improvised by the forces under General Maitland Wilson. The failure of these British attacks was undoubtedly disappointing, but provided striking confirmation of the success of 'A' Force in concentrating the attention of the Germans on the Balkans.

The retaking of Cos and Leros by the Germans in October and November and the lack of any Allied counter-measures did reveal the true weakness of British forces in the eastern Mediterranean, however, although the landings on the Italian mainland still left a sizeable and as yet uncommitted notional force in the Middle East and North Africa. This force was now more than ever required to form the basis of a successful deception plan; the quiet build-up of these notional forces according to CASCADE was therefore the most important of 'A' Force's tasks. The strategic deception plan following BOARDMAN accordingly postulated assaults in overwhelming force on Rhodes in October and Crete in November, with the aim of causing the Germans to evacuate both islands rather than reinforcing them; this plan, Operation FAIRLANDS, also involved a notional threat to Italy's coast in the area of Leghorn, the object of which was to deter the Germans from transferring forces from there to the front south of Rome. In mid-November this plan merged into Operation OAKFIELD, which postulated simultaneous landings on the Ligurian and Adriatic coasts of Italy and became the basis for all Allied strategic deception in Italy for the next nine months.

By January 1944 the centre of gravity of Allied forces in the European theatre had shifted decisively from the Mediterranean to north-west Europe. The transfer of seven divisions, their associated landing craft and experienced commanders from the Mediterranean theatre to the United Kingdom had been successfully covered by Operation FOYNES, and the entire redeployment of these Allied forces had taken place without the Germans being aware of it.

The task of 'A' Force in 1944, code-named WANTAGE, was further to inflate the bogus order of battle in the Mediterranean theatre to induce the enemy to believe that sufficient reserves existed in both the eastern and western Mediterranean to undertake large-scale invasions of Southern Europe. Real Allied strength in Italy totalled 23 divisions, and it was considered unwise to attempt to create any bogus formations there in view of the doubtful security of the area. It was therefore decided to increase notionally the 18 real divisions outside Italy to a total of 39, of which 24 would be notionally available for offensive operations, 12 of which would constitute the British 'Twelfth Army', based in Egypt, and the other 12 a US 'Seventh Army' based in Algeria. The strength of both Armies was faithfully reported by the double agents in Cairo and Algiers, and was accepted by Fremde Heer (West) in the absence of contrary indications from air reconnaissance. Overwhelming Allied air superiority meant that air reconnaissance was only intermittently possible, and the Germans were therefore increasingly dependent upon agents' reports for information concerning Allied formations outside the immediate operational area.

The overall Allied deception plan for 1944 was BODYGUARD, which had been agreed by the three major Allies at Tehran, the cover story of which was that the Western Allies would not be ready to launch an invasion of north-west Europe before the late summer of 1944, if indeed they were able to launch one at all. As a result, the main Allied effort that year would be directed at the Balkan Peninsula. The mounting of this notional threat to the Balkans was mainly the responsibility of 'A' Force, and was code-named ZEPPELIN; it comprised a threat to Crete and the Peloponnese mounted by the notional British 'Twelfth Army' from Egypt, combined with a notional attack across the Adriatic against the Istrian Peninsula and the coast of northern Dalmatia by the (real) US Seventh Army and a Polish corps from Italy. These would finally be complemented by a Soviet amphibious attack against the coast of Bulgaria.

Operations FAIRLANDS and OAKFIELD, which had been mounted by 'A' Force to both keep as many German formations as possible in the Mediterranean theatre and to pose a threat of simultaneous landings on the Ligurian coast in the region of Genoa and the Adriatic coast in the region of Rimini, were complementary to the overall deception plan, and were intended to cover the landing at Anzio on 22 January 1944. Maps and pamphlets were distributed to the assault force with details of the local art treasures which were to be preserved, visual displays of camps, aircraft, field hospitals, assault craft and roads were prepared on Corsica, the notional departure point for the Pisa assault, and prolific radio traffic was generated by the Seventh Army HQ in Sicily. Complete surprise was achieved at Anzio, but there is no evidence to suggest that this was due to the deception staffs and the double agents. Thanks to Allied air superiority the visual displays were largely wasted and were never considered seriously by the German authorities. In fact, far from expecting a pincer operation of the size projected by 'A' Force, the Germans did not believe that the Allies possessed sufficient resources in Italy even for the limited attack, four divisions strong, which they actually carried out at Anzio. The surprise achieved at Anzio thus owed little if anything to 'A' Force's activities; it was due primarily to the Germans' inability to carry out air reconnaissance, and to the excellent radio security of the Allied forces.

In March 1944 an event occurred which was to concentrate German minds on south-east Europe far more effectively than anything real or notional that the British could threaten: the opening of the major Soviet offensive on the southern part of the Eastern Front, which was to bulldoze its way through the two German Army groups defending the Ukraine and bring the war to the frontiers of Hungary and Romania. As a result, the OKW ordered the despatch to the Eastern Front of five divisions from Field-Marshal von Weichs's command and a further three, two of them armoured, from von Rundstedt's command in north-west Europe, just as the Allied invasion of north-west Europe, Operation OVERLORD, was becoming operationally feasible. An Allied attack on Greece, the Ionian Islands or Albania was considered by the OKW to be quite possible; for these operations they reckoned that the British disposed of six infantry and three armoured divisions in Egypt and Libya, with miscellaneous units amounting to five further divisions (three infantry and two armoured) which were ready for immediate action. Fremde Heer (West) appreciations in May referred to the build-up of British forces in Egypt as being of mounting significance. Neither Hitler nor von Weichs questioned the official OKW assessment of Allied forces in Egypt and Libya, about fourteen divisions, five ready for action; this assessment contrasted with the reality of three divisions, none of which was in any condition to take the field, so 'A' Force had every reason to congratulate itself. Not only was the notional order of battle which it had been projecting for so many months now firmly lodged in FH(W) files, but on the eve of OVERLORD, the threat to the Balkans which was a fundamental part of the ZEPPELIN deception was also firmly implanted in the German mind. In conjunction with the Soviet threat and that from Marshal Tito's partisans in Yugoslavia, it had forced the Germans to lock up some twenty-two divisions in their south-east theatre.

By now, the main deception aims of the Western Allies were to cover Operation OVERLORD, the landings in northern France, and its complementary landings in the south of that country, Operation ANVIL (later rechristened Operation DRAGOON). Responsibility for implementing the cover plan for the latter operation in the Mediterranean rested with 'A' Force, whose commander, Dudley Clarke, had by now been promoted to Brigadier. 'A' Force was tasked strategically with keeping German reserves from being sent to the Normandy front until at least twenty-five days after D-Day – that is until the beginning of July – and specifically with ensuring that the threat to the south of France reached its peak five days before D-Day and was held at maximum pitch thereafter for as long as possible.

The cover story for this latter deception, code-named VENDETTA and disseminated via the double agents, was that operations against Crete and the Peloponnese had been abandoned due to the actual political disturbances which had broken out among the Greek forces in Egypt, and the forces originally earmarked for these operations had been concentrated in the western Mediterranean. The notional operations for which these forces were now to be used consisted of an assault by the US 'Seventh Army' against the French coast in the area of Narbonne, a location conveniently far from the area between Toulon and Nice actually due to be attacked in August. It was also conveniently close to the Spanish frontier, with its opportunities for floating false rumours. Of the forces involved in VENDETTA, two out of the three corps headquarters and nine of the twelve divisions were wholly or partly notional; huge activity had to be simulated in the ports of Oran, Ferryville and Bône due to the large gap between the number of naval and assault craft notionally and actually available; vehicles were waterproofed and prominently displayed, dummy landing craft were floated at Ferryville and Bône, 10,000 tons of stores for the assault forces were packaged, labelled, waterproofed and stored, smoke screens were laid over all three ports, and in June a massive amphibious exercise was mounted involving the embarkation at Oran of 13,000 troops and 2,000 vehicles. Sixty naval vessels participated in this three-day exercise, including 25 destroyers, 2 aircraft carriers, 14 large transports and 30 cargo vessels. Radio traffic was intensified, and fighter aircraft attacked targets around Sète while heavy bombers attacked deep into the Rhône valley. The Spanish government was asked for Red Cross facilities to enable the evacuation of casualties incurred in the operation; the frontiers with Spanish Morocco and Tangier were closed from 11 June to 6 July, and diplomatic bag facilities were withdrawn from neutral diplomats, as they were in the United Kingdom prior to the Normandy landings on 6 June.

German sources revealed after the war that VENDETTA was only a partial success: the inflated order of battle passed in CASCADE and WANTAGE had so misled the German Intelligence staffs that they had been unable for some time to discount an Allied operation against the south of France, but German air reconnaissance of Oran and Algiers in March revealed no signs of the major concentrations of shipping in these ports reported by agents, and on 19 June Fremde Heer (West) warned that the then current wealth of alarming reports was undoubtedly fostered by the Allies with intent to deceive. Nevertheless, if 'A' Force had tended to overreach itself in this case, the Germans did not move the first Panzer division from the south of France to the operational area of Normandy until mid-June, and no other units were moved there until July. 'A'

Force had therefore been successful in tying down German forces in the south of France, which had been the main aim of VENDETTA.

A similar aim as far as German forces in the south-east theatre were concerned prompted the deception Exercise TURPITUDE in the eastern Mediterranean, which painted a picture of amphibious assaults on Salonika followed by a thrust to link up with Soviet forces which would be simultaneously landing at Varna. The Turkish authorities were more alarmed by this apparent threat to their security than the Germans, but the latter were sufficiently worried by it to retain their existing troop dispositions in the area, which had been 'A' Force's aim.

Operation ZEPPELIN came to a formal end on 6 July, and 'A' Force could feel satisfied with a job well done. It might not have achieved all its ambitious goals, but it had done all the Combined Chiefs of Staff had expected of it. The only strategic deception still to be carried out in the Mediterranean was that covering Operation DRAGOON, the actual assault on the southern French coast, due to take place on 15 August. This deception was code-named Operation FERDINAND, and was complicated by the need firstly to placate the German fears aroused by VENDETTA, and secondly by General Alexander's requirement for it to include a notional Allied landing in the Gulf of Genoa to draw German forces away from his forthcoming thrust in the centre of Italy.

The legend for FERDINAND opened with the premise that the Allies, having failed to make the Germans weaken their defences in the south of France, had abandoned all intentions in that area. Instead, they had decided to concentrate resources on the Italian theatre. An amphibious landing at Genoa, together with another on the Adriatic coast at Rimini, would enable Alexander to outflank the Gothic Line, while General Eisenhower would launch a simultaneous assault on the west coast of France in the Bay of Biscay. In the eastern Mediterranean, the British Twelfth (wholly notional) and Ninth (partly notional) Armies would be held in reserve to take advantage of any German weakening in the Balkans and to exploit any favourable situation created by a Soviet advance into Bulgaria from the Black Sea.

The story was implemented through the double agents and by diplomatic rumour. The German reaction, particularly to the notional Genoa assault, was very satisfactory. SIGINT had revealed Hitler's sensitivity to the Genoa-Leghorn area, and Kesselring duly reinforced the defences in the area as a result. By the beginning of August, German attention had been very effectively focused on Italy rather than the south of France. On 4 August, Fremde Heer (West) reported that all the information on British troop movements it had received pointed to a landing on the Italian coast in the area of Genoa, which appeared more likely than an assault on the south of France. The actual landings took place on the French coast between Hyères and Nice early on the morning of 15 August. So overwhelming was the strengh of the naval and air forces covering Operation DRAGOON and so overstretched were the German defences that surprise played a much less important role than it did in the case of Operation OVERLORD.

Nevertheless, FERDINAND was 'A' Force's most successful strategic deception operation, in which the Germans were persuaded to swallow the cover story almost whole. This was partly because Hitler tended to expect landings in the cover area, a predisposition which SIGINT had revealed to 'A' Force, and partly because the double agents through whom the cover story was disseminated had built up a reputation for reliability, and such troop movements as the Germans had been able to observe had supported them. It was some days after the landings in the French Riviera that the Germans decided that those in the Genoa area were not still pending.

Operation FERDINAND was the last strategic deception operation to be conducted by 'A' Force before the end of the war in Europe. Henceforward, 'A' Force's main function would be to carry out tactical deception in the Italian theatre of operations under the control of General Alexander. Their greatest triumph of deception after HUSKY and FERDINAND was to be the cover (Operation NUNTON) for Alexander's switch of his forces from his right wing to the left for the operation to break open the German defensive line based on Cassino (Operation DIADEM). From January 1944, tactical deceptions had been carried out both to cover actual landing operations, as at Anzio, and as amphibious feints against Italy's western coast or the head of the Adriatic. These involved plentiful displays of dummy tanks and guns, sonic deception and radio traffic, together with frenetic activity in the ports of Bari, Brindisi, Termoli and Barletta. The port of Termoli in particular was transformed in the aftermath of the Anzio landings for a notional amphibious threat against Pescara; all civilians in the neighbourhood were evacuated, docking facilities were extended, and a plentiful supply of dummy landing craft was displayed, accompanied by the usual deceptive radio traffic.

Operation NUNTON was put into operation in April, a month before DIADEM was due to start. It was accepted that so large a movement of troops could not be concealed from the enemy, so a programme of disinformation to mislead and confuse was planned, together with deception as to the date and the scope of the operation. To tie down the German armoured and infantry reserves, the threat of an amphibious operation comparable in scale to the Anzio attack against the coast of Civita Vecchia would also be projected. The deception continued until 25 May, two weeks after DIADEM had been launched. Only then did Kesselring start to commit his reserves piecemeal. Much to the gratification of 'A' Force, a German map captured during the course of the battle showed that its location of Allied units was highly inaccurate, while it overestimated Allied strength on the Adriatic wing by an entire corps and underestimated the strength on the left wing by seven divisions. 'A' Force was congratulated after the battle by General Alexander, who told them that their contribution towards the success of the operation had been enormous. He did not exaggerate.

However, after the conclusion of Operation ZEPPELIN, 'A' Force considered that deception had achieved its object in the Mediterranean theatre. Subsequent operations were an anti-climax, and in October 1944 'A' Force started to wind down. On 1 October, Brigadier Clarke had been told that there would be no more overall deception practised in the war against Germany, largely because the German Intelligence services were no longer capable of either acquiring or interpreting the information the Allies might wish to feed them: they had no air reconnaissance capability, their agents everywhere were running for cover, and their organisation at home was on the point of collapse. 'A' Force's rear headquarters in Cairo, where it had all begun, became an outstation to serve the deception authorities in Delhi in the war against Japan. The main 'A' Force HQ, which in July had moved from Algiers to Caserta, was closed down, only to be resuscitated there in December 1944, when Alexander was promoted to Supreme Allied Commander in the Mediterranean for the tactical deceptions which were to play a crucial part in covering his closing victories of the Italian campaign. Much of 'A' Force's expertise was absorbed by the London Controlling Section, where it would play its full part in the production of Operation FORTITUDE, the cover plan for the Normandy Landings in June 1944.

UNITED KINGDOM, 1943–45

As 'A' Force's contribution, its Colonel H.N. Wild had been posted back to the UK to join the London Controlling Section in the planning for the deception operations designed to cover the preparations for the Normandy Landings. He then joined SHAEF (Supreme Headquarters, Allied Expeditionary Force), which had taken over from COSSAC when General Eisenhower returned to the United Kingdom as Supreme Allied Commander. Wild was appointed head of the Ops B branch, which was given responsibility for the supervision of deception operations within General Eisenhower's command, and also became a member of the Twenty Committee. Ops B gave MI 5, MI 6 and the LCS instructions regarding the deception material to be passed via their respective channels, and was responsible for securing the necessary coordination between these channels. Another 'A' Force officer, Lieutenant-Colonel David Strangeways, was posted to General Montgomery's 21 Army Group as head of the deception staff branch G(R). The specialist deception troops under command were known as 'R' Force; these were the British men who devised the cover plan for Operation OVERLORD in the United Kingdom and advised the responsible commanders on its execution.

Operation FORTITUDE was to be the biggest, most crucial and most successful deception operation of the Second World War, its success in large part owing to the complete control which the Twenty Committee and B1(a) exerted over the double agents, coupled with the lack of any German agents in the UK outside British control. The overwhelming air superiority of the Allies in the skies over the UK and the Continent of Europe was another contributory factor, denying the Luftwaffe air photo-reconnaissance of the troop, ship and stores concentration areas and the embarkation sites around the coast.

Allied deception operations in 1943 had had their successes and their failures. For example, they had signally failed to deceive the Germans as to Allied strategic intentions. The Germans had appreciated early in the year that the main Allied effort would be in the Mediterranean, and had made their own troop dispositions accordingly, while at the tactical level neither Operations WADHAM nor TINDALL persuaded them to change their dispositions, credible though they found the notional threat to Norway. Their success in holding the Allies in Italy meant that the Allies had to maintain forces there at a level that seriously disorganised plans for the cross-Channel attack in 1944.

Despite these failures, however, the deception staffs could point with satisfaction to the acceptance by the German Intelligence staffs of the inflated order of battle so consistently fed to them. The surprise achieved in the invasion of Sicily could also be counted among their successes, as could the threat of landings in the Balkan Peninsula. In the United Kingdom in particular their successes could be judged accurately from the feedback which SIGINT gave them of the German reaction to the various deceptive ploys; particularly valuable in this respect were the intercepts which showed the degree of reliability accorded by the Abwehr to the reports of the double agents.

Deception is only possible when the operational plan has been determined, however, and with an operation of the size and scope of OVERLORD, the forming of the operational plan was a lengthy process. It was apparent from an early stage that the need to provide continuous air cover over the landing sites, the need to land over beaches of manageable gradient and the need to capture a major port early in the operation all indicated the Normandy coast in the area of Caen as the most suitable target. After the initial landings, it was thought the Allies would be able to establish their left flank securely on the Seine estuary and then to seal off the Cotentin Peninsula and capture the port of Cherbourg. This outline was sufficient to allow preliminary planning by the deception staffs. It was obviously going to be impossible to hide the preparations for so large a military operation, so the deception plan would have to mislead the Germans as to timing and point of attack. Fortunately, the plan to land in Normandy left available for deception purposes the alternative and very plausible landing site of the Pas de Calais, and this was accepted as the basis for FORTITUDE, known simply at this stage as 'Appendix Y'. Its aims were:

1. To induce the Germans to believe that the main assault and follow-up would be in the Pas de Calais area
2. To keep the enemy in doubt as to the date and time of the actual assault
3. To contain the largest possible enemy land and air forces in or east of the Pas de Calais for at least fourteen days after the initial assault.

In order to do this, it would be necessary to persuade the enemy of the existence of large amphibious forces over and above those needed for the actual assault, and this was eventually done successfully on an enormous scale.

Planning in more detail had to await the outcome of the Combined Chiefs of Staff meetings in Cairo and Tehran in November and December 1943, where it was decided that OVERLORD would be launched in May 1944, and a complementary attack, Operation ANVIL, launched against the south of France shortly afterwards. On 6 December Colonel Bevan was given instructions to prepare the necessary deception plans, which were submitted to the Chiefs of Staff Committee as Operation BODYGUARD on Christmas Eve. The problem was tackled in two stages: strategic, to persuade the enemy to dispose its forces so as to cause least interference with OVERLORD, ANVIL and operations on the Soviet front, and tactical, to deceive the enemy as to the strength, timing and objectives of OVERLORD and ANVIL. As far as the Soviet Front was concerned, it would help if the Germans could be led to believe that no major assault could be launched before late June, and that no major Allied offensive would be undertaken in the west until it had begun.

The objective of BODYGUARD was to persuade the Germans that although a cross-Channel operation was being prepared, it was not the only Allied operation being planned, and in any case it would not be launched until the late summer of 1944. Ingenious though it was, BODYGUARD cannot be said to have succeeded: the strategic deception it attempted was really a lost cause, as both Hitler and the German OKW were firmly convinced of the threat to the Channel coast, although unaware of where along the coast the real threat lay.

Operation FORTITUDE, which succeeded BODYGUARD as the deception cover plan for OVERLORD, developed as the plans for OVERLORD evolved. It consisted of two parts: the first, FORTITUDE NORTH, postulated a threat to Scandinavia, and the second, FORTITUDE SOUTH, a threat against the Pas de Calais. The legend, approved by Eisenhower on 23 February 1944, comprised two consecutive phases:

1. Before D-Day for the OVERLORD landings, the Germans would be led to believe that the cross-Channel attack was being prepared only to take advantage of any German weakening, and would take place only after other diversionary attacks had been launched, particularly against Northern Europe. Initially, operations would be launched against south Norway, with an initial assault against Stavanger, as threatened by Operation TINDALL the previous year, and then against north Norway to link up with the Red Army and obtain access to the Swedish ore fields. Only after these operations had succeeded would the assault across the Channel be launched, in mid-July in the Pas de Calais area.
2. Once the real landings had taken place in Normandy, the story would enter its second phase. It would be indicated that the Normandy landings were a feint, to draw in the German reserves before the main landings in the Pas de Calais were carried out by the main assault force currently assembling in south-east England.

Operation FORTITUDE was approved in March 1944 and preparations were soon well under way; now the deception staffs were able to reap the benefit of COCKADE the previous year, which had failed in its main purpose of strategic deception, but had been a valuable rehearsal for the big performance in 1944, thanks to the benefit of the SIGINT which had enabled the deception staffs to assess audience reaction. The other main element contributing to the credibility of FORTITUDE was the inflated Allied order of battle, both in the Mediterranean and in the UK, which had been so carefully built up since 1942 and accepted by German Intelligence as fact. In projecting this notional order of battle to the enemy, the global deployment of Allied forces had to be treated as a single entity; notional formations being notionally moved from one theatre to another had to be provided with evidence of their departure, transit and arrival, while real formations whose movements had to be concealed had similarly to have cover devised in the theatres both of departure and arrival.

An essential part of the Allied redeployment for OVERLORD was the transfer of seven seasoned divisions and some seventy landing craft from the Mediterranean to the UK, and the concealment of the latter from the Germans – who had five observation posts on the European side and another seven on the African side of the Straits of Gibraltar, with various types of detection devices – presented the biggest problem. It was covered by the story that a number of landing craft were being returned to the UK for repair, as facilities in the Mediterranean were quite inadequate. As it turned out, the deception staffs need not have worried: German air reconnaissance at this stage was so inadequate that the Germans had no idea of the number of landing craft available to the Allies in the Mediterranean or elsewhere, and they accepted that there were sufficient to cover any future needs in the Mediterranean theatre.

To cover the return of the seasoned divisions from the Mediterranean to the UK theatre of operations, the story was put out, mainly through the double agents, that personnel seen wearing the insignia of these divisions in the UK were either personnel on leave or part of training cadres sent home to train recruits, leaving all their vehicles and heavy equipment behind. At the same time it was suggested that the number of formations in the Mediterranean theatre had actually been increased by the transfer of notional formations from the United Kingdom. These deceptions were covered by Operation FOYNES, mentioned above; they had the effect of leading Fremde Heer (West) to accept the presence in the UK in January 1944 of 55 divisions, as against the actual total of 37, while by the end of May the German assessment had risen to 79 against an actual figure of only 52. It was this overestimation by the Germans that made the twin threats of FORTITUDE NORTH to Scandinavia and FORTITUDE SOUTH to the Pas de Calais appear perfectly credible to them, even after the Normandy landings had already started.

The threat in FORTITUDE NORTH was mounted by a notional 'Fourth Army', based on Scottish Command. Little use was made of visual displays of dummies in view of the vagaries of the Scottish climate, reliance being placed upon bogus radio traffic and reports from the double agents. The Soviets also played their part, putting out a great deal of information through their own channels covering the notional coordination of 'Fourth Army' operations with Soviet forces. It was not necessary to create many bogus formations as both 52 (Lowland) and 3 Infantry Divisions were already stationed in Scotland carrying out assault landing training, while there was a large concentration of Polish units in the Lowlands and a Norwegian contingent was stationed near Dingwall in the Highlands. Two notional naval forces were created to serve the notional land forces, and notional amphibious training was carried out with them, primarily through bogus radio traffic, from mid-April. The number of ships anchored in the Firth of Forth rose from 26 at the beginning of April to 71 by mid-May, by which time, to all visual and audible appearances, all land and naval forces for the landings were assembled in the Firth of Clyde, ready to sail at short notice.

The deception was successful in that it persuaded the Germans to believe in the existence of 'Fourth Army' and its hostile intentions. Fremde Heer (West) was aware as early as January 1944 of the concentrations in Scotland, but failed to accept the remaining bait, observing that the Allies were doing everything possible to tie down the German forces on other fronts while diverting attention from the decisive Atlantic Front, and never wavering from the view that the forces at Fourth Army's disposal were inadequate for anything other than diversionary operations which the existing German garrison in Norway should be able to contain. This deception failed to affect the existing German dispositions to any noticeable extent.

Before leaving the notional threat against Norway, we should mention another deception being mounted in parallel, Operation GRAFFHAM. The object of this operation was to induce the enemy to believe that the Allies were enlisting the active cooperation of Sweden in connection with the projected Allied operation against northern Norway in the spring of 1944. This was implemented almost entirely through diplomatic channels, with some useful rumours contributed by the double agents. Operation GRAFFHAM opened in February, when the British Foreign Office instructed the British Minister in Stockholm to ask the Swedish Government to allow the British to obtain meteorological reports from Sweden and to install British navigation aids at certain points on Swedish territory. At the same time, the rumour was put about that after the Allied landings in Norway, Swedish airfields would be used to supplement the Allied bombing offensive against Germany. These requests were supplemented on 4 April by more pressing ones. The British asked for the right to refuel and repair damaged aircraft in Sweden, and to operate their own reconnaissance flights over that country. The Swedish Government took these requests seriously, and discussions on the various issues raised continued throughout the spring.

The effect on the Germans was all that could have been desired, especially after the US and Soviet envoys had added their voices to those of the British. On 9 June, three days after the Normandy landings, the three Allied governments jointly demanded an assurance from the Swedes that in the event of an Allied landing in Norway, the Swedish Government would resist German pressure to allow the movement of German troops from Finland through Swedish territory. This produced a most satisfactory reaction in the Swedish press, where Allied landings in Norway were now stated to be imminent. German fears continued long after the Normandy Landings, but were not shared by the hard-headed specialists at Fremde Heer (West).

Although FORTITUDE NORTH succeeded in convincing the Germans that the threat to Scandinavia was credible, it failed to persuade them to alter their troop dispositions in answer to the threat. However, FORTITUDE SOUTH was a different matter altogether. Here the problem was to persuade the German High Command that the real Normandy landings were merely a feint to draw forces away from the notionally real invasion point of the Pas de Calais. As there was no way the Allied invasion forces massing in the south of England could be hidden, it was necessary to simulate others on a comparable scale in south-east England to represent the notional Pas de Calais invasion force. The preparations involved in simulating this threat were enormous – displays of dummy landing craft, embarkation hards, roads, dumps, camps, the evacuation of civilians, arrangements for the treating of casualties and holding of prisoners of war – and, on examination, proved to involve far too large an expenditure of manpower to be practicable. It was therefore decided that the simulation should be by means of radio traffic and reports from the double agents only, a decision made viable for two reasons. Firstly, the Allies by now had total air supremacy over the British Isles and surrounding waters, so regular air reconnaissance over south-east England by the Luftwaffe was impossible; as only the occasional lone aircraft could get through, it was deemed sufficient to have displays of dummy landing craft only, the other visual displays being rightly considered unnecessary. Secondly, the British security authorities were by now convinced that they controlled all enemy Intelligence sources within the country; the occasional leak or indiscretion might escape through a neutral source, but the credibility of the hard core of double agents had been tried and accepted according to SIGINT intercepts, and their reports were likely to be considered more reliable than the occasional contradictory report that might slip through.

After the visual display aspect had been settled, the way was now clear for the creation of a notional 'First US Army Group' (FUSAG) based on the skeleton HQ of the real 1 US Army Group, which was intended ultimately to take command of the US forces in France once they were of a size to warrant an independent command. This notional formation was to be commanded by General George S. Patton, a colourful and experienced commander who had been sidelined after an unfortunate incident in Sicily in which he had struck a soldier. The HQ of this formation was notionally at Wentworth near Ascot in Berkshire, with two real armies, the First Canadian in Kent and East Sussex, and the Third US, notionally in Suffolk and Essex, under command, each comprising two corps with a total of eleven divisions. This large and largely imaginary force of some 150,000 men opened up its radio network on 24 April 1944, which carried its administrative and operational radio traffic for some six months thereafter. Meanwhile, the double agents, under the detailed instruction of their case officers as advised by Ops B, were busy faithfully reporting the notional movements and concentrations of these formations and their subordinate units.

Security for the real invasion was a thorny problem, with many conflicting requirements. The military's prime concern was the prevention of all possible leakage of information, while the civilian authorities naturally wanted as little disruption of free movement, transport and communication as possible. The Foreign Office wanted minimum disruption of normal diplomatic channels, while the deception staffs wanted to enhance the credibility of their cover stories. Foreseeing this problem, in August 1943 the ISSB had proposed a complete severance of communications between the United Kingdom and the outside world, but that this should occur only at the last possible moment before the troops were briefed for the operation. The LCS objected to this on the very valid grounds that it would alert the Germans at the crucial moment, and Colonel Bevan proposed instead that such a ban would have to start early enough to give no indication of the real date of D-Day, and last long enough to cover the notional attack on the Pas de Calais.

Compromise was reached in February with the imposition of an immediate ban on travel between Britain and Ireland, and the imposition of a prohibited coastal zone 10 miles deep. The airmail service to Lisbon was stopped in March, all civilian travel to and from the United Kingdom was banned in April, and diplomatic mail was subjected to censorship and the use of diplomatic ciphers was banned in the same month. These last measures caused some inconvenience to B1(a) and the LCS, whose channels for misinformation of the enemy were thereby severely restricted. Despite vigorous Foreign Office objections, however, these measures remained in force, at General Eisenhower's insistence, until 25 August, well after FORTITUDE SOUTH had ended.

One of the more well-known if least effective minor ploys to deceive the Germans as to the date of D-Day was Operation COPPERHEAD, in which Lieutenant Clifton James of the Royal Army Pay Corps impersonated Field-Marshal Montgomery on a visit to Gibraltar and Algiers at the end of May 1944. The visit was duly reported by a controlled double agent, and it was noted by Fremde Heer (West), but its only known effect was to draw attention to the possibility of an Allied attack on southern France. There is no indication that this deception contributed to the tactical surprise achieved on the Normandy beaches by the Allies on 6 June.

A more useful contribution to the surprise element was the care taken to ensure that nothing was revealed by the pattern of air bombardment. Of the 49 airfields within 150 miles of Caen which were attacked before D-Day, eleven were in the Pas de Calais and only four in the area of the actual landing, while nineteen rail junctions supplying the Pas de Calais were attacked. Attacks on coastal defences and radar installations in the Pas de Calais were twice as heavy as those in the actual landing area, while attacks on bridges over the Meuse, Oise and the Albert Canal all indicated the northern area. The earlier difficulties experienced by deception staffs in persuading the air forces to divert scarce resources to 'cover' targets had at last been overcome. The Royal Navy also collaborated in simulated operations against radar stations on the Cotentin Peninsula and feint landings north of the Seine estuary and the Pas de Calais itself, and 21 Army Group employed tactical deception on a large scale in simulating air drops and landings west of St Lo and north of the Seine, as well as east and south-west of Caen.

Less than twenty-four hours before D-Day, Fremde Heer (West) had complained: 'the enemy command continues to attempt, by every method of nerve warfare, to obscure its invasion plans'. At the beginning of June the Germans had no greater knowledge of Allied intentions than they had had six months earlier. Although they correctly appreciated that the Normandy or Brittany Peninsulas were the most likely points of Allied attack, the deception of FORTITUDE SOUTH had also become firmly implanted in the mind of von Rundstedt, and caused him to delay the reinforcement of the Normandy front. Notwithstanding the threat to the Pas de Calais, by 9 June virtually the whole of the German strategic reserve in France had been thrown into the Normandy battle.

The aim of the continued playing of FORTITUDE SOUTH was therefore to delay or prevent the commitment of any of the formations of the German 15 Army in Belgium to the Normandy front, and this the deception staffs were able to do until at least four weeks after the Normandy landings. Enough of the Fremde Heer (West) situation reports were decrypted to give the deception staffs a very good idea of the success of their plans, but another equally good source was the traffic between the Japanese Embassy in Berlin, which carried regular, detailed reports from the Japanese naval and military attachés on the progress of the war. These showed that as late as 3 July, the OKW was still expecting an Allied assault in the Pas de Calais area.

By 3 August the Normandy battle had been won. Future deception operations in the European theatre would be of a tactical nature only, initiated by Ops B at SHAEF and G(R) and 'R' Force in 21 Army Group. The success of the strategic deception operations up to this date had been greater than could have been expected, achieving complete surprise for a landing operation on an enemy shore on a scale larger than any previously attempted, and successfully delaying the commitment of German reserves after the landing until Allied forces were securely established in Normandy. The lessons to be learned from these strategic deceptions, on a scale never before attempted, were many:

1. Control of military deception operations must be in the hands of one central planning body with authority to control all agencies involved.
2. This body must be part of the operational staff of the military formation planning the real operations for which cover is desired.
3. Control of all enemy agents in the planning area is desirable for planting false information.
4. SIGINT decrypts of enemy Intelligence communications are essential in order to assess the enemy's acceptance of planted misinformation.
5. Overwhelming air superiority is desirable, to prevent enemy reconnaissance of real and notional preparations and dispositions of forces.
6. Before planning deception operations, it is essential to have detailed knowledge of the real operation which has to be covered.

For all these criteria to apply is a very rare occurrence in war. The deception planning staffs were almost uniquely lucky in that they had control of all enemy agents in the United Kingdom and that GC & CS had broken the Abwehr Enigma codes so that they were able to read the enemy's Intelligence traffic and assess its reaction to the double agents' reports and other sources of misinformation. As far as the creation of a deception organisation and its relationship to the military operational staffs were concerned, the lessons had been learned the hard way, firstly in the Middle East and secondly in the United Kingdom in the earlier, darker days of the war.

There was one other important deception carried out in the United Kingdom, mainly by the double agent networks, before the end of the war in Europe. It was designed to mislead the Germans as to the accuracy of their V-weapons, the V-1 (Flying Bomb) and the V-2 (A-4 rocket) campaigns (Operation CROSSBOW) from June to December 1944. The V-1 was a small, pilotless and unguided aircraft operated from portable launching ramps by a special regiment, Flakregiment 155(W), located in the Pas de Calais area. It was the first of the two V-Weapons to be used against the United Kingdom.

British Intelligence had long been aware of German developments in the field of rocket weapons, and since receiving Intelligence reports of their activities at the experimental research station at Peenemünde, a special committee had been set up under the chairmanship of Duncan Sandys in April 1943 to evaluate Intelligence on German preparations for rocket attacks. By August of that year it seemed possible that the Germans were working on both a pilotless aircraft and a rocket projectile, and a major controversy arose as to which presented the greater threat. Air reconnaissance flights over northern France revealed a number of curiously shaped sites, known as 'ski sites', around Cherbourg and in the Pas de Calais. These were correctly identified as launching sites for the pilotless aircraft, and were subjected to heavy and effective attack from the air in December 1943. This led the Germans to devise less conspicuous sites which were not identified by Allied Intelligence until April of the following year. Although it became clear that they were being readied for action, only a limited number of aircraft could be made available for dealing with them. By June 1944 it was obvious that an attack was imminent; the first salvo was fired on the night of 12–13 June, directed against London. It was launched prematurely, imposed on the V-weapon units against their better judgment by the impatience of their High Command. The serious attacks began three nights later, when 217 missiles were launched, of which 45 landed in Central London. By the end of the month more than 2,400 weapons had been launched, their impacts being scattered very widely over the Home Counties, but some 660 had fallen in the London area, an uncomfortable 27 per cent of the total.

The Air Ministry was the department chiefly responsible for dealing with these new weapons, and its specialists had been puzzling as to how best to deal with a weapon that could not be shot down either by anti-aircraft fire or aircraft. They initially assumed that the aiming point for all launches was Charing Cross, but after ten days or so it became clear that most of the flying bombs were falling two or three miles short of this point, the mean point of impact (MPI) being calculated as being around North Dulwich station. Unpleasant though this was for the residents of the North Dulwich area, things might have been very much worse if the MPI had been in the centre of the City of London or Westminster, but luckily, many of the bombs were exploding harmlessly on the many open spaces which abound in that part of London.

The objective of the Air Ministry and the Home Defence Executive was therefore to dissuade the Germans from correcting their aim, or even, if possible, to persuade them to shorten it further by leading them to believe that many missiles were falling in North-West London. The Twenty Committee welcomed this suggestion when it met on 29 June; the Ministry of Home Security disliked the idea of persuading the Germans to shift the MPI of the flying bombs further to the south-east, but the Ministry of Production had no objection, and it was recommended that the impression should be created by 'special means' – the double agents controlled by B1(a) – that the bombs were overshooting their target, assumed to be Central London.

By 18 July, when the Chiefs of Staff again considered the situation, nearly all the double agents had received urgent requests from their German controllers to report on the time and place of V-weapon impacts, and despite the fitting of radio direction-finding devices to some 5 per cent of the weapons, after more than 2,000 launches the Germans had still made no effort to correct their aim. It was decided that the double agents should be notionally located in positions in North-West London, the better to supply the information requested by their German controllers. They would report locations of actual impacts in that area, but give the times of impacts in South-East London. It was hoped that this technique would persuade the Germans to identify the bomb which fell in South-East London with the impact reported in North-West London, and plot it there. At the same time, countermeasures were introduced to jam or distort the radio direction-finding devices fitted in some of the V-1s.

However, at a meeting with the Prime Minister on 28 July the Ministers of Production and Home Security refused to agree to the proposed action to move the MPI further to the south-east, and the argument over the action to be taken to mislead the enemy raged on until 18 August. By that time, when agreement had been finally reached, it was too late for the policy to be put into effect. The last salvo of forty-seven bombs was fired at random on the night of 30–31 August, and the launch sites were overrun by Allied forces on 1 September – the British deception policy appears to have had little effect. In any case, the V-1 was an area weapon, of little use against precise targets, and the Germans were happy to accept almost any MPI as long as the weapons were achieving their objective of lowering British civilian morale.

The threat presented by the flying bombs was in any event as nothing compared to that posed by the second of the German *Vergeltungswaffen* ('reprisal weapons'), the V-2 (or A-4) ballistic rocket missile, which the Germans brought into action at the beginning of September 1944. The development of these weapons had been detected even before that of the V-1, and because they could not be intercepted they presented a very much graver threat to London. Since the evidence indicated that their use was imminent, more than 1½ million people had left London by the end of August, but more drastic evacuation plans were not put into effect as on 6 September the Vice-Chiefs of Staff indicated that the potential launch sites would all be overrun shortly, and there would then be little further danger to the country from either of these weapons. Alas for such optimism! The launch sites in Holland and Friesland were not overrun for another six months, in which time over a thousand V-2s had fallen in England, mainly in the London area. There was little the Twenty Committee could do to affect the situation as the rockets were already being fired at their extreme range of some 200 miles, but attempts could be made to get the enemy to shorten the range. In the end, however, it was decided to let the double agents report more or less factually, giving the bare minimum of information necessary to maintain their credibility. In fact, the MPI of the rockets was altered, but evidence as to the reason for the change, whether or not it was due to the fallacious agents' reports, is now lacking. Nevertheless, in its monthly report to the Prime Minister for January 1945, MI 5 informed him of the possibility that it had been due to the deception put out by 'special means', and its report for February asserted this with some certainty.

THE FAR EAST, 1942–45

No summary of British military deception operations in the Second World War would be complete without mentioning the Far East theatre of war. As in the Middle East theatre two years earlier, the idea of military deception in the Far East was introduced by General Sir Archibald Wavell, that arch exponent of the art, who had been posted to India as Commander-in-Chief in July 1941. It was introduced for very much the same reason as had made it desirable in the Middle East – the enemy forces' superiority in training and equipment to the forces under his own command. Wavell was appointed Supreme Allied Commander of the ABDA (America-British-Dutch-Australia) Command in March 1942, and immediately requested the attachment of Major R.P. (Peter) Fleming to his command, to serve in the same capacity as Dudley Clarke had done in the Middle East.

Fleming had had some deception experience in collaboration with Clarke in the last phase of the campaign in Norway, and on his arrival in Delhi was immediately given the task of devising a deception plan designed to convince the advancing Japanese that a formidable build-up of British forces in India was taking place, on a scale which was more than sufficient to block any further Japanese advance. Fleming devised a variation of the 'briefcase containing marked maps and false order of battle' ploy so often previously used in military deceptions, under the title of Operation ERROR. It involved leaving a ditched staff car containing a briefcase carrying false documents and some of the C-in-C's personal effects on the far side of the Irrawaddy river, beside a bridge that was blown up some three hours later. There is no evidence that the Japanese even found the documents, let alone acted on them.

There was little scope for strategic deception in this theatre because of the continuing uncertainty about the Allies' real strategic intentions, so most deception was of a purely tactical nature. Nevertheless, every effort was made to conform to the overall strategic deception plans issued by the LCS and the US

Joint Inter-Service Security Board, and for this purpose Fleming organised his own small staff as GSI(d), a sub-branch of the General Staff Intelligence branch in GHQ. There was little for them to do during 1942 when contact with Japanese forces was minimal, but in 1943, when Wavell was recalled and replaced by Vice-Admiral Lord Louis Mountbatten as Commander of the new South-East Asia Command (SEAC), a more elaborate organisation became necessary. This was known as 'D' Division, with its main HQ (which became known in 1944 as 'Force 456') in Delhi, tactical HQs in Kandy (in Ceylon) and Calcutta, and an advanced HQ in Barrackpore, later moving to Rangoon. 'D' Division eventually totalled some 30 officers, 32 other ranks and 9 secretarial staff.

Tactical deception in the Far East was a very different matter from that in Europe, however. For one thing, the absence of Japanese air reconnaissance made visual deception unnecessary, while in the thick jungle of Burma, except for ground troops in contact with the enemy, there was little opportunity for the camouflage experts to practise their art. The situation was similar with radio deception: although some bogus radio traffic was mounted in India, there is no indication that this was monitored or understood by the Japanese. 'D' Division's time was therefore devoted mainly to order of battle deception, and recruiting the 'special means' with which to disseminate it. In this latter respect, Fleming had some success, particularly with the help of the Intelligence services of the Chiang Kai-shek government in Chungking, although, as with 'A' Force in the Middle East, he could not hope to achieve the degree of control over double agents achieved by the Twenty Committee and B1(a) in London. He did enjoy a fair measure of success in convincing the Japanese military Intelligence staff of the inflated notional British order of battle in the Far East theatre, but unfortunately, like many other armies, the Japanese Army placed little trust in Intelligence or in those who produced it, and therefore took very little notice of any information issuing from that source.

In the absence of any coherent and clearly stated Allied strategic plan, the best the deception staff could do was to ensure that the enemy was as confused as they were themselves. Their lasting achievement, as in Europe and the Middle East, was to build up in the minds of enemy Intelligence a completely fallacious idea of the operational forces available to the Allies in the Far East. As a result, the Japanese, like the Germans in Europe, were led to believe that available Allied forces were so overwhelmingly strong that they could deliver multiple attacks wherever required. In this respect, therefore, 'D' Division could take pride in a job well done, as could their colleagues in the LCS and 'A' Force.

Undoubtedly successful as the British and Allied strategic deception operations in the Second World War were, it is highly unlikely that similar conditions will prevail in any future war. For one thing, complete control over enemy agents such as MI 5 and the Twenty Committee exerted over the German agents in the United Kingdom in that war is an extremely rare condition, unlikely to be achievable again. For another, the sensors available on present-day reconnaissance aircraft, drones and satellites can instantly reveal the bogus nature of dummy tanks, vehicles, guns, oil storage depots and other components of the Second World War visual displays. Future deception operations, both tactical and strategic, will need very much more sophisticated measures, such as thermal camouflage and sensor-blinding devices, while darkness will no longer provide adequate cover for the surreptitious movement of forces. No doubt considerable military thought, research and development is being devoted by all the major powers to deception in the electronic and satellite age, but the results are unlikely to be made public.

CHAPTER 7

Conclusion

Over the centuries of the recorded history of British military Intelligence, we have seen that there has been a continual pattern of change in the Army's Intelligence requirements. The trend has been towards an extension of the geographical area of interest of both the commander in the field (for tactical Intelligence) and of the high command (for strategic Intelligence) forwards and to the flanks. This is the result of the continual increase in the effective range and destructive power of military weapons, from the arrow to the guided missile and from the cannonball to the nuclear warhead, and the increase in Army mobility, both tactical and strategic, arising from the invention of the steam, internal combustion, compression ignition and gas turbine engines and the fixed- and rotary-wing aircraft.

In addition to the extension of the geographical area of interest there has been a continual widening in the range of subjects in which the Army has a legitimate Intelligence interest. Apart from the basic information as to the enemy's strength, whereabouts, intentions, weapons, state of training and morale, which was all that was needed until the twentieth century, strategic military Intelligence requirements have gradually extended to include information on political, economic, troop strength, research and development, industrial, communications and other matters relating to an enemy or potential enemy.

The extension of the breadth and range of interest of the military has had the effect of impinging upon the interests of other government departments, including the other service departments, with the result that since the Second World War, Intelligence for all of them has been collated, evaluated and disseminated by a single combined organisation, the Defence Intelligence Staff in the Ministry of Defence. This has had the benefit of ensuring that Intelligence reaches the right customers rather than being compartmentalised by one department to the detriment of others. It is the obvious and most economical way of dealing with the strategic Intelligence requirements of the individual armed services.

To keep pace with the increased requirements placed upon them, Intelligence staffs have increased in numbers, while methods of Intelligence collection, collation and dissemination have changed out of all recognition since the Second World War. The rate of change has itself been accelerating, particularly since the end of the nineteenth century. Whereas one man with a quill pen could cope with the collation of military Intelligence of all kinds on one or more countries in 1900, we now have large staffs served by banks of computers to process the vast amount of information emanating from the sophisticated collection methods discussed in this book.

Generally speaking, the less a country spends in peacetime on its defence and its armed forces, the more it needs to spend on Intelligence. The better its Intelligence on potentially hostile countries, the more time it will have to prepare itself should the prospect of war against them arise. This self-evident truth has too often been ignored by British Governments in the past; their cheese-paring and parsimony towards the armed services and their equipment in peacetime has too often been applied to the Intelligence organisations as well, with the result that hostile actions have taken them by surprise and caught them with unready and ill-equipped forces. So far they have been lucky, in that they have in the end always been given enough time to build up their forces and equipment through one accident of fate or another. In 1917 the troop strength and industrial might of the USA came to the rescue, while in 1940 the obstacle of the English Channel gave the British sufficient breathing space to rearm and re-equip while again awaiting the help of the USA.

Since the invention of the guided missile, in all its tactical and strategic variations, and the nuclear warhead, this breathing space is no longer available. It is estimated that no more than a few minutes' warning of a nuclear missile attack will be available to the United Kingdom in any future war between the superpowers. There will be no time in which to redress the gross quantitative imbalance which has hitherto existed between NATO forces and those, say, of Russia and its allies. This means that our guard must be permanently up and on the alert.

An efficient military Intelligence machine is thus now more essential in peacetime than ever before. Intelligence concerning the potential enemy must be kept continually up to date and either in the hands of, or ready to be issued at a moment's notice to, the troops in the field. The watch for all indicators of possible hostile intentions must also be permanently maintained. To be able to do this, the military Intelligence organisation must be adequately funded and equipped to carry out its job. This must be one of the government's top priorities, ahead of other pressing demands for its funds from the Social Security, Health and Education budgets, for without adequate knowledge of hostile military preparations, our own defences will be hampered, the country could be laid waste or overrun, and the population killed. Money spent on more popular vote-catching services would then have been an irrelevance.

The problem really lies in the nature of democracy – it is inherently near-sighted and has a very short attention span. It is thus very difficult for a democratically elected government to do something at a time when the cost of doing it is low if there is no immediate benefit to be seen, and if it will be felt in the future, by its successors or its successors' successors.

With the development and increasing use of ever more sophisticated technical methods of Intelligence collection such as satellite IMINT, ELINT and SIGINT, the contribution of HUMINT to the overall Intelligence 'take' has shrunk. These technical methods, particularly IMINT, have also made the task of deception in war very much more difficult. Satellites are vulnerable to physical and radio attack, however, so their continued functioning in war cannot be relied upon. There will therefore always be a requirement for HUMINT, particularly as the mechanical methods of Intelligence-collection lack judgement and cannot interpret the thoughts and fears of the enemy high command. Nevertheless, the mechanical and electronic methods are inherently more reliable, current and quantifiable, when they are working, than the human agent, although their cost is many times greater, and increases as their sophistication increases.

The question of computer security is of increasing concern to Intelligence organisations. While it can be comparatively easy for a clever and determined computer expert to break into a computer system, it is very much more difficult to determine whether or not such a break-in has taken place. Experts in the City of London and in other financial centres around the world are concerned about computer fraud, and some are convinced that very large sums of money have been siphoned out of the international system, but nobody has yet proved this to be the case. It is the communications systems to which computers are connected, whether radio or landline, which present the weak point in the system, and it is on these that Intelligence services will concentrate in peacetime to obtain computer-based Intelligence concerning hostile forces.

The most important component of any technical means of Intelligence-collection is its sensor. Sensor technology has developed very rapidly during the past thirty years, and as it has developed, so has the need for visual observation declined. Sensors fall into five categories, those detecting:

1. emissions in the electro-magnetic spectrum
2. sound waves
3. magnetic anomalies in the Earth's magnetic field
4. vibrations in the ground
5. nuclear radiation

The electro-magnetic spectrum extends from very low radio frequencies up through those used for radio and radar, through millimetric and sub-millimetric wavelengths on to infra-red, visible light, ultra-violet, X-rays, gamma rays and beyond. The majority of sensors operate in this spectrum. Sensors detecting sound waves include those frequencies above and below the normal range of human hearing, while magnetic anomaly detectors (MAD), seeking geographical variations in the Earth's magnetic field, are used mainly in the detection of submerged submarines. Vibration or seismic sensors are used in the detection of tank and vehicle movements, for example; such sensors can be left behind during a withdrawal, or planted in peacetime, to give indications of enemy activity, and they are also used to detect nuclear explosions and, in peacetime, earthquakes. Radiation sensors are also used both to detect radiation resulting from nuclear explosions and to analyse the fission products resulting from them.

Electro-magnetic and audio sensors can operate in either the active or the passive mode. In the active mode the sensor derives its information by transmitting energy and then listening to the reflections of this energy, while in the passive mode it listens for external sources of electro-magnetic or audio noise.

Active sensors can be detected from their active transmissions. They can be jammed by transmitting noise on the appropriate frequencies, or confused by screening, as with radar and metallic foil ('chaff'). Passive sensors can also be confused by the broadcasting of electro-magnetic noise, thermal camouflage and spurious sounds. Both active and passive sensors are vulnerable to physical attack, the more so as their locations are discovered. All active sensors can be detected, some more easily than others, because by operating at all, they reveal their locations and become targets for jamming weapons. Jammers too, by transmitting, become targets both for passive sensors and for homing weapons, although both may be deceived by decoy transmitters. The battle between sensors and means of hiding from or deceiving them is another facet of the never-ending battle between attack and defence. Sensors seek targets; means are developed, including physical, electro-magnetic or audio attack upon the sensors, to protect targets; means are developed to protect sensors from attack, and so on *ad infinitum*. Success will depend ultimately upon the level of technology that can be afforded, and the resulting performance of the equipment.

One is tempted by all this technology to write off the Secret Intelligence Service's human agent networks as being archaic, unreliable, difficult to communicate with and having been overtaken in both quality and quantity of Intelligence by the technical sources of GCHQ and other agencies. This temptation has to be resisted, however, as there are situations in which the human agent is irreplaceable; an example is in the penetration of terrorist organisations such as the IRA, which exist in communities that nourish and succour them. Well-placed agents and counter-Intelligence are central to the monitoring of terrorist contacts and activities. In other situations where the technical collection of Intelligence is prolific there is still a place for HUMINT, if only as a back-up in case of failure of the technical sources due to hostile interference or mechanical or communications failure. The bulk of peacetime military Intelligence nevertheless continues to stem from overt sources such as the international press, defence periodicals, television and radio broadcasts, manufacturers' brochures and foreign government publications.

Several benefits have resulted in peacetime from the 'open skies' policy enforced upon nations by the land-mapping reconnaissance satellite; an obvious one is the relative ease with which arms limitation, nuclear test ban and other treaties can be monitored, and compliance ensured, while another is the availability of accurate maps of countries in which they have hitherto been banned or non-existent, such as the former Soviet Union.

As there has never, so far, been an all-out nuclear war, the prospect presents many imponderables, and no attempt will be made here to resolve them. An all-out war implies that all available resources will be committed by both sides. In such a war the United Kingdom would probably have the support of NATO and one or more Commonwealth countries in what would in all likelihood be the final world war. Even were nuclear weapons not to be used immediately, such a war would be brief and would give little chance for reinforcement or re-equipment, so that it would be fought with forces and Intelligence already in existence and *in situ* at the outset.

That being the case, the importance of military Intelligence being fully current at the outbreak of war is paramount. There will be no time to update it later, and possibly no facilities with which to do so. In fact, it must be obvious to the least initiated that with satellites orbiting in known orbits, their position at any given time is completely predictable, and they are thus easily located by hostile radar. Since they are delicate structures full of sensitive and easily damaged equipment, they could easily be put out of action by anti-satellite missiles or armed satellites, and it must be assumed that at the beginning of an all-out nuclear war, this is what would happen to all, or at least a majority of them. This would cut off at one blow not only all NATO Intelligence on enemy troop, air and naval movements, but also all knowledge of enemy missile launches, Allied missile strikes and Allied long-range radio communications. Strategically, NATO would be fighting blind; tactically, its forces would have to fall back upon their normal methods of tactical reconnaissance and radio communications. In addition, the electro-magnetic pulses generated by multiple nuclear explosions have a damaging effect upon any electronic circuits that have not been specially (and expensively) 'hardened' against them, while the nuclear radiation can destroy the lenses in optical equipment such as gun sights and laser rangefinders.

Of course, it is possible that an enemy equally reliant upon satellites might pursue a policy of 'live and let live' with regard to satellites of the opposing side, in order to retain the use of its own facilities for IMINT, SIGINT and COMINT. This would show a restraint similar to that shown by both sides in the Second World War towards the introduction of chemical warfare. If restraint is shown towards the opposition's spy satellites, why not a similar restraint with regard to nuclear weapons? In which case we are no longer dealing with nuclear war, and the conditions applying to Intelligence in a localised war would apply to a global non-nuclear war.

British national resources in SIGINT, ELINT, COMINT and HUMINT are enough to make it self-sufficient in these fields in a localised war; however, for satellite reconnaissance and the IMINT it provides, the UK is totally dependent upon the UKUSA agreement and the goodwill of the USA. In the Falklands (Malvinas) campaign, the US decided to co-operate with the UK, but if the UK were to be involved in a conflict with a country friendly to the USA, such facilities might well not be available. In such a case, the UK would be entirely dependent upon its own air photo-reconnaissance resources.

It is not only the high initial and replacement costs of the means of collection which make the gathering of military and other types of Intelligence so expensive, however; there are also the information and communication systems necessary to process the mass of covert paperwork and photographs with which the collation organisation is now inundated, and to disseminate the results to those concerned with making policy. Equipment costs are high due to the large number of high-capacity computers required, as well as the secure communications networks needed to pass information from the collectors to the collators and from the collators to their customers in other government departments and in subordinate headquarters. Staff costs are also high due to the highly skilled operators required to write their programs, to operate them, to maintain them on line and to analyse their product, as well as the large numbers of fluent linguists necessary for the translation of intercepted and decrypted foreign messages and documents. The provision of such a large skilled workforce from the limited national resources, particularly in the face of competition from industry and other more high-paying customers for these skills, is a very great difficulty, and one which is likely to grow worse as equipment becomes more sophisticated.

Security, both of equipment and personnel, is a problem that looms very large in military Intelligence organisations; it afflicts many other fields too, but in Intelligence, where it is as important to conceal what you do not know about your enemy as it is to conceal what you do know, it is even more so. This is particularly true when so much of the Intelligence product has to be disseminated over lengthy lines of communication to HQs and units in the field. If a large part of the covert Intelligence 'take' emanates from intercepted signals and messages, so, it must be assumed, does that of other countries, and every effort must therefore be made to make our computers and communication networks secure from outside interference and penetration.

Security of personnel is a difficult problem too, particularly where so many highly skilled people are employed. The current system of Personal Vetting is probably adequate to weed out the emotionally or politically weak or vulnerable characters who have caused so much damage to British and US Intelligence organisations in the past. Had the present systems been in force during and immediately after the Second World War, it is doubtful whether the many defections and serious leaks of information from MI 5, MI 6, CIA, GCHQ and the NSA would have occurred. It is, of course, essential for the checks carried out under the Positive and Developed Vetting systems to be repeated periodically as people's circumstances change.

In the UK and in British territories overseas, the maintenance of security is mainly the responsibility of the Security Service MI 5. In counter-Intelligence, HUMINT plays a larger and more important part than it does in Intelligence collection; the penetration of subversive and terrorist organisations can be highly dangerous, but is a very necessary operation, which can sometimes be achieved only by the insertion of human agents into, or the recruitment of members of, the target organisation. Technical surveillance also plays its part in counter-Intelligence work, however, and Peter Wright, a former MI 5 employee, has revealed much of the state of the art of technical surveillance as it was in 1976 in his book *Spycatcher*; such information is obviously highly classified, and would not have been made public had Wright tried to publish his book in the United Kingdom.

Much water will have passed under the bridge of technical progress in the twenty-odd years since Wright was in a position to know what was going on in his field of technical surveillance, and the rate of this technical progress, in line with the increase in the rate of development in electronics and exotic materials, has undoubtedly continued to increase. It is fascinating to speculate on the methods which might be available in the future to those whose job it is to protect the security of the nation and its armed forces by keeping under surveillance all those attempting to undermine it, but such speculation, based as it must be on conjecture and imagination, could be dangerous in revealing unknowingly a technique employed or projected by the Security Service. The future of military Intelligence will be affected by technical developments, but what these might be is impossible, as well as unwise, to predict. James Michener, in his novel *Space*, relates how President Roosevelt once assembled a meeting of leading US scientists at the White House so that they could brief him about the more important scientific developments to be expected in the future. After three days of consideration, they failed to forecast antibiotics, atomic power, the jet engine, radar, computers, xerography and rockets.

There is no reason to suppose that our abilities to predict future scientific developments are likely to be any more successful than those of Roosevelt's scientists. All that can be said with certainty is that military Intelligence of one sort or another will continue, and that the future military Intelligence organisation will avail itself of the relevant technical and scientific developments, and adapt itself to make the best use of them. However, security considerations will quite rightly prevent disclosure of these to the public until such time as disclosure cannot compromise them.

APPENDIX

Military Intelligence in Other Countries

This book so far has dealt mainly with British military Intelligence, its organisation and methods. The British way of doing things is not necessarily either the best or the only way, however, and it is therefore only right that we should consider, if only in outline, how other countries organise the collection and dissemination of military Intelligence. This appendix therefore summarises the various Intelligence services in the more important countries of the world, as far as is publicly known.

AUSTRALIA

Having paid little attention to the collection of Intelligence prior to the Second World War and relied largely on British and US Intelligence during it, the Australian Government began to think more in national terms after the onset of the Cold War, and particularly after the Gouzenko defection in Canada. The need for a security service was highlighted during the Second World War by the threat of Japanese invasion, and the Australian Security and Intelligence Organisation (ASIO) was formed shortly after the war under the guidance of MI 5. It was headed by Brigadier Sir Charles Spry, formerly the Army's Director of Military Intelligence, who established close links with both MI 5 and MI 6 in the UK. In addition to the ASIO there are Intelligence staffs in the armed forces, concerned with purely military Intelligence and security. The ASIO is overseen by an Inspector-General of Intelligence and Security, as well as by a Joint Parliamentary ASIO Committee.

The Australians have a close relationship with both British and US SIGINT organisations, their own organisation for this purpose being the Defence Signals Division at Watsonia.

BULGARIA

As one of the Soviet Union's satellites, Bulgaria came very much under the domination of the Soviet Intelligence organisations during the Cold War. It has a very sinister State Security Service (Darjavna Sugurnost – DS) which was very much influenced by the Soviet KGB and operated under its direction in the collection of Intelligence, conducting assassinations and arms smuggling. Three of their assassination attempts made headlines in the world's press. The first, successful, involved the killing of Georgi Markov, a Bulgarian dissident broadcasting to Bulgaria from the BBC in London; he was killed by being pricked in the leg at a bus stop with an umbrella which injected a small pellet containing the poison rycin into his blood stream. The same technique was used, this time unsuccessfully, in Paris on another Bulgarian dissident, Vladimir Kostov, a former member of the DS. The DS was also implicated in the attempted assassination of Pope John Paul II in Rome in May 1981.

CANADA

For a long period the Royal Canadian Mounted Police formed Canada's secret Intelligence service and security service. This was logical at the time, as the chief concern was internal security. Its scope was considerably widened in the Second World War to meet the threat of German agents being landed by sea on Canada's extensive coastline, while it also had considerable success in rounding up the Soviet espionage network in Canada revealed by the defection in 1945 of Igor Gouzenko.

As a result of an inquiry into alleged illegal wire-tapping, breaking and entering and opening of mail by the RCMP, a senior judge in a Commission of Inquiry in 1977 recommended the removal of security from the remit of the RCMP and the setting up of a separate security organisation. This was done in 1983, when the Canadian Security Intelligence Service (CSIS) was formed. This reports to the Security Intelligence Review Committee.

In addition to the RCMP and CSIS, the armed services have their own organisation for the collation and dissemination of purely military Intelligence.

The organisation for SIGINT was the Examination Unit (later renamed the Communications Branch) of the National Research Council.

CHINA

China has one of the longest traditions of espionage in the world, and comparatively little is known about its Intelligence organisation. Mao Tse-tung started the modern Intelligence service of the People's Republic of China in a modest way before the First World War, but it was greatly strengthened after Chiang Kai-shek was driven from the Chinese mainland, and given the title Central External Liaison Department (CELD). The position is complicated by the fact that, in China, each government department has its own Intelligence organisation, contributing to the central control of Intelligence by one or more of three main channels: the first is through the Communist Party, concerned mainly with internal political and organisational security Intelligence; the second is the CELD, concerned mainly with foreign Intelligence, and the third is the State Council, which is linked to the military Intelligence department of the General Staff and to the Ministry of External Trade. Personnel of the New China News Agency are also heavily involved in espionage abroad.

CUBA

As a Communist country, Cuba follows the pattern by having an Intelligence organisation much bigger and wielding greater influence than the size of the country warrants. This is because of the need in all such political systems for the government to maintain tight control of news, propaganda and political thought, and the consequent requirement for an army of informants, and a large organisation to run them and to maintain the personnel records involved.

Apart from the main secret Intelligence organisation, the Direccion General de Intelligencia (DGI), which is modelled on the former Soviet Union's KGB, the armed forces also have their own Intelligence organisation based upon the Soviet GRU (q.v.).

CZECHOSLOVAKIA

Until the break-up of the Soviet Union and the Warsaw Pact, the Czech Secret Service, the Statni Tajna Bezpecnost (STB), was one of the most efficient and most feared of the Eastern Bloc Intelligence services. Although officially coming under the ambit of the Ministry of the Interior's Intelligence Directorate, of which it was the First Section, its brief was the collection of secret Intelligence on foreign countries, and the recruitment and running of foreign agents. This it did under the direction and firm control of the KGB, although it probably scored more Intelligence coups against the UK than did its Soviet masters. In addition to the STB, the Czech Army has its own Intelligence service for the collation of purely military Intelligence.

Nothing has been publicly revealed of the Czech Intelligence organisation since the collapse of the Soviet Union and the Warsaw Pact. With the possibility of Czechoslovakia joining NATO, this information will doubtless come into the public domain in due course.

FRANCE

The French Intelligence and security services have for long been among the most efficient in the world. Before and during the Second World War, the Deuxième Bureau was the coordinating office for collating and interpreting Intelligence for the French High Command; it was so named after the Army system of organising the General Staff into four branches, of which the first dealt with administration, the second with Intelligence, the third with operations and staff duties and the fourth with supplies and logistics. The Service de Renseignements (SR) was subordinated to the Army and comprised four divisions, responsible respectively for foreign Intelligence, counter-espionage, communications and the central registry. The French SIGINT service also came under the wing of the SR.

After the fall of France in 1940, General de Gaulle formed the Bureau Centrale de Renseignements et d'Action (Militaire) (BCRA(M)), under Colonel Passy, at 10 Duke Street in London; it became the BCRA in 1942. This organisation had a somewhat evil reputation among the British, particularly after an agent suspected of having also worked for the Germans was discovered hanging in the basement after a hostile interrogation. It moved to Algiers with de Gaulle's HQ in 1943, where de Gaulle established the Direction Général des Services Spéciaux (DGSS) for the collection of secret Intelligence, under the direction of Jacques Soustelle. After the liberation of Paris, the DGSS moved there and its name was changed to Direction Général des Études et Recherches (DGER).

After the war, de Gaulle recalled Colonel Passy to run the service, which was reorganised and renamed the Service de Documentation Extérieure et de Contre-Espionage (SDECE). Since that time the SDECE has been reorganised many times until it was again renamed under President Mitterand, this time as the Direction Général de Sécurité Extérieure (DGSE). Despite many vicissitudes and however named, the service remains among the best secret Intelligence services in the world.

As in the UK and most other countries, France separates its Intelligence service from its counter-Intelligence service. Responsibility for counter-Intelligence rests with the Direction de la Surveillance du Territoire (DST), which also has a reputation for quiet efficiency. The service is subordinate to the Ministry of the Interior.

The armed services also have their own Intelligence organisations for the collation and dissemination of military Intelligence.

GERMANY

In 1939 the service responsible for military Intelligence was the Abwehr; it was subordinated to the Oberkommando der Wehrmacht (OKW), which was the equivalent of the modern British Ministry of Defence. Within the OKW, the headquarters of the Army was the Oberkommando des Heeres (OKH), equivalent to the present British MoD(Army), and the branch of the OKH responsible for the collation, evaluation and dissemination of Intelligence concerning the Western Allies in the Second World War was Fremde Heer (West) (FH(W)). Similarly, the branch responsible for Intelligence on the Soviet Union was Fremde Heer (Ost) (FH(O)).

Security was the responsibility of the Reichssicherheitshauptamt (RSHA), formed by Himmler's decree of 1939 by combining the Geheimstaatspolizei (Gestapo – Secret State Police), the Kriminalpolizei (Kripo – Criminal Police) and the Sicherheitsdienst (SD – Security Service).

After the Second World War Germany was effectively divided into two separate but related countries, the Deutsche Demokratische Republik (DDR) in the east and the Federal Republic of Germany (Bundesrepublik Deutschland) in the west.

EAST GERMANY

As with all countries with a Communist government, a very large percentage of the DDR's Intelligence effort was devoted to spying and informing on its own citizens – just how large was revealed when the majority of the files of the internal security service, the Ministerium für Staatssicherheit (MfS), were opened to the public gaze upon the reunification of East and West Germany in 1990.

Secret Intelligence was the responsibility of the Staatssicherheitsdienst (SSD, or Stasi), and a very efficient service it was, particularly against West Germany. It was largely a puppet of the Soviet KGB.

WEST GERMANY

The Security Service, known as the Office for the Protection of the Constitution (Bundesamt für Verfassungsschutz – BfV), was the first to be formed after the war, when the occupying powers realised the threat from espionage by East Germany. It was formed in 1950, subordinated to the Ministry of the Interior, and was first headed by Dr Otto John. Like the British MI 5, it has no powers of arrest.

A secret Intelligence service was not permitted by the occupying powers after the Second World War, so it was not until the granting of autonomy to the Federal Republic in 1956 that one was formed. This was known as the Bundesnachrichtendienst (BND), and was first headed by General Reinhardt Gehlen, a former professional soldier who had headed the German Army's Intelligence organisation from 1942 to the end of the Second World War, and a CIA-sponsored espionage organisation from 1945 until 1956.

There is also a frontier protection organisation organised on army lines and known as the Bundesgrenzschutz, as well as a field security organisation known as the Militärischeabschirmdienst (MAD)

HUNGARY

Until the fall of Communism, Hungary was another country whose espionage and security services operated, like those of East Germany, as an extension of the Soviet KGB. Until the end of the Second World War, Hungary had been a rabidly anti-Communist state under Admiral Horthy. In 1945, however, the new Hungarian State Police established its political investigation branch in Budapest and in 1947 this became the Államvédelmi Osztály (AVO), subordinate to the Ministry of the Interior. In 1949 it became independent and changed its name to Államvédelmi Hatósag (AVH); again as in East Germany, a large proportion of its efforts were devoted to checking and reporting on Hungarian citizens, with as many as 80,000 informers in a population of some 9½ million. Cooperation with the KGB was close until the break-up of the Soviet Union and the Warsaw Pact, but Hungary's secret Intelligence service had a poor record against the West.

IRAN

The Iranian Intelligence and security service is known as SAVAK, and under the Shah's rule, built up with the help of the CIA, MI 6 and Israel's Mossad, it acquired a justifiable reputation for ruthlessness. Since the revolution in Iran, SAVAK has been taken over by hardliners with an anti-US and anti-British bias. However, since the war with Iraq and the Gulf War, this line has softened and the new régime continues to give some help, particularly to Israel.

IRAQ

Iraq has a combined secret Intelligence and security service known as Al Mukhabarat ('The Listening Post'). In recent years it has forged close links with the KGB which have involved the former Soviet Union supplying the Iraqis with technical espionage equipment and training Iraqi Intelligence agents in exchange for Iraqi Intelligence reports on NATO installations and activities.

ISRAEL

Although only some fifty years old, Israel has one of the most efficient Intelligence services in the world, based upon and formed out of the various Jewish underground movements involved in the fight for independence in the 1940s.

Secret Intelligence is the responsibility of the Mossad Le Allyah Beth (Mossad), the Institution for Intelligence and Special Services, formed in 1949 and more or less equivalent to MI 6. The security and counter-espionage service is Shin Beth, equating to MI 5, while the military Intelligence organisation, equivalent to the British Defence Intelligence organisation, is AMAN. Both Mossad and Shin Beth have co-operated with US, British, German and French Intelligence services, a cooperation which has been mutually beneficial in most cases.

ITALY

The Intelligence services of Italy have been bedevilled by the volatile nature of Italian politics, the Italian temperament and the baleful if pervasive influence of the Mafia and other secretive organisations. They have undergone frequent reorganisations and changes since the end of the Second World War, and it is difficult to keep pace with these. SIFAR is the counter-Intelligence service, while SISME is responsible for secret Intelligence.

JAPAN

Like China, Japan's Intelligence credentials date back to ancient times, and unlike so many Western countries in which espionage is regarded as a dirty and dishonourable business, particularly by the armed services, in Japan spying is considered an honourable and patriotic duty. After Japan's defeat in the Second

World War, its Intelligence services, secret police and secret societies were banned by the Allied occupation authorities, and it was not until 1952 that the new security agency, Hoancho, was formed. Hoancho was responsible for security in the ground defence forces as well as for internal order in the country.

Hoancho was succeeded in 1954 by a new Defence Agency, Boeucho, when the new defence forces were formed; a Public Security Investigation Agency (Koan Chosa Cho) was similarly organised to replace the earlier Special Investigation Bureau (Tokushin Kyoku), and two years later the Guard Division of the Police Agency (Keisatsu Cho) followed, to keep an eye on subversive groups of both Left and Right.

SIGINT and cryptanalysis are the responsibility of the Cabinet Investigation Board (Naikaku Chosashitsu).

POLAND

After the USSR occupied Poland at the end of the Second World War, the Polish Intelligence and security services were remodelled on Soviet lines and operated largely to KGB instruction.

The secret Intelligence service was then called the Urzad Bezpieczenstva (UB), while a parallel organisation, rather on the lines of the Soviet GRU, was known as Sluzba Bezpieczenstva. Fairly successful in its operation against Western countries in the days of the Cold War, it is not known how the service has been reorganised since the collapse of Communism and the Warsaw Pact.

SOUTH AFRICA

Until the collapse of apartheid, the Republic of South Africa was ostracised by both East and West, although the tacit Soviet support of the African National Congress made the prevention of Communist subversion and penetration a prime aim of the South African Intelligence and security services. In addition, the campaigns against apartheid organised in Western countries made it necessary for the South African Intelligence services to operate in these countries as well. During this time the South African Intelligence service received considerable assistance from Israel's Mossad.

The South African Intelligence service at the time was known as the Bureau of State Security (BOSS), and was directed and run mainly by Afrikaners. As a result of a scandal involving the head of the service in 1979, the then President of South Africa, P.W. Botha, ordered a reorganisation, part of which involved changing the name to the National Intelligence Service (NIS).

Since the abolition of apartheid and the rehabilitation of South Africa in the international community, the NIS has worked with both the British SIS and the US CIA, as well as with Mossad.

SPAIN

During General Franco's régime, Spain's Intelligence service was run by the military rather than by the civilian ministries. One of the more fanatically anti-Communist governments in the world, the prime target of the service was Soviet subversion and espionage, and during the Second World War it co-operated closely with the German Abwehr.

Since Franco's death and the election of a Socialist government, the Spanish Intelligence service has been reorganised under the title Centro Superior para la Informacion de la Defensa (CESID), which also controls the Intelligence services of the army, navy and air force, as well as the SIGC, the Intelligence service of the Guardia, and SIPAN, that of the Ministry of the Interior and the National Police.

UNITED STATES OF AMERICA

Surprisingly for one of the most powerful nations in the world, the USA was a late entry into the field of Intelligence. After the First World War the USA had a highly successful radio intercept and code-breaking unit known as 'The Black Chamber', which had broken the diplomatic ciphers of France, the UK, Germany, Japan and the USSR, but this was closed down by Henry Stimson on his appointment as Secretary of State in 1929 on the pretext that 'Gentlemen do not read each others' mail.' This was compounded by the isolationist policies of Roosevelt's New Deal, when the government decided that all Intelligence-collection on foreign countries was not only ungentlemanly, but an unnecessary expense for a country grappling with the Depression. The only form of national Intelligence work permitted was that carried out by the Federal Bureau of Investigation (FBI), the counter-Intelligence and internal security organisation headed by the fanatical J. Edgar Hoover. Founded in 1910 as the Bureau of Investigation, the FBI was largely preoccupied by the fight against organised crime syndicates engaged in supplying the alcoholic liquor demanded by a country starved of it by Prohibition.

Thus, when world war loomed on the horizon in the 1930s, the USA found itself without a secret Intelligence service; the only Intelligence supplying the armed forces emanated from their own attachés abroad and the overt information gleaned by the Office of Naval Intelligence (ONI) and the Military Intelligence Department of the

Army from foreign newspapers and other publications. The nearest approach to a secret Intelligence service was 'The Room', an unofficial grouping of top Anglophile businessmen backed and partially funded by Franklin D. Roosevelt, and later, by two other equally unofficial organisations. It was not until a reluctant Roosevelt sanctioned Intelligence collaboration with the British in 1940 that the beginnings of a US secret Intelligence service could be seen. In July 1941, after a series of visits to the UK, William ('Wild Bill') J. Donovan was appointed head of the Office of the Coordinator of Information (COI), charged with securing information important to US national security. This organisation grew into the Office of Strategic Services (OSS), again headed by Donovan, in December 1942. It would have been logical for the OSS to have continued after the war as a secret Intelligence service, but this was vetoed by President Harry S.Truman, and the OSS was abolished in September 1945.

The idea of a central Intelligence organisation did not die with OSS, however; in January 1946, three months after its demise, Truman signed an order bringing into being the Central Intelligence Group (CIG) to coordinate the Intelligence efforts of the State Department and the Departments of the Army and the Navy, reporting to a National Intelligence Authority (NIA). The CIG grew into the Central Intelligence Agency (CIA) in 1948, having the secret Intelligence-collecting portions of the State Department, Departments of the Army and the Navy, and of the FBI. Now employing some 16,000 people, the CIA is a much larger equivalent of MI 6, with world-wide coverage. It works closely with MI 6 under the UKUSA agreement, and is based in Langley, Virginia, in a purpose-built complex.

For purely military Intelligence, the Intelligence agencies of the three armed services form the Defense Intelligence Agency (DIA), based in the Pentagon, just across the Potomac River from Washington, DC. SIGINT is the responsibility of the National Security Agency (NSA), based in Fort Meade, Maryland, which also works closely with the British GCHQ.

The American Secret Service is nothing to do with the collection of covert Intelligence, but is part of the US Treasury Department originally formed to counter counterfeiting of currency, but now charged solely with guarding the President and other senior members of the government.

USSR/RUSSIA

Before the Bolshevik Revolution of 1917, Russia had a much-feared Intelligence and security service within the Ministry of the Interior called the Okhrana (Okhrannye Odteleniya); this was abolished in 1917 by Lenin, and in its place he created the Cheka (Vecheka – the All-Russian Extraordinary Commission), headed by Feliks Dzherzinsky. Like the Okhrana, the Cheka recruited a nationwide network of informers, using terror and blackmail to induce people to inform on each other. In 1922 the Cheka became the State Political Administration (Gosudarstvennoe Politicheskoye Upravlenie – GPU), incorporating a Foreign Department, the INO, while the Red Army's Intelligence was organised by the Fourth Department of the General Staff, the Glavnoe Razvedyvatelnoe Upravlenie (GRU) or Chief Intelligence Administration. The GPU lasted only a year before being reorganised in November 1923 into the OGPU (Obedinennoe Politicheskoe Upravlenie – Unified State Political Administration), in which form it lasted until 1934. In that year it was changed again, becoming the People's Commissariat for Internal Affairs (Narodnyi Komissariat Vnutrennikh Del – NKVD), in which form it survived until 1941. In 1941 the NKVD's political police section became the People's Committee for State Security (Narodnyi Komissariat Gosudarstvennoe Bezopasnosti – NKGB) until 1946. From then until 1953 it was the Ministry of State Security (Ministerstvo Gosudarstvennoe Bezopasnosti – MGB) and the Ministry of Internal Affairs (Ministerstvo Vnutrennikh Del – or MVD). In 1953 these organisations were assimilated into the Committee for State Security (Komitet Gosudarstvennoe Bezopasnosti – or KGB), in which form it survived until the dissolution of the USSR in 1991.

In the reorganisation of the Russian Intelligence machine that followed the dissolution, the KGB was abolished and foreign Intelligence became the responsibility of the Foreign Intelligence Service (Sluzhba Vneshnei Razvedaki – SVR), formed from the First Chief Directorate of the former KGB. Located at Iasenovo ('The Forest') in a purpose-built complex outside Moscow, the SVR was first headed by Evgenii Primakov.

In the same reorganisation, security and counter-Intelligence were assigned to a Federal Security Service (Federal'naya Sluzhba Bezopasnosti – FSB) which grew out of the former Ministry of Security (Ministerstvo Bezopasnosti – MB), the Federal Counter-Intelligence Service (Federal'naya Sluzhba Kontrazvedki – FSK) and the FSB. It was located in the Lubianka in Moscow.

The third branch of the Intelligence tree, that dealing with SIGINT, was formed from the Eighth Chief Directorate of the former KGB and is the Federal Agency for Government Communications and Information (Federal'noe Agentstvo Pravitel'stvennoi Sviazi i Informatsii – FAPSI). It equates to the British GCHQ and the US NSA.

The GRU has remained as the Army's military Intelligence arm, but unlike the British system, has the right to recruit agents overseas and to run them alongside or in competition with those of the SVR.

Bibliography

PUBLISHED MATERIAL

Agee, Philip. *Inside the Company: CIA Diary* (Allen Lane, 1975)
Andrew, Christopher. *Secret Service* (Heinemann, London, 1985)
Anon. *MI 5 – The Security Service* (HMSO, London, 3rd edn, 1998)
Arcangelis, Mario De. *Electronic Warfare* (Blandford Press, Poole, 1985)
Berkeley, Roy. *A Spy's London* (Leo Cooper, London, 1994)
Bulloch, John. *MI 5: The Origins & History of the British Counter-espionage Service* (Arthur Baker, London, 1963)
Charteris, Brigadier-General John. *At GHQ* (Cassell, London, 1931)
Costello, John. *Mask of Treachery* (Collins, London, 1988)
Cruikshank, Charles. *Deception in World War II* (OUP, 1979)
Deacon, Richard (Donald McCormick). *A History of the British Secret Service* (Frederick Muller, London, 1969)
—. *Spyclopaedia* (Macdonald, London, 1987)
Fergusson, Lieutenant-Colonel Thomas G. *British Military Intelligence, 1870–1914* (Arms & Armour Press, London, 1984)
Foot, M.R.D. *SOE in France* (HMSO, London, 1966)
Fuller, Jean Overton. *The German Penetration of SOE* (William Kimber, London, 1975)
Furse, Colonel G.A. *Information in War – Its Acquisition and Transmission* (William Clowes & Son, London, 1895)
Gudgin, Peter. 'Phantom British Tank Regiments of World War II' (RUSI *Journal*, London, September 1980)
Hart, Captain B.H. Liddell. *History of the First World War* (Cassell, London, 1980)
Haswell, Jock. *British Military Intelligence* (Weidenfeld & Nicolson, London, 1973)
Hinsley, Professor F.H. et al. *British Intelligence in the Second World War, Volumes 1, 2 and 3 (Parts 1 & 2)* (HMSO, London, various dates)
Howard, Professor Sir Michael. *Strategic Deception in the Second World War* (Pimlico, London, 1992; previously published as volume 5 of *The Official History of British Intelligence in the Second World War,* HMSO, London)
Knightley, Phillip. *The Second Oldest Profession* (André Deutsch, London, 1986)
Lamphere, Robert J. & Schachtman, Tom. *The FBI–KGB War* (W.H. Allen, London, 1987)
Lockhart, Robert Bruce. *Ace of Spies* (Hodder & Stoughton, London, 1967)
Neave, Airey. *Saturday at MI 9* (Hodder & Stoughton, London, 1969)

Parritt, Lieutenant-Colonel B.A.H. *The Intelligencers* (Intelligence Corps Association, Ashford, Kent, 1971)
Philby, H.A.R. ('Kim'). *My Silent War* (Granada, London, 1983)
Ranelagh, John. *The Rise & Decline of the CIA* (Weidenfeld & Nicolson, London, 1986)
Strong, Major-General Sir Kenneth. *Intelligence at the Top* (Cassell, London, 1970)
—. *Men Of Intelligence* (Cassell, London, 1970)
Sweet-Escott, Bickham. *Baker Street Irregular* (Methuen, London, 1965)
West, Nigel (Rupert Allason). *MI 5 – British Security Service Operations, 1909–45* (The Bodley Head, London, 1981)
—. *A Matter of Trust: MI 5, 1945–72* (Weidenfeld & Nicolson, London, 1982)
—. *MI 6 – British SIS Operations, 1909–45* (Weidenfeld & Nicolson, London, 1983)
—. *The Branch* (Secker & Warburg, London, 1983)
—. *GCHQ: The Secret Wireless War, 1980–86* (Weidenfeld & Nicolson, London, 1986)
—. *The Friends: Britain's Post-war Secret Intelligence Operations* (Weidenfeld & Nicolson, London, 1988)
Whitby, Max. *Space Technology* (BBC Publications, London, 1986)
Wicks, Robin. *Cloak & Gown – Scholars in America's Secret War* (Collins Harvill, London, 1987)
Wright, Peter. *Spycatcher* (Heinemann, Australia, 1987)
Yenne, Bill. *Encyclopaedia of US Space Craft* (Hamlyn, London, 1985)

UNPUBLISHED MATERIAL

Drake, Lieutenant-Colonel R.F. 'History of Intelligence (B), British Expeditionary Force, France, from January 1917 to April 1919' (typescript, May 1919 – PRO WO/106/45)
Isaac, Lieutenant-Colonel (QM) W.V.R. 'The History of the Development of the Directorate of Military Intelligence, War Office, 1939–55' (typescript, 1955, MoD Central Library)
Thwaites, Major-General W. (DMI). 'Historical Sketch of the Directorate of Military Intelligence During the Great War, 1914–19' (proof copy dated May 1921, PRO WO/32/10776)

INDEX